For The Love Of God

A Tapestry of History and Heritage in Los Altos de Jalisco, Mexico

By
Liborio Gutierrez Martín del Campo
and
Jose Gutierrez Gonzalez

Copyright

© 2024 by Liborio Gutierrez Martín del Campo and Jose Gutierrez Gonzalez
All rights reserved. No part of this publication may be reproduced, distributed, or transmitted in any form or by any means, including photocopying, recording, or other electronic or mechanical methods, without the prior written permission of the publisher, except in the case of brief quotations embodied in critical reviews and certain other noncommercial uses permitted by copyright law.

Hardback
ISBN# 978-1-963925-88-3

Paperback
ISBN#978-0-9884025-4-6

E-book
ISBN# 978-1-963925-07-4

Published by New Trends Press
P.O. Box 3001, Beaumont, Ca 92223
WWW.NewTrendsPress.Com
First Edition

Library of Congress Cataloging-in-Publication Data
Names: Gutierrez Martín del Campo, Liborio, Author. | Gutierrez Gonzalez, Jose, author.
Title: For the Love of God: A Tapestry of History and Heritage in Los Altos de Jalisco, Mexico
By Liborio Gutierrez Martín del Campo and Jose Gutierrez Gonzalez.
Description: First Edition. |Beaumont: New Trends Press, 2024.
Identifiers: ISBN: 978-0-9884025-4-6
Subjects: LCSH: Los Altos de Jalisco, Mexico – History. | Los Altos de Jalisco, Mexico – Biography. | BISAC: HISTORY / Latin America / Mexico. | BIOGRAPHY & AUTOBIOGRAPHY / Personal Memoirs.
Cover design by Jose Gutierrez Gonzalez
Interior layout by Jose Gutierrez Gonzalez
Printed in the US

Contents

Prologue 2
Chapter 1 5
Chapter 2 20
Chapter 3 35
Chapter 4 40
Chapter 5 68
Chapter 6 78
Chapter 7 84
Chapter 8 98
Chapter 9 110
Chapter 10 148
Chapter 11 158
Chapter 12 181
Chapter 13 186
Chapter 14 200
Chapter 15 220
Chapter 16 226
Chapter 17 228
Chapter 18 240
Chapter 19 253
Chapter 20 271
Chapter 21 280
Chapter 22 290

"Oh Jalisco, don't back down!"
Jorge Negrete

WARNING!
Not everything written here is one hundred percent verified, but it is a collection of memories of individuals, books read, and other forms of information gathered throughout the life of **Liborio Gutierrez.**

Prologue

In life's journey, we encounter challenges that become part of our mission. This is precisely what happened to me with my father and his desire to put in writing his memories, experiences, and knowledge so that they may be passed down to posterity even when he is no longer with us.

And this is precisely the context that, as a son, brings me here with the responsibility and privilege of continuing his dream.

My father, Liborio Gutiérrez, wrote a chronicle that takes a detailed journey through the history of Mexico from colonization to the middle of the last century, focusing mainly on Los Altos de Jalisco and a beautiful exposition of the ranches of the families, the lineages, customs, and traditions of the people who occupied these places.

In addition to this work, he also wrote one with more personal anecdotes that could be considered an autobiography, which I will soon finish editing. This one you are reading today speaks more of our ancestors than ourselves.

I want to highlight two crucial points about the composition and structure of this work. First, my father, regrettably, did not witness the completion and publication of this work in his lifetime. Nevertheless, he had made a lot of progress, and it is clear that he was already compiling his notes, polishing them, and giving structure to the book.

Second, when I took on these tasks, I came across a lot of fascinating information and found it difficult to synthesize or eliminate some notes as my father would have. That's why I need to understand that if there are similar paragraphs, I've transcribed them even from manuscripts in his agendas. I wanted to respect his voice and preserve every nuance and perspective. This book is a testament to his experiences and memories, a continuation of his voice resonating through the pages. Below is an introduction my father wrote that I have decided to add to this prologue.

José Gutiérrez

Words from my father, Liborio Gutiérrez

This book unfolds a story told in three crucial segments. It is a story that I have carefully constructed using inquiry and reason to discover truths that were once hidden and unknown. The most notable of these three segments is the third, a depiction of my personal life that begins from the innocence of my early years and culminates on the threshold of my sixteenth year. Within these pages lie many revelations that offer deep insights into my journey in life. These written words now immortalize those cherished moments because as time inexorably moves forward and my health declines, I can no longer express them myself.

My Sincere Dedication

In writing the history of my life and the historical colonization of my ancestors in and around the mountainous area of Los Altos de Jalisco, Mexico, I am deeply grateful to my son, José, who has been the guiding light in this journey. His encouragement and belief in the value of my experiences have been fundamental in bringing these pages to life.

José, more than a son, you have been my anchor and wellspring of inspiration. Your support and intuition have transformed the challenge of writing this autobiography into a path of self-discovery and sharing. This book is a legacy we have created, reflecting our shared journey and the enduring bond.

To José, I owe the realization of a long-cherished dream—the immortalization of my stories. José, your unwavering patience and understanding mean so much to me, even in my imperfect moments. I hope this book brings us all closer to understanding and peace.

Above all, I extend my deepest gratitude to all my children. In moments when I have faltered, showing less warmth and kindness than they deserved, their patience and understanding have remained unwavering. The depths of my love for all of you are only known to the divine. As I reflect on the mosaic of my life, colored by triumphs and mistakes, my heart yearns for forgiveness. I hope this understanding paves the way to eternal peace with God.

With all my love and deep gratitude,

Liborio Gutiérrez

CHAPTER 1

Los Altos de Jalisco and its Castilian Descent

In the heart of Mexico lies Jalisco, a state whose capital, Guadalajara, is the prelude to an elevated region known as Los Altos de Jalisco. This area, extending about 60 kilometers east of the capital, is characterized by its altitude exceeding 2300 meters above sea level. It is surrounded by numerous localities and municipalities rich in history and natural beauty. Notable among them are Tepatitlán de Morelos, Arandas, San Ignacio Cerro Gordo, Santa Marta, San Miguel del Alto, Jalostotitlán, San Juan de los Lagos, and others.

These places, formerly chiefdoms that flourished with the arrival of conquerors and settlers, transformed into picturesque towns, each with its charm. Take Atotonilco, for instance, which is known for its hot springs and abundance of fruit trees.

Within this historical and geographical framework, I celebrate the magnificent Altos de Jalisco, my birthplace, immortalized in the iconic song, "Ay Jalisco no te rajes! Which translates to, "Oh, Jalisco, don't back down!"

This anthem gained widespread fame in the 1940s. Jorge Negrete, a renowned actor and singer and a native of Guanajuato, became an icon associated with Los Altos de Jalisco. He brought this melody to the height of its popularity through his acclaimed movies. His art reflected this region's cultural and ancestral closeness with its neighbors.

With special affection, I dedicate this book to the composer of that grand hymn to Los Altos, embodying the dream of a genuine son of this land. For the longest time, I longed for the composer to have the opportunity to read these words, written from a heart deeply rooted in the cradle of the highlands.

The Heritage of the People from Los Altos

My beloved town, Capilla de Guadalupe, was founded in 1823 in a region I now detail after almost three centuries. This land, rich in valleys and hills, stands proudly around the central and majestic Cerro Gordo, which rises 648 meters above its base and 2668 meters above sea level.

In the 16th century, with the dawn of colonization, the first conquerors arrived in Tepatitlán in 1531. Led by Pedro Almíndez Chirinos and Cristóbal de Oñate under the banner of Nuño Beltrán de Guzmán, they came with the mission entrusted in Mexico to conquer a region rumored to be robust and rich: the great chiefdom of Tonallan, inhabited by the indigenous Tonallanecas, which today is known as a suburb of Guadalajara.

Nuño Beltrán de Guzmán, upon arriving in Tonallan, found a society led by a widowed queen, Cihualpilli. A harmonious coexistence was initially established with the Tonallanecas, but this peace was ephemeral. Beltrán de Guzmán, seduced by rumors of a hill filled with silver in the northern region of Zacatecas, sent Cristóbal de Oñate and Pedro Almíndez Chirinos at the same time (1531) to verify such wealth, thus marking the beginning of an era that would change the destiny of our region forever.

A Refinement of the Preface

In an enterprise of historical scope, the expedition set off for the hills of Zacatecas, drawn by rumors of its mineral wealth. The truth unearthed was that the mountain was rich in iron instead of silver. However, the journey revealed more than mineral resources; along their way, they encountered various chiefdoms. The first was Tateposco, followed by Zapotlanejo, the land of the Tecuexes, a tribe with the same name, and then Acatic, another place of the Tecuexes. Advancing about 80 kilometers from Guadalajara, they encountered an even larger chiefdom: Tepatitlán, governed by the great chief Mapelo. The region was inhabited by the Caxcanes and the Guamares of Zacatecas, the latter being the most prominent near Cerro Gordo.

Over time, the Spaniards settled in the area, establishing captaincies and missions of friars that gradually colonized and displaced the indigenous people from their ancestral lands around Tepatitlán. Before these events, Nuño Beltrán de Guzmán had already settled in the Atemajac Valley, later founding the city of Guadalajara in 1542 after numerous confrontations and a hard struggle to consolidate his presence in the region.

This story serves as a preamble to the life and times of my father. It emerges from the depths of the past to narrate the bravery, vicissitudes, and indomitable hope of those who formed our heritage.

Establishment and Conquest in Los Altos de Jalisco

The colonization process was turbulent and full of challenges. Nuño Beltrán de Guzmán encountered resistance in Tonalá and, after facing the fierce opposition of the Caxcanes and constant attacks, was forced to relocate several times. Only after a series of failed attempts did he find a more peaceful settlement in the Atemajac Valley. In 1542, he established a plaza known today as the Degollado Theater.

Resuming the story of my region of interest, as mentioned, the conquest and colonization of Los Altos de Jalisco was a gradual process. Over the years, "captaincies," estates, and soldiers' garrisons belonging to the Viceroyalty were established at strategic points such as Tepatitlán, Arandas, San Miguel el Alto, Jalostotitlán, and San Juan de los Lagos, as well as in Yahualica. These bastions allowed control of the region, transforming chiefdoms into towns with the voluntary displacement of indigenous populations to places like Nochistlán, the homeland of the brave Caxcanes.

Migration was characterized as primarily Spanish. Since the conquest of the Los Altos region, those who settled brought their families, creating a community with roots in central and northern Spain. This outlined a cultural and demographic heritage that almost exclusively affirmed Castilian ancestry.

This is the prelude to the life of my father, whose personal story is intertwined with the broader fabric of our regional history. It reveals the layers of our collective identity forged in the crucible of cultural encounters and mismatches.

Heritage and Resistance in Los Altos de Jalisco

The region's demographic profile during colonization was dominated by Spaniards, many of whom were tall and blonde—

typical traits of the Castilians. Amidst the cultural and geographical transformation, indigenous resistance continued, particularly in the famous Cerro Gordo, the region's largest chiefdom, which remained a bastion of aboriginal resistance. The settlers initially chose to ignore this area for two reasons: first, its geographical isolation, and second, the difficulty of penetrating the rugged terrain, tenaciously defended by the astute Guamares Zacatecas.

Cerro Gordo became a refuge for those who did not move to Nochistlán with the Caxcanes, growing in population as some indigenous people chose to seek shelter in its rugged terrain rather than face displacement. Since the arrival of the conquerors in 1531, this indigenous enclave endured, resisting for more than two centuries until around 1703. No previous colonial strategy had managed to displace these inhabitants until the intervention of "special settlers" from Castile, known for handling particularly challenging cases. Their involvement was prompted by directives from the Spanish monarch.

In the 17th century, Guadalajara had already become an important city. Over the years, the Royal Road connecting Guadalajara with Mexico City was built. This route was vital, as it became a leading commercial artery, ranking among the four most important trade routes of the time, including the road connecting Veracruz with the capital.

Silver Routes and Interwoven Lives

The road network connecting New Spain with the metropolis was a vital system for the empire. Among these, the Royal Road that linked Mexico City with the viceroyal capital stood out for its strategic importance. It was the arrival and departure point for merchants and settlers from Europe and the main conduit for exports crossing the ocean to the Old World.

The significance of this road was such that it attracted admiration from the Spanish crown, particularly from King Charles V and his successor, Philip II, due to the rich silver mines of Guanajuato. These mines were the inexhaustible source that fed the constant flow of riches filling the coffers of Spain. Also, the Royal Road that stretched from Durango, Zacatecas, and Aguascalientes to the capital was another significant commercial axis, linking different points of the viceroyal geography and culminating at the foot of Cerro Gordo, near the present-day Rancho Los Sauces, after passing through the Mirandilla estate. A fork in this route led those wishing to travel to Guadalajara through Tepatitlán.

My Alteño Region and My Town

I, Liborio Gutiérrez, was born in a humble but significant little town in the heart of Los Altos de Jalisco, a region of highlands and deep cultural roots. This corner of the world, the cradle of traditions and forger of destinies, was the stage that witnessed the first chapters of my life, an existence woven between the history of a country and the simplicity of rural life. In this context, my personal story is framed within the grand narrative of a colonial Mexico slowly giving way to a new era in 1823, my beloved little town, Capilla de Guadalupe. Nestled in the municipality of Tepatitlán, this quaint town is situated to the east, approximately 20 kilometers from the endearing "Tepa," as affectionately referred to by the locals. Here, in this enclave full of devotion and traditions, our Morenita Guadalupana manifested her will through a miracle. The founder, a Castilian creole with a noble heart named Don Antonio de Aceves, received the blessing of the Virgin to erect a chapel in her honor, a reflection of the immense love he professed.

Over time, my great-great-grandfather, Don Felipe Navarro y Aceves, the grandson of Don Antonio, undertook the monumental task of transforming the modest chapel into what today stands as a majestic parish. This project was made possible through the collaboration of relatives and neighbors of the time, encapsulating within its walls a profound testimony to the faith of our people.

Upon crossing its main entrance, one can admire four imposing and beautiful murals dating from the 1940s, which narrate the apparitions of the Virgin of Guadalupe to Juan Diego and proclaim her as Queen of the Americas. These pieces, true artistic jewels, were an initiative of Mr. Cura Morales, who at that time shared with us not only his spiritual vision but also his creative impetus. All of us who lived with him remember him as a generous benefactor whose legacy transcends time. He enriched our parish with murals, endowed our altar with new beauty, adorned with exquisite decoration, and paid particular attention to every detail. The result is a sacred space that invites reflection and contemplation.

The Parish

Internally, the parish was clad in a new and magnificent style, whose finishes include gold inlays, thus enhancing its splendor. A unique dome, an architectural gem unprecedented in the state was erected, and a second tower was built, which had stood alone for years. The original vision was to erect three-story towers. The tower he built had three levels, but unfortunately, the priest passed away before he could complete the lightning rod's pinnacle.

Later, another priest took over the work, but instead of continuing the project and adding an additional floor to the existing tower, he opted to reduce the height by removing the third floor. Despite this change, the two-story towers do not detract from the structure; however, the original concept of Mr. Cura Morales, a native of

Arandas, remained unrealized. We express our gratitude to Arandas for having provided such a notable benefactor to Capilla de Guadalupe.

Regarding the geology of my region, let me explain the characteristics that define the environment of my town in Los Altos de Jalisco, from the arrival of the first Spaniards to the present day. I will describe my region from a geological perspective: its landscape is composed of beautiful and extensive plains, characterized by thick layers of red earth. Below lies a vast stratification of solid rock that, in some areas, can exceed one hundred meters in thickness. This subterranean structure is particularly conducive to dissipating the energies of earthquakes, which fortunately has kept us safe from the adverse effects of seismic events.

Earthquakes

Despite having resided here for a long time, I have not perceived any earthquakes in the region. However, this geological feature has its disadvantage: to access groundwater, it is necessary to drill through the enormous layer of solid rock.

My small town, Capilla de Guadalupe, stands at 2020 meters above sea level, and in certain areas of my region, as I mentioned earlier, the altitude even reaches more than 2300 meters. This altitude variation lends the region its apt name, "Los Altos de Jalisco."

The Great Valleys, Their Hills, and Their Mysteries

In my town, Capilla de Guadalupe, we are surrounded by vast and beautiful valleys adorned by several prominent hills. The most significant is the one located south of the Chapel—the famous and history-filled Cerro Gordo. This hill, once an inactive volcano countless millions of years ago, bears evidence of its volcanic origin through a notably enormous crater visible only from its summit.

Those of us who live in its vicinity were not aware of its volcanic origin until I began to observe several pieces of evidence on Cerro Gordo and the surrounding hills. The first time I became aware of these proofs, I was about 10 years old.

The Founders of La Capilla de Guadalupe
In 1823, the founders of La Capilla de Guadalupe chose to settle in a locality devoid of rivers due to a promise and devotion to the Virgin of Guadalupe. Faced with the need to conserve water for the periods of drought that extended for six to seven months every year—from October and sometimes until May—their ingenuity led them to create several ponds or reservoirs to store the vital liquid.
They built a great magnitude, baptized as "El Tajo," located south of the Chapel. Additionally, they expanded an existing lagoon that, in rainy seasons, became even more vast and beautifully adorned with lilies—some white and others pink—whose blooms were the visual and olfactory delight of the region. The environment was filled with the bustle of ducks, moorhens, tilos, herons, and the nightly chorus of frogs and crickets.
Delving into "El Tajo" and the volcanic indications of Cerro Gordo, a layer of distinctive black soil, about a meter and a half to two meters deep, extends around the pond and the entire lagoon—an obsidian-like blackness unlike any I have seen elsewhere. This soil was discovered during the excavation of the pond, a fertile land that perhaps holds secrets of a long dormant volcanic past.
During the construction of El Tajo, a layer of semi-hard yellow tepetate was found—a clear evidence of the lava from the Cerro Gordo volcano, which rises majestically about seven kilometers away. This pit, for more than a century, was a pillar in supplying water for the daily needs of my community. Its waters not only quenched the thirst of the cattle through tagetes but also sustained

various public laundries where, during my childhood, I observed several women laboring with clothes.

In the years 1944 and 1945, with the beginning of the construction of the federal highway to Mexico City, a new use for the tepetate was discovered: it served as the base for the road, replacing the traditional crushed stone. This practice proved to be efficient, and hence, a significant amount of tepetate was extracted, extending the extraction of El Tajo to more than 150 or 20 meters in depth. I grew up fascinated, observing the constant activity of trucks ascending and descending, loaded with this material.

The resulting quarry from the tepetate measured approximately 75x75 square meters, and within it, the drillings revealed countless medium-sized volcanic stones, a testimony of the lava flow that reached that point. The person responsible for the excavation showed us how these relics of volcanic activity, which seemed to have been forgotten, emerged among the tepetate.

Don Juan Casillas and His Contribution

The text recounts the generous contribution of Don Juan Casillas, a native of Rancho El Terrero, who decided to settle in La Capilla, bringing not only economic prosperity but also a deep commitment to the well-being of our community. Don Juan is affectionately remembered as one of the great benefactors, a friend and relative, albeit distant, whose memory endures in the hearts of the inhabitants.

In the impetus of his curiosity and service, Don Juan Casillas initiated a monumental enterprise: the excavation of a well that delved into the tenacious layer of tepetate, a task that required the displacement of thousands of tons of this material. With a vision of the future and dedication, he put a team to work with the aim of reaching the end of this stage. Even though the well reached an impressive depth of 15 meters, the end of the tepetate was not in sight, and the mystery of its depth remained intact.

After the need for more tepetate for road construction ceased, the idea emerged to transform this space into a water reservoir that would benefit the entire town. A channel was constructed from the lagoon to El Tajo, and when it was filled, the entire town celebrated; now there was a vital reservoir that ensured the water supply to meet the community's needs. The decision to convert El Tajo into a reservoir was unanimously applauded and approved—another example of the solidarity and resilience of our people.

The day we filled El Tajo is etched in my memory with extraordinary clarity; I still remember the excitement that overwhelmed my being, the temptation to dive into its clear and refreshing waters. El Tajo stood imposing, full of life, like a blue mirror reflecting the promise of better days for all of us. As evening fell, we returned to our homes, our hearts full of hope and our eyes tired from shared happiness.

At dawn the next day, still overflowing with enthusiasm, I ran towards El Tajo, eager to contemplate that communal triumph. However, as I approached, a crowd had already gathered at the site. Confusion invaded me as I perceived their faces, a mosaic of astonishment and bewilderment. And there, before my eyes, reality imposed itself with the force of a blow—El Tajo was empty, stripped of all its water during the veil of the night, as if a giant sinkhole had swallowed every drop.

Where had the water gone? That was the question floating in the air, amid murmurs and conjectures. Some speculated about underground rivers, others about hidden caverns in the depths of the earth. The mystery remained elusive, challenging.

Driven by insatiable curiosity, we decided to try once more, opening the channel that communicated with the lagoon to allow the vital liquid to pass. With renewed spirits, El Tajo was filled again, and this time, resolved to unravel the mystery, many of us stayed to watch, guarding the water. The news that El Tajo was emptying again spread like wildfire, and almost the entire town congregated, driven by intrigue and astonishment, to witness this phenomenon that escaped our understanding.

Dusk approached and with it, the revelation that our great pond had been reduced to a quarter of its original capacity. The few remaining liters began to whirl dizzyingly, forming a vortex that seemed to swallow what little was left. Among the spectators, figures such as Don Juan Casillas and Mr. Cura Morales stood out. I cannot forget Santos, the bell ringer, whose presence commanded such reverence that at some point I will tell you why I consider him the greatest in his profession worldwide.

Finally, it was decided to abandon El Tajo to its fate, and today, that same place houses residential constructions instead of the mysterious waters that once gathered us around its enigma. El Tajo and its missing water became legend, whispers of the past that still resonate in collective memory.

Regarding Cerro Gordo, on one of my expeditions to the peak, armed with a little more knowledge and experience, I was able to clearly discern the vestiges of what was once a majestic crater. At the summit, a dense forest unfolds before the eyes, populated by oaks, palo blanco, palo colorado, and a variety of shrubs, a green mantle that adorns the geography.

From the altitude of 2,668 meters above sea level, the panorama is breathtaking. In the distance, various reference points can be appreciated—a view that takes your breath away and expands the soul, offering a silent but eloquent testimony of millions of years of natural history.

Surrounded by the tranquil majesty of neighboring towns and the vibrant life of cities like Tepatitlán and Arandas, which from my natural watchtower were visible with surprising clarity, I encountered an unexpected discovery. An insect, whose presence I had never witnessed, crossed my path that day. It was a small creature, barely two centimeters long, oval and dark like a small seashell, but of such an intense blackness that it absorbed the light around it.

When disturbed, this tiny being emitted a greenish liquid that gave off an intense and peculiar aroma. My acquaintances called it "miones," perhaps echoing the liquid they released when feeling threatened. What truly astounded me was not just their presence, but their abundance—legions of them, numbering in the millions, whose collective flight formed clouds that darkened the sky, their buzzing resonating through the immensity of space.

However, what captured my curiosity and attention was the natural spectacle that takes place at sunset. A swarm of swallows descended in an aerial ballet, attracted by the innumerable "miones" that inhabited the trees surrounding the crater. The birds congregated in this precise spot, a feast in the air, a cycle of life that revealed itself before my eyes. And so, as evening fell, the swallows swooped down on their prey with precision and elegance, transforming the sky into a dynamic canvas of natural movements.

The event lasted until the last lights of the day faded, and the insects were almost exterminated, a reminder of nature's relentless but beautiful efficiency. We, the spectators, found pure entertainment in the coming and going of these birds, in their struggle for survival, and in their aerial dance to the rhythm of the wildlife of Cerro Gordo. Within the vast natural tapestry that painted the landscape around Cerro Gordo, a particular detail captured the essence of the ecosystem: the food that Providence seemed to have provided for the swallows. The "miones," that singular and dark insect I described earlier, became essential sustenance during their migration from the South and in the nutrition of their chicks. As if by a miracle, upon arrival, the birds found in the walls of our houses and in nature the ideal spaces to nest and perpetuate their species.

As I delve into the memories and stories that envelop Cerro Gordo, I pause at an almost forgotten legend: that of the green-colored snake, known as Flechilla. They say that when the Castilians ventured into the conquest of these places, they encountered this venomous snake that inhabited the heights of the trees. Its name came from the way it attacked, swiftly descending upon its prey, like a precise arrow shot from the heavens. Although today stories of encounters with the Flechilla are not heard, there are warnings about the rattlesnake, which, while remaining in the lower areas, continues to be a living testimony of the wild biodiversity surrounding the Cerro. However, another animal that once marked the natural history of the place was the wolves, which, according to the narratives, have been exterminated and are no longer sighted today.

But Cerro Gordo, with all its mysteries and legends, continues to reserve surprises for us. One of them is a phenomenon that some say is proof of its volcanic origin: a deep and muffled rumbling that emanates from its bowels from time to time. These sounds, brief but powerful, resonate like the echo of a past geological era, and although they only last a few seconds, are enough to remind us of the majestic and unpredictable force of nature. The stories passed down from generation to generation by my relatives, the Francos, are testimony to the rich cultural and natural heritage that is woven into the tapestry of our land.

CHAPTER 2

The Mysteries Surrounding Cerro Gordo

The mysteries that envelop Cerro Gordo and its surroundings are as numerous as the stories told by those who inhabit its slopes. In the intimacy of the chapels and ranches, like the famous San Antonio, the elders narrate with bright eyes that they have heard, in the stillness of the night, the deep rumblings that emerge from the bowels of the earth. Despite the noise, there is no movement in the ground, perhaps cushioned by the extensive layers of stone that dominate the region.

Cerro Gordo does not keep its secrets alone. In its company, other mountains such as Cerro Carnicero, located to the north about five kilometers away, also stand. There, too, are remnants of what appears to be an ancient crater, linked with that of Cerro Gordo by what seems to be a shared volcanic past. To the south, another hill rises with similar evidence, leading me to conjecture that perhaps, in remote times, they were united in coordinated volcanic activity, communicating through underground tunnels.

It is plausible to imagine that today there are vast caverns, a product of those eruptions that resonated through the hills in communication with Cerro Gordo hundreds of millions of years ago. Logic suggests that these underground cavities are testimony to a dynamic and explosive geological history.

There remains the hope that, at some point, explorers or the curious will discover the entrance to these great caverns, thus unveiling the long-guarded secrets. Thus, the story of the great valleys, the hills, and the mysteries that define the geography and spirit of Los Altos de Jalisco is woven, a tale passed down from generation to generation, enriching the cultural heritage of my region.

The Appearance of Humans in Los Altos

In the mists of time, when the dawn of the first millennium unfolded over our era, Nahua tribes, called "Aborigines" by some, made their appearance in the region we now know as Los Altos de Jalisco. These people, belonging to clans united by blood and language, were traveling on their long pilgrimage southward, with the Valley of Mexico as their final destination, leaving behind the mystery of their northern origins.

The chronicles recounting these migrations are varied and rich in legends, including tales of mythical cities, such as Cíbola and Quivira, whose existence has never been proven. Narratives like those of Álvar Núñez Cabeza de Vaca and the slave Estebanico, who survived the shipwreck at the mouth of the Mississippi River, weave a tapestry of adventure and mystery. They were part of an expedition led by Pánfilo de Narváez, adelantado of La Florida, whose mission failed when their ship was lost and only a few escaped the sea's fatality.

Cabeza de Vaca and Estebanico, along with other companions of misfortune, embarked on an odyssey through unknown lands, moving westward, crossing what we now know as New Mexico and Arizona. It is said that in their journey, around 1529 and after several years of hardships, they came across a city that surpassed in magnificence the City of Mexico itself, which they called Cíbola. A city that, like a vision, vanished over time, leaving its trace only in the pages of history and in the legends of those first men of Los Altos de Jalisco.

The tales of Álvar Núñez Cabeza de Vaca and Estebanico, the intrepid explorers, describe with fascination a city that, in wealth and splendor, could rival or even surpass the Tenochtitlán of their days.

They speak of a reception full of hospitality, with people who welcomed them with open arms and guided them on their pilgrimage westward, towards another metropolis of equal magnitude located in what is now the state of Arizona.

This city, near the confluence of the Gila and Colorado Rivers, was named Quivira. The narratives of Cabeza de Vaca and Estebanico are full of admiration for the cultural and material wealth of its inhabitants, painting a picture of advanced and hospitable civilizations amid unknown vastness.

Heading southward, the two men followed the ancestral routes used by the aborigines, delving deeper into the continent. They left behind Quivira, guided by natives through the Sonora deserts, where they found the Yaqui and Mayo tribes, who provided an exceptional welcome, amazed at the presence of a white man and a black man among them.

Continuing their journey southward, they reached the lands of what we now know as Durango and Zacatecas. There, Nahua tribes with established communities and chiefdoms already existed, whose social and political organization impressed the travelers. These lands, rich in culture and traditions, were a testimony to the diversity and complexity of the pre-Hispanic societies that had woven the rich history of ancient Mexico.

The adventure of these men is not only a tale of survival and discovery but also a legacy that reminds us of the greatness of the civilizations that flourished on our land long before Europeans set foot on it. These chronicles become a valuable link connecting the past with the present, thus enriching the history of Los Altos de Jalisco and its people.

The vicissitudes of Álvar Núñez Cabeza de Vaca and the slave Estebanico, after their long odyssey from the Mississippi River basin, culminated when they arrived in Guadalajara. There they met the commander and chief, Nuño de Guzmán, to whom they recounted their astonishing adventure, describing in great detail the cities they found, their immense riches, and the warmth with which they were received by their inhabitants.

However, Guzmán's twisted and ruthless nature was revealed when, without delay, he imprisoned Estebanico, claiming his status as a slave, and sent him escorted to Mexico City. Along with him, he sent the tale of the opulent cities and their magnificence, words that inflamed the greed and imagination of those who heard them.

The fervor for these lands full of promises spread rapidly, and a friar, driven by a thirst for adventure and seduced by the vision of gold, organized a contingent. This army, composed of volunteers attracted by the promise of riches, prepared to set off both by land and by sea.

In the Pacific Ocean, Pedro de Alvarado, the illustrious captain of Hernán Cortés, took to the sea with a notable group of followers. On his journey, he first arrived at what we now know as Puerto Vallarta, thus beginning another chapter in the endless quest for fortunes and glory, an echo of human ambition that still resonates in the chronicles of those times.

These narratives, intertwining brutality and hope, not only forge the history of men in Los Altos de Jalisco but also weave the rich tapestry of our regional identity, where valor and survival blend with the dreams and delusions of those who sought their destiny in the vastness of the New World.

The plot of the story intensified as Pedro de Alvarado received urgent news: Nuño Beltrán de Guzmán was besieged in Guadalajara, facing the fierce resistance of the Caxcan and Tonalteca tribes. Without hesitation, Alvarado set off for the city to aid Guzmán, and thanks to his ingenuity and cunning, lifted the siege that had lasted several days, driving the Caxcans away. However, his grave error was the arrogance of pursuing them to their stronghold near Nochistlán, between Jalisco and Zacatecas, and the Juchipila Canyon, where Guzmán had tried to found Guadalajara for the second time.

Destiny, however, was against Alvarado, as the bravery of the Caxcans and the complexity of the terrain made them invincible on their own land. And so, in the whirlwind of flight and under the cloak of torrential rains, in a desperate attempt to evade their pursuers through the enigma of ravines and natural labyrinths, Pedro de Alvarado met his misfortune. In one of these ravines, in an act of frenzied stampede, his horse lost balance, and both fell into the abyss.

The tragic end of Pedro de Alvarado was sealed near Yahualica, today a beautiful city to the north of the Los Altos de Jalisco region. There, the dream and ambition of this conquistador of distant lands found an abrupt end, in a land that, though beautiful and welcoming, also knows how to be implacable and fierce.

Thus, the story of men in Los Altos de Jalisco is woven with acts of bravery and episodes of tragedy, in a land that has been a silent witness to human tenacity and frailty through the centuries.

The search for the legendary cities of Cíbola and Quivira, those metropolises wrapped in riches and mysteries, eventually faded into the pages of history. Returning to my native region, Los Altos de Jalisco, the first settlers who planted life in these lands were nomads from the north, who, during their migrations to the Valley of Mexico, found a home in places that captivated their hearts, settling at different times.

After the fall of the Toltec civilization around the year 1200, witnesses to the decline of an era were the seven Nahuatlacas tribes who, originating from a place known as Aztlan-Chicomoztoc —the abode of the herons—, began their exodus. This is one of the versions regarding the origins of the tribes that eventually settled in the Valley of Mexico, traveling from distant places located to the north, in what is now Arizona and New Mexico in the United States. The first tribe to settle in the Valley of Mexico was the Xochimilcas, followed by the Tepanecas, the Tlaxcaltecas, and finally, the Mexicas or Aztecs. It was with the Aztecs, in the year 1323, that the greatness of their culture began to take shape on an islet of Lake Texcoco, where they erected their first temple dedicated to the god Huitzilopochtli. Acamapichtli was proclaimed their first tlatoani, lord of a people destined to forge an empire that, for centuries, will resonate in the memory of humanity.

Through the migrations that intertwine like a tapestry in the vast canvas of time, various tribes that crossed these lands at different times, left behind small groups that settled and dispersed throughout the territory. In their beginnings, these groups were nomadic hunters, collectively known as Chichimecas, a term that denoted those who ceaselessly move from one place to another.

However, over the years, they began to take root and form chiefdoms at different points in the state of Jalisco, and in my region, Los Altos de Jalisco, where some of the most significant ones settled, highlighting the one located in Cerro Gordo. This chiefdom prospered and became one of the most powerful in the region, known as the Zacatecas-Nahuatlacas. The community of Cerro Gordo is remembered for its organization and advances in various aspects of daily life, as well as for the bravery and cunning of its warriors. There is a legend that encapsulates the bravery and spirit of these inhabitants, a story both beautiful and melancholic, transmitted by my uncle Silviano Gutiérrez, my father's brother. He dedicated his life to unraveling the ancient parish archives of Tepatitlán, and it was there where he came across this legend that so fascinated me every time, he narrated it.

This ancestral story, which dates to times before the arrival of the Spaniards, is a testimony of the rich cultural heritage that I have inherited and that forms an inseparable part of the identity of Los Altos de Jalisco. The legend, alive in family stories and in ancient documents, remains as an echo of the traditions and courage of those who forged with their effort and their blood the history of our land.

The Legend of Cerro Gordo and Its Princess

It was the time of the first Spaniards in the region of Los Altos de Tepatitlán in 1531. Long before the first Spaniards marked their footprint in Los Altos, the chiefdom of Cerro Gordo flourished at the height of its splendor. The organization of its society was such that it had a robust and meticulously trained army, whose purpose was the defense of the region. In alliance with neighboring chiefdoms, they remained in constant vigilance against the incursions of the Tarasco Indians of Michoacán, who besieged their lands seeking prisoners to offer in sacrifice to their gods in what they called "Flower Wars."

The Guamare, cunning and brave, had their armed forces arranged in an admirable structure, under the direction of a great chief, a renowned cacique whose leadership was unquestionable. This supreme leader, seen as a king, was deeply respected for his courage and his strategic ability to command and organize quickly in times of crisis.

This cacique, whose name resonated like an echo of power and wisdom, was Tlaloc. His name, shared with the deity of rain, was an omen of his influence and strength. Alongside him, a princess of incomparable beauty, whose name has been lost in the mists of time, rose as the most precious flower of the chiefdom.

Tlaloc, along with his caciques, faced persistent conflicts with the Tarascos, defending their land and their people with iron determination, cementing his legend in each battle, in each strategy deployed on the board of war. This is the story that is narrated with reverence in my land, a glorious and immortal chapter in the chronicle of Los Altos de Jalisco.

Near the State of Jalisco, to the south, lies Michoacán, the cradle of the fierce Tarasca race, with a language and customs different from those of the tribes of Los Altos. In the heart of these Jaliscan lands, there existed a princess of unparalleled beauty and indomitable spirit, known as Mesmo Pensil. She was not only a vision of grace but also a consummate warrior, whose prowess in battle surpassed that of many warriors of her time.

Mesmo Pensil, who had triumphed in several confrontations against the Tarascos, was the living image of bravery. Under the orders of her father, Tlaloc, she launched into combat with such daring that she instilled confidence and admiration in all the warriors she commanded. Her strategy and valor were so remarkable that Tlaloc swelled with pride and placed full trust in his daughter in all contests. Alongside her valiant princess, Tlaloc and his army ventured on expeditions to Michoacán, challenging the Tarascos. With surprise attacks and cunning tactics, they inflicted defeats and captured enemies, in a ceaseless series of skirmishes between both sides. The Tarascos, for their part, knew well the risk of facing the Guamare in their stronghold, Cerro Gordo, as it was a challenge in which defeat was almost certain.

The valley that extends to the north of Cerro Gordo, reaching my town, Capilla de Guadalupe, was then a battlefield and is now a testimony to the history and courage of those who inhabited it. This legend, imbued in the land and in the soul of the Altenses, resonates like a hymn to bravery and the unbreakable heritage of our people. In the chronicles of ancient times, a Tarasca expedition to the valley of Cerro Gordo became legendary. The vigilant Lamare quickly detected the invaders. Like a torrent anticipating the storm, the sound of the conch shell resounded, a cry that swiftly spread throughout the hill and the allied chiefdoms. The messengers, with a speed that defied the breath of the wind and strategically placed relays, transmitted the alert signal, preparing the warriors for the imminent battle in the valley that loomed under the shadow of Cerro Gordo.

The ensuing confrontation was of an epic scale, with thousands of combatants from both sides, emerging from the multitude of chiefdoms surrounding the region. This story, flowing from the depths of time, was transmitted orally by the natives, who lacked writing until their tales were finally documented and safeguarded in the archives of Tepatitlán, and perhaps also in Arandas.

Returning to the contest waged between the Guamare and the Tarascos, it is said that the Guamare were already in position, waiting with strategy and warrior ardor. That confrontation, according to the voices that have endured, could have been the last of its magnitude. Although the Tarascos attacked on all fronts, they encountered the indomitable resistance of the Guamare, defending their land with immeasurable valor.

In those times of conflict and strategy, the Guamare found themselves on the brink of combat, with almost complete ranks and attack plans already outlined. The garrisons, alerted by the war signal, activated with an efficiency that bordered on the supernatural. The warriors, far from succumbing to lethargy, mobilized with an uncontrollable energy, organizing and summoning the chiefdoms with a speed that defied understanding, preparing for the imminent arrival of the Tarascos.

The warriors were gathering, and it was evident that a significant mission was approaching. The call for mobilization had been given, and although the distance determined the response time of each chiefdom, the closest ones, such as those of San Ignacio Cerro Gordo, Arandas, and Tepatitlán, quickly assembled due to their proximity to the Hill.

At the epicenter of this alliance stood Tlaloc and his daughter, Princess Mesmo Pensil, who descended with their elite warriors, eager to prove their valor in the heat of battle. These warriors were the cream of the militia, selected for their physical strength, cunning, and rigorous training that turned them into war machines.

The battle commenced without preamble; the Tarascos launched their offensive with the intention of giving no respite nor allowing the arrival of reinforcements. But the Guamare, led by the combative ardor of their leader and his valiant princess, presented themselves on the battlefield, determined to face the challenge and defend their home and honor against the enemy onslaught.

In the strategy of war, time is either an ally or an enemy. The distant chiefdoms, whose reinforcements were slow to arrive, left a gap that the Tarascos, astute in their art of war, hoped to exploit. They estimated it was the opportune moment to attack, knowing that the number of warriors present was fewer than theirs—a numerical advantage they could not afford to miss.

The battle intensified, and amid the fray, Princess Mesmo Pensil stood out at the forefront, under the watchful eye of her father, the great cacique and leader of the Guamare. The fight was fierce, and the warriors, though brave and resilient, began to falter against the overwhelming tide of Tarascos outnumbering them. The hope of the Guamare lay in the prompt arrival of reinforcements from more remote places like Jalostotitlán, San Miguel el Alto, Yahualica, Mezcala, and San Juan de los Lagos, some more than 80 kilometers away.

In a dramatic twist of fate, during an advance of the Tarasca forces, the brave Princess Mesmo Pensil was captured, but not before demonstrating her bravery by killing several enemies. The Tarasca commander, aware of the symbolic and strategic value of the princess, immediately ordered her transfer, knowing that her capture was a devastating blow to the spirit of the Guamare.

In the bloody battle, the capture of Princess Mesmo Pensil emerged as the masterstroke of the Tarascos—a blow they hoped would deeply wound the heart and pride of Tlaloc and the Guamare. The princess, a symbol of the struggle and hope of her people, had been kidnapped in a tactical advance, engulfed in the chaos of a confrontation that left casualties on both sides.

The Tarascos had meticulously planned this strategy, considering the princess not only as a war trophy but also as the soul of the enemy resistance, whose bravery and ingenuity elevated the morale of the Guamare troops. Her capture was not only a strategic triumph but also an effort to demoralize the opposing warriors.

When the allies of the Guamare began to arrive in large numbers, the Tarascos, recognizing the imminent tide change, quickly retreated, ensuring they took the princess with them. Tlaloc, desperate at losing sight of her, launched into a frantic search to rescue his daughter.

The pursuit extended, with Tlaloc and his warriors following the trail of the Tarascos, determined to recover Princess Mesmo Pensil. In a long and exhausting chase, Tlaloc's forces dispersed across the terrain, each driven by urgency and hope to return their princess to the bosom of their community.

The cunning of the Tarascos, in their strategic retreat, disoriented and confronted the Guamare in scattered skirmishes, avoiding large-scale direct confrontations until they finally vanished on the horizon. Tlaloc, weighed down by the absence of hope, returned to Cerro Gordo with the weight of desolation darkening his spirit. However, his resolution did not waver in the face of adversity; he organized two vigorous expeditions, in alliance with the allied chiefdoms that shared the mourning and determination to rescue the beloved princess.

One expedition would focus on gathering intelligence, while the other would be armed with an offensive strategy to attack and recover the princess. Tlaloc, driven by his desperation, ascended to the highest point of Cerro Gordo, from where his gaze reached as far as Lake Chapala, the largest body of water in Mexico, situated between Jalisco and Michoacán, about 60 kilometers away.

From that vantage point, the great cacique Tlaloc, father, and leader consumed by anxiety, remained vigilant day and night. He scrutinized the vast panorama in search of any sign that could indicate the return of the expeditions sent to Michoacán. With hope clung to his heart, he awaited the moment when his eyes would witness the victorious return of his warriors, bringing Princess Mesmo Pensil with them.

Tlaloc, consumed by anguish and longing, remained motionless on the summit of Cerro Gordo, tirelessly watching through the night, hoping that dawn would bring some sign of his daughter. He barely tasted a morsel, only doing so at the insistence of his loyal assistants, who watched over him with growing concern. As the days passed, hope faded, and sadness took deeper root within his being.

Tlaloc wasted away, day after day, languishing not from lack of sustenance, but from the relentless pain of a father. Eventually, his spirit succumbed to sorrow, and his life extinguished on that solitary and elevated lookout, always gazing southeastward, where his beloved daughter Mesmo Pensil had been taken. His love for her was such that it proved more powerful and tenacious than life itself. The news of his death traveled with the speed of the wind, announced by the sounds of conch shells that, with their unique keys, communicated the mournful event to all corners of the territory. Soon, the caciques and their people converged upon Cerro Gordo to pay homage to the fallen great leader. So many came to show their respect and share the mourning that the hill seemed incapable of accommodating all the grieving who arrived.

And so concluded the story of Tlaloc. This tale's painful beauty has endured through generations, serving as a poignant reminder of the depth of paternal love and the unbreakable spirit of the ancient inhabitants of Los Altos de Jalisco.

The departure of Tlaloc, the revered sovereign and leader, marked the beginning of a final journey to his eternal resting place. It was decided, for reasons that escape my knowledge, to transfer his remains to another hill in the vicinity of Arandas. The funeral procession that accompanied his body was of unprecedented magnitude, forming a funeral procession that stretched for kilometers.

According to the traditions and rites of the Nahuas, Tlaloc was buried with honors and respect, accompanied by clay utensils filled with food offerings to sustain him on his journey to the beyond, in accordance with native beliefs. Alongside him, various figures of deities, called "idols" by the ancients, and some precious gold objects were deposited, as narrated in the writings my uncle Silviano had studied.

Although I did not pay due attention to the exact location of the hill mentioned near Arandas where Tlaloc rested, I now feel the call of curiosity and duty to explore those lands of Los Altos de Jalisco to discover the underlying truth in this beautiful land.

And so, concludes the legend of Cerro Gordo, its illustrious inhabitants, the Guamare of Zacatecas, their great chief Tlaloc, and his brave princess Mesmo Pensil. This narrative, bittersweet in its essence, must contain great truth, supported by the written chronicles of the 19th century, which have survived to this day.

The story of our great cacique Tlaloc and his daughter, Princess Xochitl, was preserved in the memory and tales of my uncle Silviano Gutiérrez. Inspired by his passion and divine will, I have dedicated myself to the task of transcribing this legend, in the hope that its reading reveals the cultural richness of my beloved Jalisco to those who approach these pages. The intensity of Tlaloc's love for his daughter was so immense that it transcended life itself, a feeling that he could not bear her departure.

With your respect and permission, I dedicate this legend to my uncle, Silbiano Gutiérrez, from whom I learned not only this moving story, but also many others that form the fabric of our past.

The Guamare Indians of Cerro Gordo

Following the events that marked the history of the Guamare, I cannot affirm if they had more confrontations with the Tarascos of Michoacán. However, what I can assure is that they maintained their bravery and cunning until the arrival of 47 Spanish families from the region of Castile in the year 1703 marked a new chapter. This arrival was the consequence of a grave conflict that took place on the northern slopes of Cerro Gordo, on the route of the Camino Real that led from Guadalajara to Mexico City.

In the heart of the slope of Cerro Gordo, where today the Rancho de San Antonio is located, the renowned Franco family, national champions of charrería, whose fame transcends borders, celebrated both in Mexico and the United States, settled. In the dawn of the 18th century, specifically in 1702, the Guamare still dominated the chiefdom of Cerro Gordo, immovable due to their bravery and sagacity.

The tenacity of the Guamare was such that, unable to be banished by conventional means, it is said that they were victims of a betrayal by the Viceroy of Mexico—a story I promise to narrate later. In response to this conflict, the Viceroy requested help from the King of Spain, Philip V, appointed by France, whose story I will also detail in its moment.

Attending the urgent call, Philip V decided to send a select group of Castilian families, reserved for the most arduous situations. Thus, these 47 families arrived in Los Altos de Jalisco, with their wives and children. To fully understand this episode, we must go back to the origins of Spain, known then as the Iberian Peninsula, and its inhabitants, the Iberians.

CHAPTER 3

The History of Spain and Its Invaders

My fascination with the history of Spain, and particularly Castile, land full of legends and historical facts that still resonate with the presence of the spirits of my ancestors, grows day by day. It is in Burgos where the figure of the immortal hero, Rodrigo Díaz de Vivar, known as El Cid, emerged, whose name became synonymous with bravery and honor in the battles fought against the valiant Moors. His legacy endures in the songs and poems that, over the centuries, have been a hymn to Castilian and Spanish glory.

Spain, like many nations, saw its first inhabitants in nomads and hunters. The oldest evidence of their presence is found in the Altamira caves, prehistoric sanctuaries dating back more than 17,000 years.

These caves, located in northern Spain, near the Cantabrian Sea, and north of the city of León, in what was the ancient kingdom of León, house a rich collection of cave paintings representing felines, wild bulls, bison, and other animals, a testament to the rich cultural heritage that precedes us.

In the vast chronology of primitive art, the Altamira caves in Spain are an essential chapter, with their murals of bison, wild horses, and other animals that, as I mentioned, date back about 17,000 years. But it's not just the Spanish caves that captivate with their relics of the past; in neighboring France, the Lascaux caves boast similar wonders, even older, with approximately 20,000 years of history, according to scientific studies using carbon-14 dating.

In France, since the 19th century, more than twenty caves adorned with ancestral images have been discovered. However, one of the most momentous revelations occurred in 1994, almost like a gift from time, with the discovery of the Chauvet cave. Located in southeastern France, near the borders with Spain and Italy, this cave houses treasures that double the antiquity of those in Altamira and Lascaux.

Amateur explorers found in Chauvet underground chambers full of paintings, engravings, and drawings dating back about 35,000 years. On its walls, more than a dozen species are depicted, including felines represented alongside murals of an astonishing variety of prehistoric life. These findings are a window into the artistic and spiritual expressions of our most distant ancestors.

The Chauvet Cave

The Chauvet cave, named after its discoverer in 1994, stretches about 300 meters and houses an invaluable collection of prehistoric art on its walls. Among the most fascinating representations is the image of a bison, outlined by human palms imprinted in red paint, a technique that highlights its presence in the darkness of the cave. This mural is a testament to the creativity and spiritual connection of our ancestors with the world around them approximately 35,000 years ago.

Within the sacred darkness of Chauvet, figures of mammoths, bison, wild horses, rhinoceroses, leopards, mane lions, elephants, and even the rare appearance of a human figure, make up a total of 73 representations evoking the rich biodiversity of southern Europe at that time.

These discoveries have shed light on the deepest roots of the shared history between Spain and its neighbor France, revealing the oldest and most precious evidence of humanity. Over the millennia, the Iberian Peninsula saw the arrival of the Iberians, extending their influence throughout the region. The Basques, with their distinctive and ancient culture, and later the Celts, who flowed through France, settled in the region a thousand years before Christ.

Furthermore, the Mediterranean coasts were frequently visited by the Phoenicians, who came in search of trade and contact with the diverse peoples of Iberia. These interactions wove the rich fabric of what would eventually be known as Spain.

The history of Spain is an amalgam of cultures and dominions that have left their indelible mark over the centuries. The Carthaginians, sailors and city founders, left their legacy in Barcelona, which today is one of the most vibrant cities in Europe.

With the arrival of the Roman Empire, about 200 years before Christ, Spain entered a new era that would last for approximately 700 years. The Roman influence imbued the peninsula with its language, laws, and architecture, leaving a legacy that would later be assimilated by the Christians.

However, in the year 711 A.D., the Moors crossed from Morocco, initiating a period of conquest and settlement that would change the face of the peninsula. At that time, Islam was already firmly established, having begun with the revelation of Muhammad in the year 610 in Mecca, located in the kingdom of present-day Saudi Arabia. It was then that the Quran, the sacred book of Islam, was codified, and practices such as love and devotion to Allah were established.

Moors, Christians, and My Ancestors

Continuing with the historical narrative about the Moorish and Muslim presence in the Iberian Peninsula, I resume the thread from times when, long before the 12th century, intense battles were waged between Moors and Christians. Castile, along with other kingdoms like Aragon, Navarre, León, and Asturias, which would later join León, faced the Moors with tenacity from the first military contacts.

The Moors, crossing the Mediterranean, invaded the south and east of Spain, driven by a fervent desire for territorial expansion. The bloody struggles did not diminish the valor of the Christian kingdoms, which defended their land with exemplary bravery. Over time and the vicissitudes of history, as you will see, the Moors were eventually expelled by the Castilians and their allies.

Despite the Moors having an extensive nation and a flourishing civilization, their ambition for more territory was not satisfied, despite nearly 800 years of presence on the peninsula, sometimes insisting by force. However, during the long period they lasted in Spain, the Moors left an indelible mark on the culture, architecture, science, and gastronomy, a legacy that endures to this day, enriching the historical and cultural heritage of Spain.

The Moorish Cultural Splendor and the Ancestry of My Ancestors

The presence of the Moors on the Iberian Peninsula left a legacy of an elegant and advanced culture, contributing their refined mathematics and acting as a channel for the reintroduction of Greek knowledge into Spain and, by extension, into Europe. Their marvelous architecture continues to be a source of admiration. It was in this context that, in the 12th century, the Christians intensified their campaign to expel the Moors, forming powerful armies composed of select and well-trained warriors. The battles that were fought were fierce and challenging.

It is in these confrontations where, without fear of being mistaken, I perceive the presence of my ancestors fighting in the fearsome battles alongside the immortal and famous Cid, Rodrigo Díaz de

Vivar. Speaking of the Cid, I sense a great interest in you in knowing the life of this hero, for I feel that my roots, from those times when the Cid lived, are intertwined with the struggle for the expulsion of the valiant Moors.

My ancestors, settled in Castile, lived near the nobility, sharing life and battles with figures like the Cid, and were involved in the armies of the century of the 'Ghosts,' a nickname given by the Moors to the Christians due to the way the Cid and his army attacked, with strategies that reflected their determination and audacity.

Chapter 4

El Cid, The Champion

Rodrigo Díaz, known as El Cid, was not only a legendary hero but also a historical figure whose life inspired "El Cantar de Mio Cid," an epic poem narrating his feats. He was characterized by a noble spirit and unwavering loyalty to the royal family, as well as by his religious fervor, which set him apart from his contemporaries.

Born in a village near Burgos around the year 1040, the son of a Castilian noble and linked to the high nobility through his maternal line, El Cid grew up under the influence of King Sancho II, known for his nobility towards his subjects but implacable in the fight against the Moors. His reign began in 1038, and two years later, he witnessed the birth of who would become a great leader and warrior, an unparalleled swordsman, and supreme champion among all the defenders of Castile.

From an early age, El Cid demonstrated his worth in battle, especially in a crucial confrontation against the Moors in Zaragoza, where he stood out as the best among all. In the heat of the fight, the Moors were often taken by surprise by his speed and strategy; he was like lightning, a ghost with incredible reflexes that instilled fear in the hearts of his enemies.

Liborio Gutierrez on His Horse!

El Cid, The Warrior and the Lineage of My Ancestors

Rodrigo Díaz, known as El Cid, was a man of tall stature and notable strength, whose skill in combat was unparalleled. His intelligence in battle was complemented by his ability to wear light armor, which did not hinder his mobility, and his horse, equally trained to confront the intensity of armed clashes, defended itself with the same cunning and bravery as its rider.

The Moors nicknamed him "The Ghost" due to his capacity to attack from unexpected angles, causing significant losses and demoralizing their ranks. This is the historical moment when my ancestors begin to emerge. Logic leads me to this conclusion, as it is from Castile where my roots originate.

The great King Sancho II proudly observed the feats of El Cid, but after a fierce battle in Zaragoza in 1072, the monarch's life came to a tragic end. After this event, El Cid entered the service of the new king, Alfonso VI, known as 'The Wise,' in 1081. Rodrigo Díaz de Vivar proved on numerous occasions to be the supreme swordsman, consolidating his honor and glory.

Later, in a crucial battle for the conquest of Valencia in 1094, a city strongly defended by the Moors, El Cid demonstrated his skill and bravery in capturing the fortress, adding another chapter to his already legendary reputation.

El Cid, whose name will resonate forever in the annals of history, led his ghost army from victory to victory, showcasing his expertise in the art of war. However, in a battle in 1097, surrounded by a relentless tide of Moors, he met his fate. An arrow, shot with deadly precision, found the only unarmored spot on his left flank, wounding his heart. Despite efforts to save him, the wound was fatal, but his legend as an immortal hero beloved by his people endures. Rodrigo Díaz de Vivar, El Cid, was enshrined as the hero of a hundred battles, an eternal symbol of valor and honor.

More than a century later, in the 13th century, Castile saw the ascension of Alfonso X to the throne, a king no less great and intelligent, whose reign began in 1252 and culminated in 1284. He was succeeded on the throne, in the 14th century, by Don Juan Manuel, a king of distinguished lineage, nephew of Alfonso X and descendant of Saint Dominic of Guzmán.

Before the ascension of Don Juan Manuel, the 13th century witnessed a significant event: in 1215, Saint Dominic of Guzmán founded the Order of Preachers, known as the Dominicans, a fraternity dedicated to teaching and preaching, and which left a deep imprint on the religion and society of Europe at the time.

Saint Dominic of Guzmán and the Holy Inquisition

In the 15th century, specifically in 1478, the Holy Inquisition was established, an organization that by contemporary standards, sought to intensify the process of expelling Jews and Muslims from the Iberian Peninsula. The Christian kingdoms, in their mission to reconquer the Iberian Peninsula—then known as Iberia or Hispania—began to redouble their efforts in the mid-15th century. The Muslims, who had been settled in the region for approximately 750 years, since the year 710, found themselves increasingly pressured by the growing Christian influence.

The turning point in this dynamic came with the marriage of Ferdinand of Aragon and Isabella the Catholic of Castile in 1469, a union which consolidated what became known as the union of Christian kingdoms. This alliance was crucial for the reconquest and the subsequent formation of Spain as a nation.

It was under the reign of these Catholic Monarchs that the Inquisition was established in 1478, appointing Tomás de Torquemada as the General Inquisitor, who was born in 1420 and died in 1498, and not in 1478 as mentioned in the original text. During the twenty years he wielded his power, Torquemada was feared by both Jews and Muslims, carrying out a harsh and controversial persecution of those who refused to convert to Christianity.

The Reconquest of Spain

The Reconquest of Spain was a time when exceptional armies were forged, composed of brave and meticulously trained men and women, as confrontations with the Moors were characterized by being particularly fierce and generating numerous casualties. In this wartime context, my Castilian ancestors emerged, who's cunning and bravery were indispensable in the fight. There was no doubt that the blood of those ancestors still lived in the veins of those who, generation after generation, remained immersed in the nobility and armies due to their innate warlike disposition.

These families never withdrew from the Kingdom of Castile, reflecting an unbreakable caste. As the saying goes: "From tigers come spots," indicating that the offspring reflect the qualities of their predecessors. Thus, successive generations maintained their status and were possibly very involved in the nobility. This is the reason why, in 1703, King Philip V of Anjou sent 47 families of his trust to resolve a major problem that had arisen in my region, Los Altos de Jalisco. The evidence of their legacy still resonates in the region, and I will unveil it little by little, as I have extended myself a bit beyond the 15th century.

Emblematic Figures of the Reconquest and the Lineage of My Ancestors

In the context of the stern Inquisition established in Spain, the great General Inquisitor Tomás de Torquemada stood out for his relentless attitude towards Moors and Jews. Alongside him, another figure of great military relevance was Gonzalo de Córdoba, known as the Great Captain, who reformed combat tactics and consolidated the formidable Spanish infantry, which became the queen of the battlefields.

My ancestors, guided by the logic of their bravery and passion for victory, were undoubtedly present in these combats, fighting with the firmness of those who are willing to triumph or die. In their private lives, they were leaders faithful to their beliefs, humble in their daily life, and obedient only to their superiors: God and the King were their unconditional symbols.

Throughout the centuries, the cunning and bravery of figures like Rodrigo Díaz de Vivar, El Cid, were inherited and refined by their descendants, keeping alive the flame of warrior nobility. Over time, although the memory of the colonization of Los Altos de Jalisco became dispersed, what remained unaltered in my ancestors was the internal fire, the bravery, and the warrior ardor that they carried in their blood.

The Humility and Valor of My Ancestors and Their Foray into History

My ancestors were always characterized by their intrinsic humility and joyful nature, enjoying the wonders created by God on Earth. And, if any circumstance threatened their happiness, they did not hesitate to act to restore normality.

Returning to the 15th century with Gonzalo de Córdoba, known as the Great Captain, he formed a formidable army that, victory after victory, pushed the Moors towards the south of Spain. Concurrently, Jews began to migrate to Morocco, seeking refuge from the growing hostility.

The infamous General Torquemada, in 1492, presented an ultimatum to the Jews: leave Spain, convert to Catholicism, or face death. Despite a brief reprieve of nine days for deliberation, the weight of their decision loomed heavy.

In that crucial year, the figure of Christopher Columbus also emerged, supported by Queen Isabella the Catholic. Columbus, coming from an exhausting struggle to validate his theory about a new route to the Indies, finally obtained the necessary backing for his expedition.

Christopher Columbus and His Quest for Support

There is a theory that Christopher Columbus, born around 1451 in Genoa, Italy, had Jewish ancestry. His father, Domingo Colón, is a lesser-known figure in the vast narrative of the discoverer. However, the life of Christopher Columbus and his journey into the unknown would mark a before and after in world history.

Christopher Columbus, the son of Domingo Colón and Susanna Fontana Rossa, and the brother of Bartholomew and Diego, was immersed in the task of convincing some European power about the viability of a new route to India. Initially, he tried to gain the support of Spain but encountered the indifference of the Catholic Monarchs, who were focused on resolving the matter of expelling the Moors from Spanish territory, a project led by the Great Captain, Gonzalo de Córdoba, whose invincible army was triumphantly advancing in the Reconquest.

Seeing the lack of interest in Spain, Columbus decided to take his proposal to Portugal, where King John II reigned. Fortunately, he managed to secure an interview with the monarch, who offered him some hope, though without firm commitments. During this period of uncertainty and while awaiting a decision from the Portuguese king, Columbus met a beautiful woman named Felipa Moniz de Perestrelo. The navigator fell in love and married her, starting a new stage in his personal life.

Christopher Columbus and the Genesis of His Journey

After marrying Felipa Moniz de Perestrelo, Christopher Columbus settled for a time on the island of Porto Santo. Later, he lived on the island of Madeira, where his marriage bore fruit with the birth of his son Diego, whom he named after his brother.

Disappointed by the lack of support from King John II of Portugal for his expeditionary plans, Columbus returned to Spain in search of a new opportunity with the Catholic Monarchs. There, he met Beatriz Enríquez de Arana, with whom he also had a son, baptized Fernando, in a gesture that reflected his cunning and perhaps a subtle strategy to win royal favor.

His persistence bore fruit when he finally managed to get an audience with the Spanish sovereigns. Although he initially did not convince the monarchs, Queen Isabella, after thoroughly studying his proposal, became convinced of the potential of Columbus's plan. Days later, Isabel called Columbus again to agree to financially support the project. In an act of faith in the ambitious plan, the queen sold almost all her jewels to finance the expedition.

When everything was ready, Isabel sent for Columbus to order him to prepare for the great enterprise that lay ahead.

Organizing Columbus's Historic Mission

Christopher Columbus, in his meticulous task of organizing the planned mission, obtained the necessary caravels for his expedition. One of them was named La Niña and the other, La Pinta. The owners finally agreed to participate in the enterprise after being convinced of the advantages and benefits the expedition promised. These caravels, although not distinguished by their size or speed, sailed at an average of 10 kilometers per hour, sufficient for the planned voyage.

Columbus's plan required a third caravel, leading him on a search through various ports until he arrived in Galicia. There he met Juan de la Cosa, a Basque passionate about adventure and owner of a robust ship he had built in a Galician port. Juan de la Cosa, known for his solvency and skill, had designed his ship to face the open sea and the harshness of navigation.

Juan de la Cosa's vessel was christened La Santa María, but it was also known as La Gallega. With a capacity to reach speeds of up to 16.5 kilometers per hour, it was a valuable addition to the fleet. Juan de la Cosa was not only the owner but would also serve as captain of his ship.

Once the agreements were in place and everything was ready, the expedition was set to embark on one of the greatest adventures of the 15th century. Christopher Columbus, ready to start his great voyage, was not satisfied with the name of his ship, La Marigalante. After an agreement with Juan de la Cosa, they decided to rename it La Santa María. With the ships prepared and the crew aboard, they set sail on August 3, 1492, from the port of Palos, located at the mouth of the Tinto River, venturing westward into the vast expanse of the Mediterranean.

On their voyage, they encountered a flotilla of 25 ships transporting Jews expelled from Spain, who, crossing the Mediterranean to Morocco, sang jubilantly at the new hope offered by the Moroccans, providing them asylum. The number of Jews was considerable, adding to those who had already crossed earlier, which explains the notable Spanish-speaking community in Morocco today.

Later on, Columbus's expedition crossed paths with a corsair known as Pedro Cabrón, who was sailing east in the Mediterranean. His reputation was such that his name became immortalized in popular lexicon, especially in Mexico, where "cabrón" has evolved to become a colloquial expression with negative connotations.

The Dawn of America: Columbus's First Voyage

After sailing for several days, Christopher Columbus's expedition reached its first stop: the Canary Islands. There, on the island of El Hierro, they experienced a setback when one of the caravels suffered damage. After a month dedicated to repairs, they resumed their westward course, following parallel 28. Uncertainty about finding land led Columbus to adjust his route slightly southwest.

On October 12, 1492, an exciting shout resonated in the air: "Land! Land!" The island visible on the horizon was known to the natives as Guanahani, in the archipelago of the Lucayas, now the Bahamas. Columbus, upon setting foot on this land, named it San Salvador, thus marking the beginning of a series of discoveries.

Subsequently, the expedition headed towards Cuba, arriving on October 27. After exploring the coasts of Cuba and Hispaniola (now Haiti and the Dominican Republic), Columbus returned to Spain. He was received with great joy and presented tangible evidence of his discoveries. He even brought with him a native, whom he mistakenly called an Indian, believing he had reached the Indies as per his original plan. This mistake led to the use of the term "Indian" to refer to the original inhabitants of the American continent, a term that, although incorrect, has persisted to this day in the region's name: America.

Christopher Columbus and the Post-Discovery Challenges

After his historic arrival in America, Christopher Columbus found that the news of a New World had aroused the interest of European powers such as France, England, and Portugal, which quickly embarked on exploration and conquest.

Columbus made several trips to the New World. He left his brothers, Diego and Bartholomew, in charge of the explored territories. Despite King Ferdinand's promise to grant him a viceroyalty, Columbus faced difficulties in settling in the discovered lands due to disagreements and tensions with his subordinates, exacerbated by his irascible character and sometimes inconsiderate behavior.

Later, he chose to support his brothers in managing the jurisdictions granted over the newly conquered territories.

On his last trip, and back in Spain in 1506, Columbus followed King Ferdinand to Valladolid. It was in this city where, plagued by illnesses that worsened over time, he spent his last days. He died at the age of 55, in solitude, poverty, and bitterness, without realizing that he had not found a new route to India but had discovered an unknown continent. He died believing his voyages had been extensions of Asia, not recognizing the magnitude of his discovery.

Christopher Columbus and the Naming of the New Continent

Christopher Columbus, after his transoceanic voyages, did not live to see the New World named in his honor. In his conviction, he never wavered from the idea that he had found a new route to India. For this reason, and due to the circumstances of his death, the continent was not initially named after him. It was later that a nation in the south of the American continent was named Colombia, changing the original name of New Granada.

America, on the other hand, received its name from Amerigo Vespucci, another Italian explorer. Vespucci was born in 1454 and died in 1512 at the age of 58. From 1497, during his own expeditions, Vespucci became convinced and managed to convince others that the lands found constituted a continent unknown until then by Europe. A German cartographer named Martin Waldseemüller, in 1507, accepted the idea that Vespucci had discovered the new continent and, therefore, used the name America on one of his maps, giving rise to the denomination we know today.

This account is a part of the story of Christopher Columbus and the subsequent conquest of America, an extensive narrative that contains countless events and anecdotes. My intention is not to elaborate on every detail of the conquest but to continue with the historical narrative in the context of the 16th century, while also acknowledging the relevance of my ancestors in the fabric of our history.

The Mosaic of Peoples of the Iberian Peninsula and the Emergence of the Hispanic Kingdoms

In the north of present-day Spain, long before the Muslim invasion from Morocco, kingdoms formed by peoples already settled in the region, then known as Iberia, and their inhabitants were called Iberians. The Iberian Peninsula, the cradle of various peoples, saw its first significant settlement in the north with the Basques, whose ancestral presence leaves no clear evidence of their arrival in the region.

The Celts, crossing France, migrated in large numbers to the peninsula. To these were added the Phoenicians, natural traders who frequented the ports of the Mediterranean. We cannot forget the Carthaginians, who, 200 years before Christ, established their presence in part of the nation.

With the fall of Spain under Roman rule, more than 700 years of Roman influence ensued, during which creole families were formed that would never return to Rome. It was after the Visigoths expelled the Romans, in the 5th century, that the kingdoms in the north of Spain really began to take shape. History tells us that the Visigoths, once they displaced the Romans, were assimilated by the Christianized peoples of the peninsula.

The Christian Kingdoms and the Reconquest

With the decline of Visigothic rule, various Christian kingdoms consolidated on the Iberian Peninsula, which, with increasing power, began to establish their domains and reaffirm their influence in the region. Two centuries later, the Moors crossed from Morocco and conquered the Visigoths. This event marked the beginning of a long and complex struggle between Moors and Christians. The Moors aspired to conquer all of Spain, intending to displace the Christians in the north and take over the entire nation.

The Christian kingdoms, aware of the threat, quickly responded to the invasion. In particular, the Kingdom of Castile, strongly backed by France and supported by other peninsular kingdoms such as Asturias, Leon, Navarre, and Aragon, began to receive military reinforcements from its allies. France, considering Castile a brother kingdom, sent soldiers specialized in large numbers to initiate the offensive that would seek the expulsion of the Moors.

The migration of French and other Europeans from the south to the north of the Iberian Peninsula was notable during this period. Later, in the 16th century, nations from central Europe, such as Germany, Austria, and even England, joined the cause and contributed to the fight that Castile and the coalition of Christian kingdoms were waging. This confluence of support and resources was decisive for the development and success of the Reconquista.

European Unification Through Emigration and Royal Marriages

The 16th-century emigration to the Iberian Peninsula was not coincidental but a reflection of the power of the Union of Spanish Kingdoms. With their formidable armies, they succeeded in expelling the Moors, culminating in 1492 with the surrender of the last Muslim stronghold in Granada. This migration was driven by strategic alliances through royal marriages, fostering a rich blend of blood and culture among various European nations.

Particularly, England adopted a significant Latin influence in its language, with a notable contribution from Spanish. This cultural and linguistic exchange was intensified by the marital union between the crowns of England and Spain, exemplifying the connection between the two nations.

The result of these marriages and the emigration of Europeans to Spain led to the creation of a cosmopolitan nation that lasted for many years. Surnames adapted and evolved: some took Spanish forms, while others extended. For example, 'Martín del Campo' added 'del Campo' to a common surname, and 'De la Tour' from France transformed into 'De la Torre'. 'Franco' is a surname of clear provenance, resonating in both France and Germany and finding its place in Spain.

Juana of Castile and the Hispanic Dynastic

Continuing the narrative with the history of my ancestors, whose lineage extends to Los Altos de Jalisco in Mexico, it's essential to mention the legacy of the Catholic Monarchs. Following their union in 1469, Princess Juana was born, known for her beauty and royal lineage. In the 1490s, Juana married Philip, the Archduke of Austria and Prince of the German lands, son of Emperor Maximilian.

This marriage, celebrated with great splendor, soon faced difficulties. Philip, known as "the Handsome" for his physical attractiveness, was besieged by the attention of many ladies. His inability to reject such attentions caused deep emotional instability in Juana, whose love for Philip transformed into jealous hysteria, sometimes resulting in intense episodes.

This union was significant not just for personal repercussions but also for its political and dynastic impact, marking the beginning of a new era in Spanish history and, by extension, in that of Europe and the New World.

Juana the Mad and the Tragedy of a Royal Love

The story of Juana, later known as "La Loca" (The Mad), is a tale of love and tragedy. Her marriage to Philip the Handsome was marked by passion and controversy. From this union, a son was born in Ghent in February 1500, a boy who would carry the legacy of two crowns: Spain and the Holy Roman Empire. Named Charles, he would become one of the most prominent monarchs in European history.

Philip, enchanted by feminine beauty and oblivious to his future duties as heir to the Spanish kingdoms and his father Maximilian I's empire, succumbed to the charms of his admirers, neglecting his wife's needs. Philip's infidelity and inability to reject other women drove Juana to a state of sickly jealousy.

Philip's licentious behavior eventually cost him his life, dying young from a venereal disease, without having taken advantage of the opportunity to reign. Juana, sunk in despair and madness, died shortly after, leaving her young son orphaned and under the care of her parents, the Catholic Monarchs, Fernando and Isabel, regents of Spain and the vast German empire.

The Consolidation of an Empire and the End of the Reconquest

In times of discoveries and conquests, the New World began to reveal its riches, and galleons crossed the Atlantic loaded with gold and silver to Spain. These newfound treasures began to fill the royal coffers, heralding an era of unprecedented splendor and power for the kingdom.

Meanwhile, a promising future was brewing with young Charles, heir to the grand legacy of the Catholic Monarchs. However, in the peninsula, a chapter in Spanish history persisted: the famed Granada. This last stronghold, ignored for a time in the fervor of overseas riches, remained firm in the south, between Malaga and Almeria, on the shores of the Mediterranean.

It was in 1503 that the definitive decision was made to expel the valiant Moors. The invincible armies of Castile now reinforced both in numbers and economy, perhaps even with silver armors reflecting the abundance of the New World, managed to liberate Granada from Moorish presence.

Just a year later, in 1504, Queen Isabel the Catholic died, leaving a void on the throne and in the heart of Spain. King Fernando continued his royal duties, facing the challenge of governing a kingdom in mourning but harboring hope in his grandson Carlos, who would soon become the symbol of the unification and expansion of the Spanish empire.

Hernán Cortés and the Call of the New World

In 16th-century Spain, amidst apparent peace, a movement of exploration and conquest began to stir, fueled by the riches arriving from the New World. Ships laden with precious metals ignited the imagination and adventurous spirit of Europeans. Among them was a young man of noble birth and strong character named Hernán Cortés, poised to make his mark in history.

Hernán, son of Martín Cortés, initially pursued ecclesiastical studies at his father's behest. However, the lure of adventure and fascination with the newly discovered lands in America proved stronger than his contemplative life. Around 1510, driven by unstoppable impulse and without formally bidding farewell to his family, he embarked for Cuba, eyeing unknown opportunities and horizons.

Hernán Cortés: The Conquistador

In Cuba, Hernán, seeking purpose and fortune, became a key figure in the conquest enterprise. Attracted by rumors of lands beyond, rich in wealth and ancient civilizations, he quickly became integral to the Spanish Crown's efforts to conquer and establish new cities.

Hernán Cortés' Arrival in Cuba

Upon arriving in Cuba, Hernán found an essential ally in Diego Velázquez de Cuéllar, the commander of the island's conquest and his future relative. Velázquez enthusiastically welcomed the newcomer, who quickly integrated into the conquistadors' ranks. Hernán and Diego's relationship strengthened when Hernán married Diego's sister, forging family ties that seemed unbreakable for a time.

Together, in 1511, Diego and Hernán completed the conquest of Cuba. However, the brutal treatment of the native Indians, forced into labor and killed if resistant, began to cast a dark shadow over Velázquez's achievements.

By 1515, Diego Velázquez was appointed Cuba's first governor. Yet, tensions arose between Cortés and his brother-in-law, strained by disagreements and hardened hearts due to greed. Discontented and estranged from his wife, Hernán decided to part ways with both his political family and Diego.

Fatefully, these tensions led Cortés to a new mission. Diego Velázquez tasked him with exploring Mexico in search of gold. In 1517, yearning for redemption and wealth, Hernán Cortés set sail for the unknown, landing at Cape Catoche and beginning one of the most momentous adventures in the New World's history.

Crucial Encounters in Yucatán

On the Yucatán Peninsula, Cortés met two Spanish castaways assimilated into the local culture. One was the priest Jerónimo de Aguilar, who, after a shipwreck years earlier, had learned the Maya language. The other was Gonzalo Guerrero, who had started a family with a Maya woman and chosen to live as part of the indigenous community.

Aguilar joined Cortés's expedition, invaluable as an interpreter due to his knowledge of Maya. Symbolically and practically, Aguilar served as a bridge between the conquerors and the original inhabitants.

The Mayas gifted Cortés a slave, Malintzin, also known as Malinche, of Nahuatl origin but given to the Mayas. Like Aguilar, she spoke two languages. Her intelligence and linguistic skill became key in communication between Cortés and various indigenous peoples. Recognizing her importance, Cortés baptized her as Doña Marina.

This linguistic trio, with Aguilar and Malintzin as interpreters, allowed Cortés to advance his conquest. Doña Marina became central in the encounters between the Spanish and Mexicas, playing a crucial role in the fall of Tenochtitlán, the great city of the Mexica empire.

The Communication and Alliance Strategy

Effective communication was essential in Hernán Cortés's expedition. Doña Marina, also known as Malintzin, became Cortés's voice, translating Nahuatl to Maya for Jerónimo de Aguilar, who then translated it to Spanish. This interpretation system was a crucial cog in the conquest.

After returning to Cuba, Cortés planned his strategy for the conquest of Tenochtitlán, the imposing city of Mexico. Rumored to be originally gifted to one of Cortés's captains, Doña Marina's role as an interpreter and advisor became indispensable to Cortés, who took her under his direct protection.

The expedition resumed, and in route to Tenochtitlán, they passed Orizaba, Mexico's highest peak, and arrived at Tlaxcala. There, Cortés forged an alliance with the Tlaxcaltecs, natural enemies of the Mexicas. Doña Marina was instrumental in these negotiations, facilitating communication and strategic connections.

The next stop was Cholula, a significant Nahuatl religious center, where distrust of the Spanish was evident. It was in Cholula that Doña Marina acquired the nickname "La Malinche," which over time became synonymous with betrayal for some and adaptability and survival for others. Her intermediary role was key to Cortés's interests, firmly establishing her as a central figure in the events leading to the fall of Tenochtitlán.

The Encounter in Tenochtitlán and the Sad Night

History narrates that upon arriving in Tenochtitlan in 1519, Hernán Cortés and his men were met with a mix of reverence and suspicion. Moctezuma II, the powerful Mexica tlatoani, extended hospitality to the foreigners, though a current of discontent and suspicion grew among his people.

The Spanish, with their fair skin and thick beards, riding their imposing horses, were initially seen by some Aztecs as emissaries of deities, mistaking the horse-rider duo as a single divine entity. However, this perception soon faded. Anticipating possible intentions to return to Cuba by his captains, Cortés ordered the burning of the ships in Veracruz, committing his troops to the conquest.

Tensions in Tenochtitlan escalated to a burst of violence when Moctezuma attempted to pacify his people and was fatally wounded by his own subjects. His death cleared the way for Cuauhtémoc to assume leadership and challenge Spanish rule.

The situation became untenable, and the conquistadors faced the fury of the Aztecs in a battle that would be known as the Sad Night. Hernán Cortés and his men barely escaped the city in a critical moment that nearly ended in their total defeat.

The Sad Night and the Reconquest of Tenochtitlan

History is tinged with melancholy when narrating the legendary Sad Night, where Hernán Cortés, defeated and humiliated, found refuge under the branches of an ahuehuete tree. That night, the tears of the conqueror mixed with the rain, symbolizing the bitterness of a forced retreat from the great Tenochtitlan.

With urgency marking his destiny, Cortés sought the support of his Tlaxcalteca allies, eternal adversaries of the Aztecs. In an act of strengthening bonds and military strategy, a plan for reconquest was drawn up, beginning with the acquisition of sulfur from the heights of Popocatépetl. The volcano, imposing and serene, stood as a natural fortress surpassing five thousand meters in height. The mission of the conquerors was not simple, but the precious mineral was obtained, essential for the manufacture of gunpowder for their arquebuses.

Finally, well-supplied and with renewed vigor, Cortés and his men positioned themselves on the shores of Lake Texcoco. Before them, Tenochtitlan rose on an island, the nerve center of Aztec power. It was time to begin the siege that would define the future of the valley and its inhabitants. The Aztecs, now under the leadership of Cuauhtémoc, prepared to defend their city against the imminent Spanish siege.

The Conquest of Tenochtitlan and the Birth of Mexico City

The siege that Hernán Cortés imposed on Tenochtitlan lasted an unusual 72 days, a period that stands out in the annals of history for its extensive duration. The tenacity of the Aztec resistance and the determination of the conquistadors collided in an unparalleled confrontation. Cuauhtémoc, the last tlatoani, attempted to evade the encirclement in a swift boat, steered by expert rowers, but Cortés, with his military inventiveness, had prepared a flotilla of light boats to ensure the blockade.

The capture of Cuauhtémoc marked the end of the Aztec resistance and in 1521, Cortés victoriously entered the city of Tenochtitlan. Then began the foundation of Mexico City, built upon the foundations of a fallen civilization. The grand pyramids were demolished to make way for symbols of Spanish dominion: the Metropolitan Cathedral, the Viceregal Palace, the Bishopric, and various monasteries. Thus, the imposing Presidential Palace and the vast square known as the Zócalo were erected, marking the beginning of the viceroyalty with Don Antonio de Mendoza at the helm.

In his first shipment to Spain, Cortés included an unprecedented treasure, highlighting among its riches two gold necklaces, one embellished with 185 emeralds and the other with 172, reflecting the opulence of the conquered lands. This was Spain's strategy to appropriate the treasures of the New World: extraction, marking, and shipment of gold to the metropolis.

Shortly thereafter, Cortés's personal life took a new turn as he became a father, marking another chapter in his legacy.

Hernán Cortés and the Birth of Martín Cortés

From the union of Hernán Cortés with Doña Marina, known as La Malinche, a son was born whom they baptized as Martín Cortés, in honor of Hernán's father. This birth is inscribed as a key event in the narrative of the Conqueror of Mexico's life.

Now, returning to the Iberian Peninsula and going back in time to around 1510 when Hernán Cortés embarked for Mexico, and advancing about five years, we encounter another crucial event in world history that occurred shortly before the death of King Fernando of Spain, which I will mention shortly. In the year 1515, a young German monk of the Order of Saint Augustine visited Pope Leo X in Rome, who at that time was Leo X. However, this young German monk did not like what he saw.

Martin Luther

Although Martin Luther is not directly part of Spain's history, his influence resonates worldwide, including Spain. Luther, born in 1483 and dying in 1546, entered university in 1501 at his father's will but abandoned it in 1505 to enter an Augustinian monastery. He was ordained a priest in 1507 and by 1512 was already a professor of Theology.

Martin Luther and the Criticism of Indulgences

Martin Luther, endowed with vast culture and a doctorate in Theology, made a critical visit to Pope Leo X in 1517. He was deeply displeased that the Pope was selling indulgences to finance the construction of St. Peter's Basilica. This act seemed to him a manifestation that salvation was being offered easily to the rich, something he strongly questioned upon returning to Germany. He considered such a practice a serious error that did not reflect the essence of the Church of Jesus Christ, which, in his opinion, should remain pure in its commandments and teachings, as Christ had left them through the gospels and his disciples.

Luther held the belief that the Church of Christ would inherently remain pure, despite some of its representatives trying to distort its teachings. History shows that, from its beginning with Saint Peter, considered the first Pope, the Church has walked with its successive Popes constantly facing the influences of evil. Evidence of this struggle is reflected in the approximately thirty antipopes that have arisen throughout history. The first of them was Hippolytus in the year 217, marking the beginning of a series of internal challenges that the Catholic Church would face.

The last recognized antipope, recorded in 1439, was Felix V. Since then, there have been no more recognized antipopes. Leo X occupied the papacy from 1513 to 1520 and, although his proposal of indulgences for the financing of St. Peter's Basilica may have been misdirected, his intention was to honorably dignify Saint Peter with a symbolic and splendid monument. There might have been more suitable alternatives to gather the necessary resources without resorting to indulgences, although this would have meant more time to complete the work.

On the other hand, Martin Luther expressed his firmness and discontent when Pope Leo X rejected his 95 theses, which he had nailed to the doors of the church in Wittenberg in 1517. After 13 years of searching without finding a solution that would alleviate his displeasure with the practices of the Church, Luther initiated a protest that would lead to a schism with the Catholic Church. This rupture was consolidated after the death of Leo X in 1522, and during the brief papacy of Adrian VI, who ruled between 1522 and 1523 and was the last non-Italian Pope to date, being of Spanish origin.

Till date, we have witnessed the influence of Pope John Paul II and, going back in time, after the death of Adrian VI in the same year of his ascent to the papacy, Clement VII was appointed, whose pontificate extended until 1534. During his mandate, in the year 1530, Martin Luther starred in one of the most significant religious events of the era by forming the new current of Lutheranism, whose followers initially called themselves Lutherans and later opted for the term Evangelicals.

Soon, other figures of the Reformation emerged, such as John Calvin and the English reformer Thomas Cranmer. In response to these movements, figures of the Counter-Reformation emerged, among them Saint Ignatius of Loyola, who made a vital contribution in this period between 1545 and 1563. Previously, in 1534, he founded the Society of Jesus, better known as the Jesuits. Alfonso Maria de Ligorio, another important Counter-Reformer and Catholic philosopher, played a crucial role until his death in 1787, contributing to the Catholic Church's response to the religious explosion caused by the Reformation.

The Emergence of Martin Luther

With the emergence of Martin Luther, various Christian denominations began to arise, such as the Evangelicals, who branched off from the Lutherans. From the latter, the Anglicans emerged, and in turn, from them came the Methodists. Later, from Methodism came the Salvation Army and the Pentecostal movement, distinguished by emphasizing the lived experience of the day of Pentecost, where, according to tradition, the apostle Saint Peter spoke in unknown tongues. This movement strongly believes in the gifts of the Holy Spirit, including the healing of the sick.

On the other hand, the Seventh-day Adventists advocate the observance of Saturday instead of Sunday, awaiting the imminent return of Christ.

Over time, the number of Christian denominations has increased considerably, today counting more than 1500. Each of them claims to be the reflection of the true church of Christ. Although they diverge in certain doctrines and practices, most share the fundamental belief in Christ. However, some of these denominations tend to overlook the figure of Mary, the mother of Christ, which raises varied opinions among the faithful. Nevertheless, it is not my place to judge this religious revival, but it is a subject open to reflection and respect for each believer.

Maria de Jesus and Her Influence on Christianity

In this theological debate, some criticize and seek to diminish the importance of Mary, questioning God's ability to grant her the power to intercede for humanity and perform miracles. Asserting that Mary was a human woman, just like any other, overlooks the fact that she was chosen by God for a divine mission. It was through the announcement of the Archangel Gabriel that she knew she would be the mother of the Son of God, conceived by the Holy Spirit. Mary accompanied Jesus from his infancy, sharing in the sufferings and persecutions, until the moment Jesus gave his life for the redemption of humanity. She witnessed Jesus's sufferings, his flagellation, his painful march to Calvary, and his agony on the cross. Mary's powerlessness in seeing her son subjected to such extreme suffering and being unable to alleviate his pain tore at her heart.

Yet, Mary remained steadfast in her faith and commitment, an example of resignation and strength in the face of adversity. Her role was not only to be the mother of Jesus on earth but also to become a symbol of hope and comfort for many believers. Therefore, to question her relevance in faith is to overlook her uniqueness as the mother of God and her perpetual influence in the history of salvation. In heaven, Mary understood that all that sacrifice was necessary for the salvation of humanity and for God the Father to forgive our sins. By her special role as the mother of Christ and by divine will, she was endowed with singular privileges. According to Catholic beliefs, by the disposition of the Father and His Son, Mary was assumed into heaven in body and soul, an event celebrated in the Church on August 15, known as the Assumption of the Virgin Mary.

With the consent and love of God and Jesus Christ, Mary has dedicated herself to helping and protecting humanity, appearing on numerous occasions in different parts of the world. In each appearance, she insists on the importance of kindness and love, interceding for us before her son and asking for compassion to stop the punishment, distressed to see that many stray from the righteous path. Mary, in her infinite maternal concern, observes how each day, unfortunately, souls are lost and fervently wishes that humanity finds redemption and peace.

The Apparitions of Mary

In these times, the apparitions of Mary are more frequent, a call to kindness and the correction of our actions, warning about the consequences faced by those who choose the wrong path. Mary, whose knowledge of justice is surpassed by her unconditional motherly love, offers us immense love, and it is this love that I wish to highlight in these lines, based on my personal experience.

I have had the opportunity to attend several of her apparitions in California, USA, and have witnessed her presence in Santa Maria, California, since 1987. I have heard with my own ears and seen with my own eyes various miracles that have reaffirmed my faith in Mary. Each year, at the convention held on the last weekend of March, the local government provides several high school auditoriums for the event, culminating with a mass on Sunday at 5 p.m. to close the convention.

After the mass, as a token of gratitude, it is said that the Virgin gifts us a miracle with the sun. Everyone goes out to contemplate it as it begins to 'dance' and change colors. The first time I witnessed this phenomenon, some people fainted from emotion. For the three consecutive years that I attended, the miracle repeated itself, leaving an indelible mark of faith and wonder in each one of us.

For Those Skeptics Who Do Not Believe in the Apparitions

For those skeptics who do not believe in the apparitions, I can only say that perhaps they have not had the opportunity to be present at one. Some may not be interested, but I invite those who are curious to visit Santa Maria, California, or any other place of renowned apparitions. Personally, I recommend the sites where I have been and have been able to verify for myself.

Leaving aside religious explanations, I return to the story of my ancestors and the historical context of Martin Luther and Pope Leo X, whose pontificate between 1513 and 1521 was the catalyst for Luther's protest.

CHAPTER 5

Charles of Spain

I continue with Castile in 1516, the year King Ferdinand died, leaving his kingdom to his grandson Charles. Thus begins the chapter of Charles I of Spain and Charles V of Germany. In 1516, following the death of King Ferdinand, young Charles, just 16 years old, began his empire. Despite his youth, he had the support and counsel of capable mentors to maintain control of the vast empire. In 1519, at the age of 17, he began to fully exercise his responsibilities as emperor.

Charles, I began to enjoy the riches coming from the New World, and the coffers of his treasury swelled with gold and silver mainly extracted from Mexico. Over time, he immersed himself in the royalty of Castile, learning to govern his kingdom effectively, proving to be a competent emperor. He married and had two sons, Philip, and Ferdinand, who grew up enjoying the vastest empire the world had known, a legacy that would be difficult to surpass.

Under the reign of Charles I, Spain enjoyed a long period of peace and stability, managing its domain with intelligence. However, the situation in America, especially in Mexico, was different. The indigenous people suffered under the yoke of conquest: their gold and silver were stolen, and they were often killed without justification, often in the name of the Inquisition. Among them, Friar Diego de Landa, who despite destroying the idols of the Maya and burning most of their codices in an act of religious fervor, later regretfully narrated the history of the Maya, trying to preserve some of the culture he had helped to eradicate.

Today, in a drastic 180% change, we can look back and contemplate contrasting figures in the history of the conquest. On one hand, we have characters like Nuño Beltrán de Guzmán, with an ungodly heart, founder of Guadalajara in Mexico, and on the other hand, Diego Velázquez, the first governor of Cuba, among others whose names would fill entire pages if they were given the due attention.

Emperor Charles, immersed in the tranquility of his reign in Spain, seemed oblivious to the atrocities committed by his conquerors in the Americas, who sent galleons loaded with gold and silver to further enrich his treasury. Meanwhile, in peaceful Castile, my ancestors had no immediate conflicts that required their military attention. It is likely that some retired to country life, enjoying agriculture and the quiet life near the Tagus River in Toledo, not far from the splendid castles and nobility, always ready to be called upon in case of emergency.

It is plausible that in those times of calm, the surname Martín del Campo was born, reflecting the movement of many families from Old Castile in the north of Spain to New Castile, seeking new opportunities and perhaps a more serene life near the court of Charles I and V, who often resided in those regions.

Castles and Crowns: The Legacy of Charles I in Toledo

In the region of Toledo, near Madrid, to this day, impressive castles can be admired that witnessed the coexistence of kings, their nobility, and their great armies. As mentioned earlier, nearby flows the Tagus, Spain's most important river, flowing into the Atlantic after crossing Portugal.

The story continues with Charles I, who around 1540 faced his neighbor, King Francis I of France, defeating him in battle and challenging the Pope of Rome at the same time. After these conflicts, he enjoyed a period of peace and joy with his sons Philip and Ferdinand for about 15 more years. Already mature, in 1556, Charles I, feeling ill, decided to retire to a monastery in Yuste, leaving the empire divided between his two sons: Philip II received the kingdom of Spain as the eldest, and Ferdinand, the kingdom of Germany.

Two years later, in 1558, the great emperor Charles I, king of Spain and emperor of the Holy Roman Empire, passed away. With the disappearance of this key figure in history, Philip II ascended to the throne of Spain, marking the beginning of his own reign.

Philip II, King of Spain

After the death of his father, Charles I, in the same year, Philip II married, following the tradition of alliances and power that characterized the European royalty of the time.

Mary Tudor: A Bridge between England and Spain

Mary Tudor, daughter of King Henry VIII of England and his first wife, Catherine of Aragon, who was part of the distinguished Spanish family linked to Charles I of Spain, became the wife of Philip II. Catherine, of Spanish nobility, had strong ties to the powerful empire of her time.

King of England

Henry VIII, son of Henry VII and Queen Margaret, ascended the throne of England in 1509, following his father's death. Shortly after, he married Catherine of Aragon, from which union Princess Mary Tudor was born. Over time, Henry VIII and Catherine faced marital difficulties, and Henry sought annulment of their marriage from the Pope in Rome. When the Pope refused, Henry VIII, frustrated at not obtaining the annulment, decided to separate from papal jurisdiction. He divorced Catherine in his own way and, taking advantage of the emerging Lutheran Reformation, joined it for convenience, subsequently entering another marriage.

This action not only changed the political and religious dynamics of England but also impacted international relations of the time, especially with Catholic powers such as Spain, where his daughter Mary Tudor later married Philip II, thus strengthening ties between the two nations.

With Anne Boleyn, Henry VIII married for the second time under the auspices of the new religion, defying the opposition of figures like Thomas More, who, resisting the divorce and new royal marriage, was executed. From the union with Anne Boleyn, a princess named Elizabeth was born. However, the marriage did not last: Henry VIII, accusing Anne of infidelity, ordered her execution.

After the tragic end of his second marriage, Henry VIII remarried Jane Seymour in 1536. From this union, a son, Prince Edward, was born. Unfortunately, the marriage with Jane also ended, and Henry VIII continued his pattern of marriages, marrying a total of six times, with his last wife being Catherine Parr.

Henry VIII, one of England's most popular and controversial monarchs, died in 1547. He left the kingdom to his young son Edward VI, born in 1537. Following his father's death, Edward, just a child of ten, ascended the throne. However, his reign was brief; he died in 1553 at the young age of sixteen. The circumstances of his death are unclear, but his early demise marked another tumultuous chapter in English monarchy history.

Eduardo VI, Hastened by a Kick from a Pinto Donkey

It was rumored that the premature death of young Edward VI had been hastened by a kick from a pinto donkey. Following this tragic event, Mary Tudor ascended to the English throne in 1553, reigning until 1558. Her fervent Catholicism led her to attempt to revert the kingdom's religion to Catholic faith, creating tensions and discontent. In 1558, Mary Tudor died suddenly, leaving the crown to her half-sister.

That same year, Elizabeth I was proclaimed Queen of England. Her reign would be noted as one of the most illustrious and transformative. Elizabeth, known for her intelligence and culture, mastered multiple languages besides English, including Greek, Latin, Italian, and French. The relationship between Spain and England remained complex, but at that time, Spain enjoyed great military power and a rising economy, fueled by the constant shipments of riches from the New World.

Affluence of the Old World

During the 16th century, the Old World witnessed a significant influx of gold and silver from the Americas. In particular, in Mexico, in the region we now know as the capital of the State of Guanajuato, a silver mine of unimaginable proportions was discovered, considered by King Charles I of Spain and later by his son Philip II as a heavenly gift.

Philip II, in the 1560s and 1570s, had consolidated an unrivaled naval fleet and formidably equipped land armies. By the 1570s, another formidable power emerged on the international stage: the Ottoman Empire, confident in its military strength, almost comparable to Spain's, though not exactly on equal footing.

The Ottoman Empire, underestimating the skill and audacity of Philip II and the strength of Spain, the most powerful nation in Europe at that time, was driven by ambition. Believing they could invade and conquer Spanish territory, the Ottomans faced a great challenge, underestimating the power and resolve of the Spanish monarch and his nation.

Spain Expelled the Moors

In those times, Spain had succeeded in expelling the Moors, who were Islamic brothers of the Turks, and for such reasons, the Ottoman Empire wished to claim the Spanish nation. Their intention was not only for revenge but also to seize the immense treasure accumulated by Spain, a booty overflowing with gold and silver that flooded the national treasury. However, often, dreams of conquest are nothing but illusions.

Faced with the imminent threat of the Turks, Philip II took preventive measures and prepared promptly and diligently. In the same way, my ancestors, imbued with enthusiasm and courage, enlisted for the defense of the homeland. They inherited the bravery and valor of past generations, like those who fought alongside Gonzalo de Córdoba and his invincible Castilian army in 1489. Thus, when the

Moors faced adversities, the formidable and invincible infantry had already been consolidated thanks to the brave Castilian warriors.

In 1570, the descendants of those same warriors, with the legacy of the caste and bravery running through their veins, prepared to face the Turks with equal or greater bravery. As the saying goes, "from tigers come spots," ready to conquer or die in the attempt to defend their beloved homeland.

In the turbulent year of 1571, Philip II faced the possibility of an armed conflict with the Ottoman Empire—a formidable force that threatened the coasts of his kingdom. With faith in God and trusting in the maritime supremacy of his kingdom, the Spanish monarch had an imposing naval fleet and land armies ready for combat.

The thunderous Battle of Lepanto erupted, the cannons of both fleets clashing in a titanic struggle over the Mediterranean waves. The Duke of Alba, with unwavering cunning and valor, led the Spanish forces in a fierce fight. The Turks, with their ferocity and determination, seemed at times close to victory, but never managed to break the resilience of the Spaniards.

It was in this historic confrontation where Miguel de Cervantes Saavedra, who would later become one of the most celebrated writers in universal literature, suffered severe injuries that would mark his life forever. Despite his injuries, Cervantes miraculously survived, and his bravery was immortalized in the pages of history.

Finally, the skill and courage of the Spaniards prevailed, and Philip II achieved a decisive victory over the Ottomans. This battle not only saved Spain from a possible Muslim invasion but also consolidated its reputation as an indisputable naval power. The Battle of Lepanto was etched as a milestone in the history of the struggle between the West and the Ottoman Empire.

Miguel de Cervantes Saavedra (1547-1616)

Miguel de Cervantes Saavedra, the eminent writer, first saw the light in Alcalá de Henares, a picturesque suburb of Madrid, Spain, on September 29, 1547. At the young age of 21, in 1568, Cervantes enlisted in the army and had a prominent role in the famous Battle of Lepanto in 1571, where he was gravely wounded, miraculously surviving.

His military career later took him to North Africa and other Mediterranean enclaves. In 1575, he fell into the hands of pirates and was turned into a slave, during which captivity he began to conceive his masterpiece, "Don Quixote de la Mancha." After his release, he returned to Madrid in 1580 and in 1585 published "La Galatea," a romantic pastoral novel.

The first part of "Don Quixote" was published in 1605, a work that would immortalize him as one of the greatest writers in the Spanish language. Cervantes, now blind and in solitude, became an indefatigable activist of letters, and in his last three years, dedicated his genius to the creation of stories imbued with realism and satire. In 1615, he published the second part of "Don Quixote," during the reign of Philip III. The printing of this work was carried out at the University of Alcalá, where the new grammatical castes of Spanish were gestated, thus consolidating Castilian as the official language, and granting Miguel de Cervantes Saavedra the deserved recognition as the great reformer of our rich Spanish language. At this same university of Alcalá, Cervantes is remembered and revered as a true bastion of literature in Spanish.

William Shakespeare and Miguel de Cervantes: A Parallelism in Literary History

William Shakespeare, the immortal bard of Avon, was born on April 23, 1564, and, by a twist of fate, also died on his birthday, April 23, 1616. This curious fact resonates in the annals of literature, as in that same year, another giant of letters, Miguel de Cervantes Saavedra, closed his eyes forever in the city where he was born, Madrid, on April 22, being buried the following day. The coincidence of dates between the deaths of these two pillars of world literature has been a subject of fascination and study.

The University of Alcalá, founded by King Ferdinand of Aragon in 1508, became a beacon of knowledge and culture. It was here where, in 1522, the Polyglot Bible was printed, a monumental work compiling sacred texts in Latin, Greek, Hebrew, and Aramaic, reflecting the intellectual richness of the era.

The Naval Battle of Spain with England and the Decline of the Spanish Armada

The Invincible Armada of Spain, which once dominated the seas and was the symbol of Spanish power, suffered a critical setback in its confrontation with England. Philip II, after having triumphed over the Turks, faced a declining economy. In 1588, Philip II of Spain launched a naval campaign to invade and conquer England. However, much like the Turks who underestimated Spanish might, the Spanish Armada, confident in its invincibility, was defeated. This marked a turning point in naval history and the beginning of the decline of the Spanish empire.

The Challenge of the Invincible Armada in 1588 and British Defense

In the year 1588, the pride of Philip II of Spain drove him to conceive what seemed to be a certain invasion against the British kingdom. With a fleet of 130 ships armed to the teeth with cannons and soldiers, the Invincible Armada set sail towards what would be an epic battle in the annals of maritime history.

The British response, led by Admiral Howard of Effingham, was fierce and cunning. Taking advantage of naval skill and adverse weather conditions, the defenders wreaked havoc on the Spanish fleet, sinking and scattering their ships.

There is often reflection on divine will in human affairs, and in this case, it seemed that fate did not favor the pride of Philip II. The storms that ravaged the Armada contributed to its ruin, as if they were a divine message rejecting Spain's imperialist ambitions.

Queen Elizabeth I of England, on the other hand, was a monarch admired for her justice and humanism. Divine protection seemed to lean towards her just cause, helping to thwart Philip II's plans for conquest.

The failed expedition marked a decline in Spanish hegemony, and although Spain continued to be a respected power, that event in 1588 outlined the beginning of its descent as the dominant empire on the global stage. The British victory not only saved England from invasion but also paved the way for its future as a naval power.

Chapter 6

The Inexhaustible Wealth of Guanajuato

Since time immemorial, when galleons sailed the seas filled with treasures from the New World, one precious metal stood out among them, flowing from the depths of Guanajuato. This mine, a blessing from heaven according to Carlos I, seemed like a divine miracle; the deeper the miners dug, the more silver they found. Today, Guanajuato is not only the capital of the state bearing its name but also a place of great historical and cultural significance.

The Fascinating History of Guanajuato's Name

One of the most interesting stories of Guanajuato revolves around its name, which in Nahuatl means "Mountain of Frogs." This was the name that the indigenous peoples gave to the place when the conquerors arrived on their lands. These early Spanish explorers, hungry for wealth and glory, wasted no time in putting the indigenous people to work in the silver mines, starting the famous mine that never stopped producing silver from one generation to the next, shaping the history and fortune of the region.

Guanajuato: The Silver Boom

In the year 1541, the first Spanish conquistadors made their presence known in what we now know as Guanajuato. With unprecedented fervor, they discovered several veins of silver and began to excavate, extracting large quantities of the precious metal. They established the Royal Road that connected Guanajuato to Mexico City and from there to Veracruz. Laden galleons constantly set sail for the Atlantic, filling the coffers of King Charles V of Spain. The mines, including Mellado, Rayas, and above all, La Valenciana, operated for centuries. Between 1750 and 1810, it is estimated that these mines produced more than three-quarters of the silver circulating in the world.

As the conquerors settled from 1554 onwards, Guanajuato emerged almost spontaneously. There is no urban logic in its initial development; houses were erected wherever space was available, rising without order or concert. Access routes were built to adapt to the whims of the topography, creating labyrinths of narrow streets that, to this day, defy any attempts at organization. This uniqueness has given the city a charming, albeit complicated, character that persists to this day.

The Urban Configuration of Guanajuato and Its Heritage

Guanajuato's structure arose in response to the need and limitations of the terrain: streets that sprouted spontaneously and plazas that were delineated through urban coincidences. The city, subject to its own freedom and geographic constraints, developed into a peculiar and enchanting configuration.

In the early days of 1554, King Charles I of Spain, along with his son Philip II, granted Guanajuato the title of "The Very Noble and Loyal City of Santa Fe of the Mines of Guanajuato." In 1557, just a year before the death of Charles I, the city received a sculpture of the Virgin Mary. This image, believed to date from the 8th century, was later housed in the Basilica of Our Lady of Guanajuato, built between 1672 and 1676, and is recognized as the city's patron saint. Some claim it to be the oldest Marian image in the Americas.

Today, Guanajuato continues to honor these traditions with tributes every Friday of Sorrows. Although the official name of the basilica is the Church of San Cayetano, its facade, masterfully carved in pink quarry stone, is a testament to the baroque style at its finest, a living testimony to the city's cultural richness.

Guanajuato's Peculiarities: The Mummies and the Rayas Mine

Guanajuato harbors among its mysteries a unique cemetery, famous for its naturally preserved mummies, whose exact origin is lost in history. This place, now converted into a museum, houses an astonishing collection of mummified remains. The specific soil conditions, rich in minerals, have preserved these figures with expressions and gestures that seem to narrate stories of the past.

Another underground wonder of this city is the Rayas Mine. At a depth of 300 meters underground, an altar stands where miners used to entrust themselves to heaven before facing the darkness and risks of the underground. This mining sanctuary, nearly aligned with the iconic Juarez Theater, is a testament to the faith and hope of those brave men.

The heroic saga of Guanajuato also intertwines with the beginning of Mexico's struggle for independence. It was in the nearby town of Dolores where Priest Miguel Hidalgo y Costilla called for rebellion against colonial oppression with the historic "Grito de Dolores" in the early hours of September 16, 1810. This call for freedom resonated in the hearts of indigenous people and mestizos, who joined together to break free from the abuses of some Spaniards, while criollos watched with suspicion the awakening of a people seeking emancipation.

Heroism in Mexico's Independence: Guanajuato and its Emblematic Figures

In the heat of Mexico's independence movement, Guanajuato became the stage for heroic acts that would shape the country's history. Figures like Josefa Ortiz de Domínguez and Priest Miguel Hidalgo, as well as the noble Agustín de Iturbide, who would later briefly become Mexico's first emperor, played crucial roles in the struggle for liberation from Spanish rule.

Guanajuato's spirit of resistance reached its zenith at the Alhóndiga de Granaditas. This fortress, then in the hands of the Spanish army and local authorities, seemed impregnable. The stronghold, with its strategic position, resisted any assault... until a volunteer known as "El Pípila" appeared. This man, of robust stature and unwavering courage, offered to set fire to the main gate. Covered with a slab to shield himself from enemy bullets, he advanced fearlessly with his torch to fulfill his mission, allowing the insurgents to take the fort in an act of bravery etched in the nation's soul.

This narrative is just a glimpse of Guanajuato's rich history, a place where the struggle for independence and the passion for freedom are felt at every corner. The city not only preserves the memory of its heroes but also continues to resonate with the culture and indomitable spirit that characterize it.

From Victory at Lepanto to Defeat against England

The figure of Philip II is contradictory in the history of Spain, marked both by victory and defeat. While he demonstrated unwavering Christian faith and a legacy of triumphs inherited from his predecessors, Ferdinand and Isabella, his miscalculation in the conflict against England tarnished his reign.

Philip II, educated in victory after the Battle of Lepanto where he saved Spain from the Turks, found himself challenging the nature and cunning of Queen Elizabeth I. His determination to keep Spain at the pinnacle of power led him to underestimate his opponent's capabilities. This desire for conquest, blinded by pride rather than statecraft, led the Invincible Armada to a catastrophic defeat, exacerbated by devastating storms.

The lesson that Philip II leaves us is complex: a king can be deeply Christian and yet fall into the trap of his own arrogance. In the pursuit of maintaining the economic splendor of his empire, Philip II forgot that true cunning in politics lies not in aggression but in wisdom and discernment, something that in this case failed, culminating in the humiliating Spanish defeat by the English.

Philip II: The Decline of a Reign and the Dawn in America

Philip II, who was advised by counselors of great wisdom, seemed to ignore their warnings or succumb to his insatiable thirst for wealth. Despite the defeat against England, providence was not entirely cruel; life in Spain continued its course, and the economy began to recover gradually. My ancestors, always at the forefront and in the service of the Crown and its nobility in Castile, may have been close to the war events against the English, although it is unlikely that they directly participated in the naval battle.

With the death of Philip II in 1598 and the ascent of Philip III to the Spanish throne, the country maintained its course without major upheavals. In the New World, cities began to flourish; just 75 years after the foundation of Mexico City by Hernán Cortés in 1523, explorers like Vasco Núñez de Balboa ventured into Central America, paving the way for colonization and rapid Spanish settlement. Meanwhile, in 1531, Mexico witnessed an event that would forever mark its religious devotion: the apparitions of the Virgin of Guadalupe to the indigenous Juan Diego. This transcendent event still resonates strongly in the identity and faith of the Mexican people.

Chapter 7

Celebrations to the Virgin of Guadalupe

Every year, on December 12, the Basilica of Guadalupe becomes a center of faith and devotion. This day, officially a holiday in Mexico, brings together millions of pilgrims from around the world, surpassing the two million visitors who come to pay homage to the Virgin. In a miracle that defies time, the cotton ayate that holds the image of the Morenita has remained intact since 1531, defying its natural lifespan of only a few decades. The representation of the Virgin with dark skin as a beautiful indigenous woman is a powerful display of identity and cultural unity. As a prelude to the grand celebration, in the days leading up to December 12, traditional dances of various ethnicities take place. Dancers, dressed in typical clothing and adorned with colorful feather headdresses, decorate their ankles with shells that resonate to the rhythm of their coordinated steps. These dances continue for 24 hours a day, with shifts that allow the celebration to continue, a testament to the deep love and veneration that the Mexican people feel for their Guadalupana.

The Queen and Empress of Mexico and America: The Virgin of Guadalupe

Consecrated as the patron and queen of all Mexicans, and proclaimed Empress of the American continent, the Virgin of Guadalupe reveals herself with dark skin, an echo of her identification with the indigenous population. To those who may harbor doubts about this miraculous phenomenon, I extend a cordial invitation to visit Mexico City on December 12, to witness this phenomenon and judge for themselves whether what is narrated is true or mere fantasy.

The celebrations in honor of the Morenita Guadalupana are not limited to the Basilica in the capital; they extend throughout Mexico, in every city and town, as well as in Central and South America, and in the United States, wherever there is a Latin Catholic community.

The day begins with "Las Mañanitas Guadalupana" at dawn, followed by pilgrimages filled with singing and jubilation, and the burst of fireworks that resound in the sky. The day culminates with a solemn Mass and the enjoyment of traditional dishes like tamales and posole, symbolizing a true celebration of faith and heritage.

In the year 1531, the conqueror, Nuño Beltrán de Guzmán, hailing from Guadalajara, Spain, arrived in Tonalá, which is now in the state of Jalisco, with the firm intention of founding the city of Guadalajara in Mexico. Despite three failed attempts due to the fierce resistance of the brave Tonaltecans and the ferocious Cazcanes, he finally managed to establish the city in 1542, thus marking another important chapter in the history of Mexico.

The Settlement in the Atemajac Valley and the Proliferation of the Highlands of Jalisco

It was in the Atemajac Valley where, for the last time, the founders of what is now known as the second most populous city in Mexico settled. Not long after, the colonization of my region, the Highlands of Jalisco, began. Places like Tepatitlán, Arandas, San Miguel el Alto, Jalos, Tototlán, San Juan, and Yahualica. Spanish settlers arrived, forming charming villages with the style and customs of Spain.

These places, which are now prosperous small cities and municipal seats, were once known as captaincies. Around these captaincies, the colonizers began to establish rancherias, introducing livestock and animals of all kinds for breeding and agriculture. They used oxen to till the land and as transportation, a tradition that endured for many years. They also brought in wild cattle for their bullfights and fighting roosters, giving rise to the famous charreadas that initially emerged from cattle branding.

These events, turned into rough and dangerous sports, were the entertainment and pride of the people in that region. The people who arrived in the Highlands of Jalisco probably came from northern and central Spain since they were mostly blond, fair-skinned, light-eyed, and robust in build. This has marked the region's identity and tradition, preserving to this day a rich cultural heritage reflected in its festivities, art, and way of life.

The Lineage and Character of the Highlands of Jalisco

In the Highlands of Jalisco, an intrinsic bravery and characteristic simplicity manifest, inherited from the typical Castilian spirit. Although it is rare to find Arab features among us, they exist because during the long stay in Spain, many Arabs lived and integrated with the Christians, even adopting Catholicism. This mixture has left its mark on us, preserving not only Jewish blood in some cases but also certain family customs in daily life and a particular knack for business. It is true that these characteristics are not erased; especially in my picturesque town, where generosity is the norm, and they are willing to give the shirt off their back if necessary. They are extraordinarily charitable, but when it comes to business, their shrewdness is unmatched. I can assure you that in a business deal, they never come out on the losing end. And don't be surprised if, in a moment of distraction, you leave even without the shirt you were wearing. Such is the negotiating skill of my people, a legacy of a rich and complex history.

Felipe III, King of Spain
Continuing with the history of the Spanish monarchy, after the death of Philip II, his son, Philip III, ascended to the throne in 1598. Under his reign, Spain continued its expansion and consolidation in the New World, while on the peninsula, life went on amidst the opulence of gold and silver flowing from the colonies.

The Reign of Felipe IV and the Paths of Colonial Mexico
In the year 1621, Felipe IV ascended to the throne of Spain, marking a new chapter in the history of the crown. Meanwhile, in Mexico, more than a century after its conquest, it had become a well-structured colony, with cities like Guadalajara firmly established. The first viceroy, Don Antonio de Mendoza, understanding the importance of communication routes, ordered the construction of the Grand Royal Road that connected Mexico City to Guadalajara, as well as another essential road that linked the capital to Veracruz. Additionally, the renowned Camino Real of Guanajuato became a

vital artery through which shipments of silver from the rich mines of the region flowed incessantly.

We must not forget the Camino Real from Puebla to Mexico and, above all, the one that came from Zacatecas to Mexico City, which led to the famous Cerro Gordo. At this crossroads, travelers had to choose their destination: to the right for Guadalajara, to the left for Mexico City, skirting the slope of Cerro Gordo, always under the looming threat of the Guamares of Zacatecas. These indigenous people, settled at the summit, were known for their cunning and bravery. The hill, at that time, was a dense jungle, whose secrets only they knew.

The Legacy of the Royal Roads in Historical Memory

These roads, more than mere trade routes, became the veins through which colonial life flowed, interconnecting destinies and shaping the history of a growing nation. Over time, they have been etched into historical memory, not only as trade routes but as witnesses to a past where the courage and determination of its people prevailed over the challenges of the terrain and the challenges of the time.

Colonial Expansion in Tepatitlán and the Challenge of the Guamares

During the reign of Felipe IV, the colonization of the Highlands of Jalisco continued its inexorable march, especially in Tepatitlán, which became one of the first Spanish enclaves in the region. The colonists, mostly Spanish families, arrived with unwavering determination, establishing extensive ranches to the south, west, and north of Tepatitlán. This region was freed of indigenous people, not by force but because they, realizing they could not coexist with the newcomers, voluntarily moved to Zacatecas and Nochistlán, to the land of the Caxcanes, their kindred people.

However, to the east of Tepatitlán, a considerable challenge stood: the jurisdiction of the Guamares of Zacatecas, who had taken refuge in Cerro Gordo and resisted any attempts at colonization. For this reason, the vast and fertile valley now known as Capilla de Guadalupe and its surroundings, extending to Arandas and San Miguel el Alto, remained uninhabited. The first Spanish settlers avoided settling in that region, aware of the ongoing problems they would face with the valiant Guamares, whose resistance was well-known.

Tension between Colonial Advancement and Indigenous Resistance

This scenario reflected palpable tension between colonial expansion and indigenous resistance, a reminder that territorial expansion was neither a peaceful nor unanimous process. The imposing presence of the Guamares on Cerro Gordo symbolized a last bastion of resistance, a constant reminder of the complexity and diversity of the peoples that made up the fabric of colonial Mexico.

The Vicissitudes of the Highlands of Jalisco and the Challenge of the Guamares

In the highlands of Jalisco, during the transition between the 16th and 17th centuries, the royal road that crossed the northern slope of Cerro Gordo became a place of constant apprehension. This trail, connecting Mexico City to Guadalajara, was frequently stalked by the Guamares, an indigenous group known for their surprise raids on unsuspecting travelers. Furthermore, the region was disturbed by bands of criollo bandits who plunged passersby into disorder. The detachments of soldiers stationed in the nearby captaincies were unable to contain these assaults, in part because their attention was divided, focusing on the management of their vast ranches.

Although they were of strong character, the Guamares wisely avoided approaching the more populated areas, like Tepatitlán, where the presence of the Spanish criollos, equally brave and ready to defend, posed a significant danger. Over time, this scenario of conflict and challenge became integrated into the daily life of Mexico, maintaining its rhythm until 1665, when a chapter closed with the death of Felipe IV, leaving a legacy of strength and resilience in the inhabitants of these lands, who continued their development under the cloak of Spanish history and the emerging Mexican identity.

Consolidation and Transition in the Spanish Crown: From Carlos II to Felipe V

The royal succession in Spain underwent a decisive phase in the late 17th century. After a lengthy reign of 44 years, Felipe IV abdicated the throne to Carlos II, known in history as "The Bewitched" due to his fragile health and the complexity of his reign, which spanned from 1665 to 1700.

This period was marked by internal difficulties and a series of conflicts with France, which took advantage of Spain's weakness to seize several provinces in the northern peninsula. With no descendants to ensure the continuity of the House of Austria on the Spanish throne, Carlos II sought a solution to appease tensions with France. To safeguard the stability of the kingdom, he handed over the crown to Felipe de Anjou, the grandson of the French monarch Louis XIV.

The death of Carlos II in 1700 marked the end of an era and the beginning of the reign of Felipe V, the first king of the House of

Bourbon in Spain. Under Felipe V, the Spanish monarchy began a period of recovery and governmental strengthening. Despite reservations and discontent in other European nations about how the Spanish succession was resolved, Felipe V began to rule with firmness and a vision for the future.

Meanwhile, in the New World, problems persisted in Mexico with the indomitable Guamares of Zacatecas, who continued to defy colonial power from their stronghold in Cerro Gordo, attacking those who traveled along the Camino Real and thereby leaving a resilient chapter in the history of indigenous resistance.

The Assault of the Guamares: A Challenge in the Highlands of Jalisco

At the dawn of the 18th century, the trade routes of New Spain were vital arteries for the flow of wealth extracted from its rich mines. Zacatecas, a city renowned for its rich veins, regularly sent caravans loaded with gold and silver to the heart of the viceroyalty. However, these roads were not without dangers, including the Guamares of Zacatecas, an indigenous group that had made Cerro Gordo their unbreakable bastion. Spanish soldiers, aware of the risk, strengthened their detachments and outposts along critical routes, but the cunning and bravery of the Guamares posed a constant threat.

In an event that left its mark on local history, at the beginning of 1710, a caravan consisting of 30 mules, five of which carried gold and the rest silver, approached Cerro Gordo. The assault by the Guamares was swift and devastating. The caravan, which had departed from the mines of Zacatecas and had crossed the Estancia de Mirandilla, was heading south with the intention of skirting the slopes of Cerro Gordo, near a ranch mentioned in the documents of the time.

The audacity of the Guamares in this event was such that it remained engraved in the collective memory of the region, serving as a reminder of indigenous resistance and the challenges faced by Spanish settlers in the Highlands of Jalisco.

The Assault in Los Sauces and the Viceroyal Response

The tragic event in Los Sauces, where the Camino Real traced its route from Guadalajara to Mexico City, was inscribed in the annals of history as a reminder of the relentless bravery of the Guamares. On that day, while a viceroyal detachment escorted a valuable cargo of gold and silver, the indigenous ambush not only deprived the viceroyalty of treasure but also of brave lives. At the foot of Rancho San Antonio, owned by the renowned Franco family, the viceroyal soldiers fell victim to the sudden and ruthless assault.

The Guamares, known for their numerical superiority and tactical prowess in the region, left no survivors, and the fate of the treasure became shrouded in the mystery of Mexican soil. The news of the attack resonated strongly in the Viceroyalty of Mexico, prompting the Viceroy to send an urgent message to the King of Spain, Felipe V, pleading for assistance. Aware of the seriousness of the incident, the monarch pledged to send reinforcements, selecting the best from his reserves to bolster the military presence in New Spain. This royal commitment underscored the importance of protecting vital trade routes for the imperial economy and set a precedent for defending the crown's interests in the American lands.

The Royal Commission and the Foundation of Los Altos de Jalisco

In the annals of history, a matter of great significance was recorded when King Felipe V, alerted by the urgency of the Viceroy of Mexico, decided to send the most distinguished and valiant families from Spain to confront the situation in CERRO GORDO. This decision, made promptly as the case required, resulted in the dispatch of 47 carefully selected families renowned for their skill and valor to face the formidable challenge posed by the indomitable Guamares of Zacatecas.

These families, who embarked on their journey to the New World in 1762, were the seed of what we now know as the region of Los Altos de Jalisco. In this rugged land, their descendants forged enduring bonds, creating a united and robust community that would eventually become one of Mexico's most emblematic and prosperous areas. At that time, despite Spain enjoying relative peace and many of its soldiers and nobles being inactive in the military, the monarch's call was answered without hesitation. These men and women, far from the luxuries of castles and the comforts of cities like Toledo, embraced the noble task of establishing a new frontier in American territory, thus demonstrating their loyalty and courage. It was a time of bravery and honor when the word of the king and the needs of the crown summoned the boldest to write new pages in the history of their nation.

The Legacy of Toledo and the Foundation of Capilla de Guadalupe

In the surroundings of Toledo, where rivers meandered and castles stood majestic, stories of royalty and nobility were born and still resonate in collective memory. It was an era when the Kings of Spain, like Carlos and his son, Felipe II, not only ruled but also lived in opulence, surrounded by the wealth provided by the Americas. Gold and silver flowed, adorning everything from the grandest castles to the most luxurious attire, reflecting an era of opulence and magnificence.

In this context, the royal commission emerged, leading a select group of Castilian families to the New World with the purpose of establishing new roots and expanding the empire. Among them were those who served in castles near Toledo, others who cultivated fields, or traded skillfully in nearby towns and villages.

The Tajo River, a witness to their life and effort, flowed like a vital vein through the region, being the most important in Spain and a source of inspiration and sustenance. Beyond the ocean, in Mexican lands, these brave Castilians founded what is now known as Capilla de Guadalupe. In honor of their roots and remembering the land they left behind; they baptized a pond built next to a natural lagoon with the name "El Tajo" in 1823.

This symbolic act linked their new home with the old, an invisible but indelible bridge between the past and the present, between Spain and Mexico. "El Tajo" in Capilla de Guadalupe is not just a body of water but a mirror reflecting the heritage and spirit of those pioneering Castilians who, with vision and courage, wove a fundamental part of Mexico's cultural tapestry.

The Decision and Adventurous Spirit of the Castilians

The roots of my lineage are firmly anchored in the region of Castile, as evidenced by family records and narratives. In the 1770s, a group of Castilian volunteers, driven by the adventurous spirit already running through their veins and the promise of new lands to colonize, eagerly began to enlist. There was a burning desire in them to explore and claim these virgin lands, motivated also by the enticing bonus offered to them as initial incentive for their work as farmers and laborers.

However, they were presented with an inescapable condition: they had to resolve a challenge in Mexico before they could fully commit. They candidly and openly explained the situation and the problems they would face upon arrival. This honesty was crucial to ensure that the decision to embark on such an enterprise was made with full awareness.

The prospect of facing dangers and adventures evoked the legacy of their ancestors, who had engaged in encounters against the Moors in times past. The possibility of being involved in such a significant enterprise was appealing, especially since many felt stagnant due to the lack of action in their daily lives.

Therefore, these 47 Castilian families, from whom I am honored to descend, chose to embark on a radical change in their lives. With the same fervor their forebears had shown in past battles, they set out to face this new challenge with a mix of courage and hope, seeking in the New World not only a change of scenery but also the opportunity to forge a promising future.

The Beginning of the Journey: The Castilian Families and Their Voyage to the New World

With the conviction that Divine Providence would guide them and supported by their proven courage and warrior experience, the Castilian families diligently began preparations for the great journey. Aware that only the essentials could accompany them on the voyage, they carefully selected their belongings, leaving behind everything that tied them to their homeland. This was the beginning of a new stage, marked by promise and the mystery of the unknown.

The Long Farewell

The moment of departure finally arrived. With heavy hearts but their gaze fixed on the future, they gathered to form a caravan united by hope and mutual support. Men and women of mercantile spirit, they knew the future was uncertain, but the determination to forge a new life was stronger than any fear. United in a single cry, "Let's go!" they set off southward toward the port, perhaps that of Cadiz or maybe that of Palos, the latter immortalized by Christopher Columbus' journey in 1492.

The first stop on their journey was the region of La Mancha, where they may have taken a break in Ciudad Real to rest. The next day, they resumed their march, crossing the Sierra Morena without mishap. The caravan continued its route to Cordoba and Seville, following the course of the Tinto River to its mouth in the

Mediterranean Sea, near the historic Port of Palos. From there, ready and determined, the Castilian families set sail for the New World, carrying with them their dreams, their courage, and the legacy of a land that would always be part of their identity.

The Departure to Mexico from the Port of Spain

Finally, after a long journey, the extensive caravan consisting of 47 families, possibly totaling over 200 souls, gathered at the port. The vastness of the group surely required more than one caravel, and after a well-deserved rest and final preparations, in 1712, they entrusted themselves to divine providence and embarked. Not without a silent concern shared by all, due to the uncertainty of the future unfolding before them, they set sail from the port, perhaps from Cadiz or Palos, and took the same route that Christopher Columbus had charted centuries ago.

CHAPTER 8

The Voyage to the New World

They sailed in silence, each immersed in their thoughts and concerns, as the caravel plied the waters of the Mediterranean. It was inevitable to recall Columbus's historic route, and like him, they made a stop in the Canary Islands to replenish supplies and fresh water. There, in the middle of the ocean, they found a moment to rest and regroup before facing the longest and most challenging leg of the journey. With their holds full and a renewed resolve in their hearts, they resumed the voyage with a refreshed spirit, now accustomed to the constant rocking of the sea and life on the open ocean.

Arrival in America from the Mediterranean Port

They departed from the Mediterranean to the Canary Islands, where, with songs of praise to God, they reflected their devout Catholic faith, considering Christ their protective shield. With sails unfurled and following parallel 28 towards America, and then descending to parallel 20 between Cuba and Haiti, they headed for Veracruz. The journey across the vast Atlantic was not without difficulties, and although we do not know if they made a stop in Cuba for a break, they finally arrived at the main gateway to Mexico City, Veracruz.

From Veracruz to Mexico City

Grateful for a safe and incident-free arrival, they rested in the charming port of Veracruz. After a few days of rest, they prepared to undertake the last leg of their journey to Mexico City. Accompanied by guides and personnel sent by the Viceroy of

Mexico, they ventured onto the Royal Road, comforted by the hospitality and encouragement provided to make the journey less arduous and to facilitate their acclimatization to the new land they were gradually getting to know.

Arrival and Reception in Mexico City

After their departure from Veracruz, the new world unfolded before them. The meticulously organized caravan began its journey towards Mexico City. The emotional burden lightened as they were captivated by the impressive flora and tropical vegetation of the state of Veracruz, a spectacle of beauty that lasts throughout the year.

Prepared with horses, mules, and mounted personnel, the caravan traversed iconic landscapes, such as Cerro Gordo and the majestic Pico de Orizaba, the highest point in Mexico. Despite the fatigue, joy prevailed when they finally arrived in Mexico City.

Before entering the city, they were received with great enthusiasm. The streets were lined with soldiers ready to offer a warm welcome by order of the Viceroy himself, who expressed his jubilation at the arrival of these families who, with great hope, were beginning a new chapter in their history.

Stay at the Bishopric and Colonization Planning

During their temporary stay at the Bishopric, the families received hospitality befitting their royal recommendation. Comfortable accommodations were provided for them to recover from the wear and tear of the long journey, and special attention was given to wives and children who required care and attention.

During this period of adaptation, the ecclesiastical authorities provided them with detailed information about the region they were colonizing, offering them a comprehensive view of their future home and the responsibilities it entailed. They were assured that the vast, uncolonized region would be at their disposal for equitable distribution among all the families.

They took advantage of their time in Mexico City to visit the Basilica of Guadalupe, where they immersed themselves in the history and meaning of the apparitions of the Brown Virgin, undoubtedly strengthening their faith and giving them courage to face the challenges of colonization that awaited them. With renewed spirits and a deeper understanding of their mission, they prepared for the next step in their journey.

Departure to Los Altos de Jalisco and Reverence to the Virgin of Guadalupe

With hearts filled with devotion and souls imbued with the stories of the celestial appearance of the Virgin of Guadalupe, the Castilian families prepared for their departure to the Los Altos de Jalisco region. Their love and respect for the Virgin Mary, who appeared in Tepeyac as the Morenita, patroness and symbol of unity between indigenous and Spanish peoples, foreshadowing the birth of a new Mexican identity, were palpable in them.

As these families stood on the brink of a new era in 1703, they were inspired by the message of the Virgin: a call for integration and equality that would flourish in the mixing of races and cultures that characterizes the Mexican nation today.

Before embarking on the journey to their new life, they made sure to carry not only provisions and belongings but also the most cherished memories of the Guadalupan Virgin. A sacred image, likely a replica of Juan Diego's tilma, was taken as an amulet of blessings and protection on their journey, symbolizing the faith and hope that guided them.

With this sacred symbol, the Castilian ancestors set out to leave Mexico City. They were not only departing for an unknown destination but also carrying with them the promise of a mestizo future, forged under the gaze of the Morenita Guadalupana, whose love and desire for unity would become the essence of their new community in Los Altos de Jalisco.

The Enrichment of the Spiritual Heritage in the Foundation of a Town

In the sacred delivery of the paintings by the bishop, our ancestors received a portrait of the Virgin of Guadalupe, a semblance of the original image venerated in Mexico City. This sacred icon was destined to preside over the parish of the town founded by Don Antonio de Aceves, initially known as Guadalupe. Devotion to the Morenita took root in the heart of the community from its beginnings, and that portrait that accompanied the Castilian pioneers endures to this day, serving as a silent yet eloquent witness to the faith and cultural heritage established back then.

Likewise, a Divine Face painted in silver was also part of this spiritual legacy, placed at the foot of the main altar as a replica of the one found in the Basilica of Guadalupe, thus recalling the celestial proximity that the inhabitants of this new settlement desired to feel with the miraculous image of the Virgin. The resemblance of this work to another one in the old Basilica, dated 1675, was so striking that in current comparisons through photographs in specialized books, the almost twin-like similarity between both representations is evident.

The original LITTLE CHAPEL, which housed these relics, made way for a larger construction to accommodate the growth of fervor and population. However, the images that were venerated in it, especially the Virgin of Guadalupe, have maintained their preeminent place, symbolizing not only the religious identity but also the unity between two worlds that gave rise to the mestizo spirit of the town.

Heritage and Devotion: Family Tradition in the Custody of Sacred Relics

In the early days of our parish, my great-grandfather, a direct descendant of the founder, Don Antonio de Aceves, undertook the venerable task of safeguarding the sacred images that were part of the foundational spirit of our town. Among these, the Portrait of the Virgin and the Divine Face stood out for their spiritual significance, being moved with reverence to the new temple once it was erected. The canvas of the Morenita, representing the Virgin of Guadalupe, was placed again on a majestic altar, continuing its legacy of faith and devotion. On the other hand, the portrait of the Divine Face found a new sanctuary in my great-grandfather's house, where it remained as a family relic and object of special veneration.

I grew up within these walls steeped in history and faith, where the narratives of my grandmother, a direct heir to this tradition, resonated with the wisdom and fervor of past generations. She, Doña Mariquita de la Torre Aceves, widow of Don Felipe Navarro Aceves and cousins to each other—a common practice in those times—kept alive the flame of our lineage and its convictions.

Upon my grandmother's passing, my father inherited the house and with it, the Divine Face, passing it on to my hands later. Today, this venerable object is kept on a home altar, where I care for it with the love and respect it deserves. It is not just a piece of religious art; it is a living testimony of the spiritual odyssey of my ancestors from

Mexico City in 1702 and a tangible reminder of our Castilian heritage and Mexican identity.

Exodus to Los Altos: The Journey of the Castilians to Tepatitlán

The time had come: my Castilian ancestors had to embark on the journey to the Los Altos de Jalisco region. The journey, expected to be long and arduous, demanded meticulous planning. It was estimated that the journey would cover about 600 kilometers—a distance not without challenges and hardships.

In a meeting that brought the entire community together, various strategies were debated, and a crucial decision was made: the men would depart first. The uncertainty of their destination and the situation that awaited them in Los Altos required prior exploration. Thus, with the determination that characterized our ancestors, they prepared to depart.

However, before their departure, they sent a message to Tepatitlán, using the diligence that routinely traveled the distance between Mexico and Guadalajara, passing through Tepatitlán. The purpose was to ensure that everything was ready for their arrival.

Equipped with horses, mules, and wagons, and even some diligence that allowed for a more comfortable journey for some, they set out on the Royal Road. Accompanied by a mixture of excitement and natural caution towards the unknown, they began their departure.

The duration of the journey is uncertain, as the pace of their progress was marked by necessary breaks at each stop. These pauses served not only for rest but also to strengthen the spirit and conviction that each step brought them closer to their new destination, where the hope of a prosperous future intertwined with the promise of keeping their rich cultural heritage alive.

The Odyssey of the Castilians: The Final Stretch to Tepatitlán

The caravan of Castilians, carrying the inheritance of their homeland's resolution, advanced along the Royal Road, nearing their destination: the Captaincy of Tepatitlán. It was not a journey devoid of dangers; they had to pass through Arandas, an intermediate point marked by the presence of Cerro Gordo, a summit that dominated the region of Los Altos de Jalisco and was the stronghold of the indomitable Guamares.

The last 80 kilometers before reaching Guadalajara were filled with tension. Although a considerable escort of soldiers accompanied the Castilians, they did not rely solely on others for their safety; they were armed with their Spanish muskets, period sabers, and the occasional crossbow, useful in case reloading firearms took longer than available in a potential confrontation.

As the caravan snaked along the foothills of Cerro Gordo, the new colonists received an explanation of the persistent threat posed by the Guamares, entrenched in that place for nearly two centuries. Despite the years and various attempts to dislodge them, this last bastion of indigenous resistance stood firm, a testament to the indomitable spirit of those who inhabited the heights of Jalisco.

Expectations grew with each step that brought them closer to Tepatitlán, where a new life would be established, built on the perseverance and bravery that these Castilians carried with them from the Iberian Peninsula. With the blessing of their faith and the strength of their lineage, they were ready to forge another chapter in the rich history of their lineage in the New World.

Colonization and Challenges in Tepatitlán

The first Spaniards who settled in Tepatitlán after the conquest of 1531 soon realized that colonization would bring unexpected challenges. The natives, who once populated the surrounding chiefdoms, voluntarily retreated. Some, merging with the tenacious Guamares in Cerro Gordo, fortified a formidable chieftaincy, while others dispersed to Zacatecas and nearby regions, finding affinity and alliance with the fearless Cazcanes, sharing both race and Nahuatl language.

This was the situation that the Castilians would face upon their arrival, a scenario narrated in detail as they approached Tepatitlán. However, their fears dissipated when they were received with joy and celebration. The news of their arrival, announced in advance by diligence is that regularly traveled to Guadalajara, had solidified favorable expectations. The community was already aware of the royal recommendation supporting these new colonists destined to populate the vast valleys still barren and desolate due to the Guamares' threat.

It was precisely this absence of settlements in those valleys, due to the persistent shadow of Cerro Gordo and its indigenous inhabitants, that was the reason for the warm welcome. The existing residents of Tepatitlán, driven by the promise of new neighbors and the prosperity they would bring, gathered at the town's entrance to receive the Castilians with joy and open arms. Their journey had been blessed by the Spanish crown, and they were now on the verge of a new life in the highlands of Jalisco.

Celebration and Reception in Tepatitlán

The arrival of the Castilians in Tepatitlán was an event that stirred great excitement among the already creole descendants of Spaniards, who had been eagerly anticipating the arrival of people directly from Castile, bearers of news from the old world and the land of their ancestors. The news of their coming had circulated widely, creating an atmosphere of anticipation and curiosity about learning more about the homeland of their forebears.

The reception was effusive and colorful, marked by festive paper flags and accompanied by a music band that evoked the Spanish bullfighting tradition, with the drumbeat of the tambora in the background. The visitors were treated to a celebration that marked their arrival, offering them a sumptuous meal and time to recover from the journey, accommodating them in various resting spaces: from the local inn, comparable to modern hotels, to the captain's estate, the monastery, and the rectory inhabited by the Franciscan friars.

The warmth and innate hospitality of the region's residents were evident in how they welcomed the newcomers, with some finding lodging in private homes where they quickly felt at home. The next day, with dawn still stretching on the horizon, the community eagerly gathered to interact with the newcomers, asking questions and observing them with admiration and respect, weaving bonds that would soon become an integral part of Tepatitlán's social fabric.

The Foundation of the Castilian Town

The arrival of the Castilians in Tepatitlán was met with a mixture of astonishment and curiosity; the local community was eager to learn everything about Castile and Spain, as well as about the experiences of the newcomers in their journey. The days were filled with lively and enriching exchanges, where the Castilians openly shared all the information and details, they could, enjoying the opportunity to establish new friendships and camaraderie.

A committee was quickly formed to organize and plan the settlement of the newcomers. They identified land north of Tepatitlán that was suitable for the construction and development of a new community. Inspired by their roots, they decided to name this new settlement "Villa," thus evoking the small towns of Castile. With the collaboration and enthusiasm of the people of Tepatitlán, bricks and tiles were started to be manufactured to build this promising "Villa." They focused not only on building homes but also on creating a chapel in honor of San José de Basarte, a name that still evokes a mysterious connection to Castile and has not yet been in records. The chapel was erected not only as a place of worship but also as a symbol of joint effort and shared heritage of this community, which still takes pride in its name and legacy.

Departure from Castile and Settlement in Tepatitlán

Upon leaving Castile, the 47 families embarked on a crucial mission, not only for themselves but also for the history of Tepatitlán. After a short period of hard and dedicated work, they managed to build enough houses to accommodate all the families in the Villa of Tepatitlán. With the basic structure already established, some members of these families returned to Mexico City to bring the rest of their loved ones, who eagerly awaited the reunion.

Once all the relatives gathered in the Villa, celebrations and meetings multiplied. It was a moment of joy and also of planning, as the task of dislodging the Guamares from Cerro Gordo still loomed over them. Fortunately, they had the support of the Viceroy of Mexico, who instructed that they be provided with everything necessary for their mission, including access to military detachments if necessary.

With everything prepared and in no hurry, in the idyllic Villa, the families devised a meticulous attack plan, employing stealth and surprise strategies that they mastered perfectly. The seriousness of the situation was evident to the inhabitants and ranchers of

Tepatitlán, and in a gesture of solidarity and bravery, hundreds of them volunteered to support the mission.

This chapter of history not only reflects the determination and bravery of those Castilians who crossed the ocean in search of a better future but also the spirit of community and cooperation that prevailed in those times. The Villa of Tepatitlán, built with effort and hope, became a symbol of unity and resilience in the face of challenges.

The Exile of the Guamares in Cerro Gordo

The presence of the Guamares in Cerro Gordo posed a significant challenge for the newly arrived Castilians and the inhabitants of Tepatitlán. The Guamares, upon realizing the arrival of these new and powerful people, initially showed indifference towards the muskets, as they were skilled in handling similar firearms. However, they soon understood that these newcomers were not ordinary; they must have had something special to have been specifically brought for this mission.

The Castilians, with the support of the locals and ranchers from the surrounding areas, strengthened their military strategy. They agreed to establish three fronts of attack: one visible and two invisibles. The visible front, the largest one, was backed by a part of the Viceroyalty's soldier detachments. In addition to their weaponry, the Castilians also brought Danish dogs, a key tool in their strategy.

The other plan, called "Ghost," involved stealth and surprise tactics. The people of Tepatitlán, known for their bravery and fondness for combat, played a crucial role in this approach. They were enthusiastic about the opportunity to confront the Guamares, showcasing their skills and courage.

This chapter illustrates the tenacity and ingenuity of the Castilians and the inhabitants of Tepatitlán, who, despite facing a formidable and well-established enemy in the region, were willing to use all tactics and resources at their disposal to achieve their goal and ensure the peace and security of the region.

In Cerro Gordo, the Guamares, aware of the challenge posed by the new Castilians and the population of Tepatitlán, prepared to face any attack. However, the meticulous and clever strategy of the Castilians, along with the collaboration of the brave inhabitants of Tepatitlán, was crucial in changing the course of events.

The plan devised by the Castilians and their allies involved a surprise attack from the rear, while another group, dressed simply but effectively to go unnoticed, slowly advanced to the front of Cerro Gordo. The objective was to capture any indigenous lookout to ensure a surprising and effective assault.

With caution and precision, the soldiers, and the people of Tepatitlán managed to capture several lookouts. At the crucial moment, when the Guamares were focused on repelling the frontal attack, the soldiers, and the people of Tepatitlán, like "ghosts," appeared from the rear, taking the Guamares by surprise. The shouts and shots caused confusion and disorder among them, missing the opportunity to organize an effective defense.

The Guamares, surprised and uncontrolled, did not have time to react properly and began to flee downhill among the trees, pursued by the Castilians and their allies. Despite the rapid escape of the Guamares, the effectiveness of the surprise attack was decisive for the victory of the Castilians and the inhabitants of Tepatitlán, marking a milestone in the process of colonization and pacification of the region. This chapter highlights the bravery, ingenuity, and determination of the Castilians and the locals to establish a new order in the region.

CHAPTER 9

The Consolidation of Los Altos de Jalisco

Following the successful exile of the Guamares from Cerro Gordo, the Castilians and their descendants embarked on a new stage of organization and settlement in the region of Los Altos de Jalisco. This process marked a significant change in local history, leading to the formation of stable and prosperous communities.

The Viceroy of Mexico, recognizing the valor and determination of these settlers, granted them generous "sites' ' of land, each covering approximately 22 square kilometers, a considerable expense for agricultural and livestock development. This distribution of land facilitated the establishment of new ranches and the flourishing of the region.

In this vast and fertile land, extending from the vicinity of Arandas to San Miguel el Alto and the Valle de Guadalupe, my Castilian ancestors dedicated themselves to agriculture, cattle breeding, and the construction of their homes and communities. This is how the heart of what is now known as Los Altos de Jalisco was formed.

The legacy of these brave and visionary Castilians is reflected in the rich culture and traditions of the region. Their effort and dedication not only transformed the physical landscape but also shaped the character and identity of Los Altos, a region that takes pride in its Spanish heritage and entrepreneurial spirit.

The Capilla de Guadalupe, my town, is a living testament to this history. Founded by these pioneers, it became a symbol of perseverance and the spirit of community that characterizes Los Altos de Jalisco. This story, woven with bravery, faith, and hard work, remains a source of inspiration for current and future generations.

The Colonization of My Region and the Ranches

By the year 1713 and 1714, with the challenges of the Guamares under control, a directive was formed to begin the planning and distribution of extensive lands in Los Altos de Jalisco. Although the specific details of the distribution process are not clear, it is evident that each family received their share, contributing to the foundation and development of various ranches in the region.

One of the first settlements was established on the northern slope of Cerro Gordo, where the royal road and the feared Guamares had previously been located. Today, this area is known as the Rancho de San Antonio of the famous champion charros, the Gueros Franco. The Torres, Galván, and Paredes families were among the first to settle in this area, possibly due to their bravery and willingness to face risks, or perhaps because of a draw.

However, despite the overall tranquility, problems with bands of bandits persisted. These groups attacked on roads and streets, and even in towns, becoming a constant threat to the safety of the settlers. Their ability to blend in with the population and disappear quickly made their capture difficult, creating an atmosphere of uncertainty and challenge for the newly formed communities. These circumstances demonstrated the strength and resilience of the early settlers in my region.

Despite obstacles and difficulties, they persevered in their effort to build a better life, leaving future generations with an example of tenacity and community spirit. This era of colonization and the formation of ranches is a fundamental chapter in the history of Los Altos de Jalisco, marking the beginning of an era of growth and prosperity in my homeland.

Rancho Cerro Gordo and El Cedazo

After the establishment of Rancho San Antonio, to the east and along the same Royal Road towards Arandas, Rancho Cerro Gordo was founded. This area was mainly colonized by the Hernandez families, along with other surnames that I cannot recall at this moment. To this day, Rancho Cerro Gordo is a picturesque town known for its people with fair features and the remarkable beauty of its women.

Not far from there, almost adjacent to Cerro Gordo, another ranch was established, El Cedazo, which retained that name for over 200 years. The renowned Barba family settled here, a very popular family throughout the Los Altos de Jalisco region. Over time, El Cedazo evolved into a larger and more significant town, now known as Los

Dolores. This place stands out for its commercial dynamism and modern productive infrastructure.

The name changes to Los Dolores coincided with the construction of a beautiful temple dedicated to the Virgin of Los Dolores. This church houses an impressive figure representing the Virgin Mary, a symbol of faith and devotion for the community. According to chronicles, in the 17th century, some friars passed through the region, leaving an indelible mark on the spirituality and traditions of the place.

These two ranches, Cerro Gordo and El Cedazo, are examples of the growth and development of the Los Altos de Jalisco region, reflecting the history, culture, and faith of its inhabitants. Over time, these communities have preserved their roots while adapting to the changes of the modern world, representing the resilient and entrepreneurial spirit of my land.

Rancho El Espino and Other Settlements in the Region

In 1943, a group of friars in transit from Guadalajara stopped to rest in El Cedazo. There, they encountered familiar families and gifted them a beautiful figure representing the Virgin of Dolores. Inspired by this gift, the residents built a charming temple dedicated to the Virgin, as well as a spacious square adorned with a kiosk. My visits to El Cedazo have always been welcoming; the people there are hospitable and simple, typical characteristics of the inhabitants of Los Altos. Additionally, the beauty of its women and the joy that the community radiates are noteworthy.

Rancho El Espino

This beautiful ranch, located in a picturesque plain, was founded by the distinguished Castellanos family. I fondly remember my visits to Don Eufodio Castellanos' large house, which had a lush fruit orchard.

It was there that, alongside his grandson Sisto, of my same age, I learned to ride a horse. We spent great moments together, departing from my town, La Capilla, on a horse named Panzón. However, there is a sad story associated with this place, which I will share later.

Continuation to Other Ranches

The history of my region does not end with Rancho El Espino. Over the years, other settlements and ranches have developed, each with its own history and contribution to the cultural tapestry of Los Altos de Jalisco. The richness of these lands and the strength of their inhabitants have woven an impressive legacy, marking every corner with stories of bravery, tradition, and progress. I will continue to narrate these stories, carrying them with me as a treasure of my heritage and my land.

The Legacy of Ranches in the Region - Las Teposas and Los González

In the northeast of El Espino lies Rancho Las Teposas, owned by the González family. I vividly remember visits to this place with Arturo González, the owner's son. One particularly cherished memory is when I caught my first fish in a pond on the ranch, using a hook borrowed from Arturo. Although it was just a small sardine, the excitement of that moment has endured in my memory. The González family settled in Las Teposas, creating a significant legacy in the region.

Los Palos and Los Ascencio

Further northeast lies Rancho Los Palos, founded by the influential Ascencio family. This ranch is recognized for its significant contribution to the development and wealth of the region, leaving an indelible mark on the local heritage.

La Loma de los Gorditos and Los González
To the north lies La Loma de los Gorditos, another prominent ranch under the management of the González family. This place is known for its grand temple and an impressive water reservoir. The González family, famous for their wealth, owned extensive cattle and land. They were known for their distinguished personality and for having many employees in their service, reflecting the prosperity and social status they had achieved in the region.

Each of these ranches, with its own unique stories and characteristics, contributes to the rich cultural tapestry of Los Altos de Jalisco. Their legacies continue to live on in the memory and traditions that persist to this day.

La Tinaja de los Navarro: A Corner of Stories and Memories
La Tinaja de los Navarro, a ranch near my town, holds a wealth of anecdotes and memories. This place, originally inhabited by the Navarro family, is special to me because of the numerous stories I have from there. I met some members of the De La Torre family, who likely migrated from San Jorge, an old ranch near San Miguel el Alto. La Tinaja represents a microcosm of the history and traditions of the region, reflecting how families have shaped the social and cultural landscape of Los Altos de Jalisco.

Every corner of this land, every ranch, and every family, tells a unique story that intertwines to form the rich tapestry of our regional heritage. In La Tinaja de los Navarro, as in many other places, the living history of those who forged their path in these lands can be felt.

Expansion and Prosperity in Ranches Near San Miguel el Alto

In the region near San Miguel el Alto, various families settled and, over time, achieved remarkable economic development. They became prominent landowners, cattle ranchers, farmers, and merchants, while also standing out for their high culture. Among these families are the Lozano, de Anda, Padilla, Gutiérrez, and Ramírez families, whose contributions significantly enriched the region.

Mirandilla: The Birthplace of Founding Families

Mirandilla, a picturesque little village, has its roots in my ancestors: the Martín del Campo, Franco, and Aceves families. This estate, already established long before the arrival of the 47 Castilian families in 1720, served as a resting and relay point for travelers and stagecoaches traveling from Durango, Zacatecas, and Aguascalientes along the Royal Road.

With the arrival of Castilian settlers, the Mirandilla area experienced a new boom. The Franco family, one of the first families to settle near the estate, soon moved south, near Cerro Gordo. There, they acquired extensive lands, starting near Cerro Gordo and stretching across the region. Over time, the Franco family and other families transformed these lands into prosperous estates, significantly contributing to the economic and social development of the region. This story of growth and prosperity in ranches near San Miguel el Alto is a testament to the tenacity and entrepreneurial spirit of these families, whose roots run deep in the history and culture of the region.

The Legacy of Juanacatlán and Mirandilla

Near Tepatitlán, along the Royal Road and extending to the foothills of Cerro Gordo, lies Rancho Juanacatlán, a land that bears witness to the perseverance and labor of our ancestors. Not far from there, in Mirandilla, the Martín del Campo and Aceves families emerged, along with the Casillas in Rancho El Terrero.

Mirandilla, now part of the municipality of San Miguel el Alto, reflects in its people the Castilian legacy: they are humble, hospitable, and faithful to their traditions and religious beliefs. The church of Mirandilla, though modest in size, stands out in the community with its splendid square where San Isidro Labrador is venerated, a saint with roots in Spain.

During my visit in 1990 to Mirandilla, I experienced a profound connection with the land of my ancestors. My great-grandfather Don Gerónimo Martín del Campo and my grandfather Antonio Martín del Campo were born here. The emotion of stepping on the same ground as them was indescribable. A cousin, Martín del Campo, who owns the old estate, showed me how he had renovated and preserved this important vestige of our family history, keeping alive the spirit and legacy of our Castilian ancestors in this region of Mexico.

Traditions and Legacy in Mirandilla

In Mirandilla, a town where echoes of the past resonate, I had the honor of meeting dear relatives bearing surnames such as Martín del Campo, Aceves, Cachos, and Gutiérrez. This place, steeped in history and traditions, still retains the charm of its Castilian heritage. The estate, with its original roof of ancient bricks known as "tablones," reveals inside its painted historical dates, a testimony to a past that still endures. The architecture and decoration of these structures reflect the influence and lifestyle of our ancestors.

My cousin showed me family relics, including old wolf spurs that belonged to my great-grandfather Jerónimo and his brothers. These were times when horsemanship was not only a means of transportation but also a symbol of status and tradition. The Martín del Campo family, farmers, and ranchers, enjoyed a solid economic position and were distinguished by their elegant attire, blending Spanish style with "chinaco," a characteristic fashion of 19th-century Mexico.

In Mirandilla, festivities and social events were the essence of community life. Bullfights, horse races, and cockfights were events that brought everyone together in a festive and celebratory atmosphere, keeping alive the customs inherited from Spain. These traditions, which began to merge with the emerging "charro" style towards the end of the 19th century, remain an integral part of local culture, uniting the community in the celebration of its rich historical and cultural legacy.

Musical Traditions and Family Settlements in the Altos de Jalisco

In the Altos de Jalisco, music is an essential part of the cultural fabric, a heritage that is kept alive through local bands. These groups, with their Spanish and European repertoire, enliven the plazas with the vibrant sound of the "tambora," performing paso dobles and marches that resonate in the afternoon air. It is a tradition that, even today, is preserved, offering towns and cities a living connection to their past.

In bullfighting events, these bands are a fundamental element, starting their performances with rhythms that mark the beginning of the bullfights. This custom, deeply rooted in the region, is a testament to the love for music and celebration, central elements of the local culture.

Speaking of attire, the ladies and gentlemen of yesteryears adorned themselves in their finery at these events, a practice that has evolved over time. Today, it is mainly the "charros" and "chinas poblanas" who uphold this tradition, proudly wearing their typical costumes in various celebrations.

Returning to the history of the colonization of the region, in the years following 1731, each family settled in their own ranch, creating a network of communities that extended along the Royal Road. In places like El Cedazo (now Los Dolores) and Mirandilla, my ancestors and other settlers forged their homes and lives.

Further south of Mirandilla, about 30-40 km away, lies the Presa de Gómez. Here, the Gómez family, known for their physical and moral stature, settled, and reflected in their simplicity and humility the essence of their Castilian heritage. These families, with their strong cultural identity, have contributed to the rich tapestry of the Altos de Jalisco, preserving and enriching the culture and traditions of the region.

Presa de Gómez and the Culture of Joy

In Presa de Gómez, a community rooted in deep values of faith and hospitality stands. Here, prominent families like the Gómez and Aceves manifest their devotion and love for God in a genuine and experiential way. This community is characterized by its human warmth and a sense of family unity that extends even to those who work with them, creating an environment where mutual support is the norm.

Music occupies a central place in the lives of these families. Their passion for the guitar and other musical instruments is more than a pastime; it is an expression of their joy of living and their rich cultural tradition. It is common to find men and women of all ages playing and singing, bringing joy to every corner of their community.

The Aceves, with roots in Mirandilla, have gradually intertwined with the residents of Presa de Gómez, creating bonds that go beyond neighborly relations. They share festivities and celebrations throughout the year, where music always takes center stage. These gatherings become true parties, where singing and music serve as the backdrop for community interaction and rejoicing.

In this community, any reason is sufficient to celebrate. The festivals are not just events; they are the manifestation of a culture that values joy, unity, and tradition. Presa de Gómez, with its enthusiastic and talented people, becomes a symbol of the joy of life, a place where music and fraternity form the fabric of its identity.

Traditions and Festivals in the Community

In the community, the arrival of the corn season is celebrated with a tradition known as "Elotadas." These celebrations, which extend throughout August and part of September, are a true expression of local culture and their love for communal gatherings. During the evenings, neighbors gather at any house, playing their instruments with great joy while preparing tender corn. These are cooked in a special way, often accompanied by tasty cheese adoberas, creating an exquisite and unique combination.

Grilled meats are not missing, or on special occasions, a fried suckling pig prepared in a copper pot, resulting in golden and delicious carnitas. Mentioning these dishes is enough to make anyone's mouth water, evoking the taste and joy of these gatherings.

If there are agave plants nearby, fresh pulque is brought, a traditional drink that complements the meal perfectly. Tacos are also prepared, filled with these delicious stews, enjoyed by everyone present.

Another notable tradition is the "Herraderos," especially in times of drought. These events involve gathering to brand cattle, but they also turn into a big celebration known as "Jaripeo." During these events, attendees could ride bulls, throw lassos, and perform charro maneuvers, showcasing their rope skills. Jaripeos are a day-long celebration, full of excitement, music, and of course, pulque to liven up the atmosphere.

These traditions reflect not only the cultural richness of the community but also its spirit of unity and fraternity. Through these festivities, the legacy of ancestors is preserved, and the social fabric of the region is strengthened.

Unforgettable Memories and Continuing the Journey

Throughout these festivities in La Presa de Gómez, music is always present, with guitars and accordions setting the mood. Typical meals, such as grilled meat or crispy carnitas tacos, are accompanied by beans, fresh cheese, and the inevitable jalapeño peppers. These elements combine to create a memorable culinary experience, capable of whetting the appetite just by remembering it.

These gatherings extend throughout the day, culminating with some attendees limping after being thrown by steers or colts during the jaripeo, and others feeling dizzy from the excess of pulque. At the end of the day, each one returns home, promising to meet again next year to continue this tradition.

Leaving behind the pleasant memories of La Presa de Gómez, I continue my journey westward, approximately four or five kilometers away. Here, I am greeted by other dear friends and the promise of new experiences. Although the passage of time and distance may impose limitations, memories remain vivid in my mind. I reflect on what the world would be like if everyone shared the generosity and community spirit of the people of La Presa de Gómez. I am convinced it would be a much warmer and more welcoming place. With this idea in mind, I continue my journey, carrying with me the warmth of hospitality and the joy of shared experiences.

The Alcalá Family, a Legacy of Respect and Tradition

El Cacalote, a charming corner of the region, became the home of the Alcalá family, who have preserved respect and kindness as their core values. This family, possibly originating from Alcalá in Castile, Spain - a city known for its prestigious university founded in 1508 by King Ferdinand of Aragon - has kept their legacy alive in this Mexican land.

The Alcalá family, possibly linked to the city of Alcalá, shares a historical connection with the city of Guadalajara in Spain, where Nuñez Beltrán de Guzmán, the founder of Guadalajara, Jalisco, Mexico, in 1542, hails from. This connection to their Spanish roots has profoundly influenced their way of life and work.

In El Cacalote, the Alcalá family, like other settlers, began their life in Mexico by engaging in agricultural work and cattle development. However, they stand out particularly for their skills as merchants. Their proximity to Mirandilla has allowed them to establish family ties with the Martín family, further enriching their history with shared anecdotes and experiences.

In their day-to-day lives, the Alcalá family reflects their entrepreneurial spirit and commitment to the community. While they maintain a low profile, their influence and respect in the region are notable. They are known for their ability to react firmly, when necessary, always maintaining a respectful demeanor towards others. In future chapters, we will continue to explore the stories and anecdotes surrounding this fascinating family, whose life mirrors the rich cultural and social heritage of their Castilian ancestors.

Rancho La Cruz and El Centro: The Gonzales and Estrada Families, Pillars of Tradition and Courage

In the heart of the Los Altos de Jalisco region, Rancho La Cruz, the ancestral residence of the Gonzales family, stands as a bastion of equestrian and charro tradition. The Gonzales, recognized for their cordiality and social prominence, have been fundamental pillars in the Charro Association of Tepatitlán. This ranch, located east of Rancho El Cacalote, symbolizes the rich cattle heritage and strong sense of community that characterizes the area.

To the east, lies El Centro, a place that has witnessed the settlement and flourishing of the Estrada family. Descendants of a revered communal defender, the Estrada family has maintained their legacy in El Centro to this day. Florencio Estrada, the brother of my great-grandfather Demetrio Estrada and the uncle of my grandmother Doña María de Jesús (Mamá Chita) Estrada, is still remembered as a man of unwavering courage, dedicated to both his community and his deep Catholic faith.

Catholic devotion, intertwined with a spirit of courage, has been a distinctive feature of the Estrada family. Their fervent veneration of the Virgin of Guadalupe has marked generations. The stories of my grandmother Mamá Chita, recounting her childhood and her spiritual relationship with the Virgin, highlight how this devotion has been a cornerstone in family and community life.

These tales not only illustrate the cultural and spiritual richness of my lineage but also emphasize the crucial role of faith and traditions in shaping the regional identity of Los Altos de Jalisco. The blend of courage and spirituality in figures like Florencio Estrada and his descendants has indelibly permeated the cultural legacy of the region.

The Navarro Family and Their Legacy

In the pages of family history, the figure of Demetrio Navarro emerges with strength and character. His mother, Doña Matilde Navarro, belonged to a lineage of resilience and conviction. The Rancho de San Antonio, located on the slopes of Cerro Gordo and mentioned earlier, housed the house that Don Simón, my great-great-grandfather, built in the 19th century, a residence that symbolizes the tenacity and effort of generations.

Demetrio, always accompanied by his only daughter Matilde, used to travel on horseback from the Capilla de Guadalupe to the ranch. During these journeys, the rosary was a constant, reflecting a deep family devotion. Demetrio, always vigilant against the dangers of the time, never failed to carry his faithful carrillera and pistol, indispensable tools in an era marked by the presence of bandits.

The Estrada family, according to memories shared by my grandmother Chita, were not part of the Castilian families that originally arrived. Their origin seemed to be external, perhaps adventurers or travelers who found a new home in our land. Of medium stature and robust constitution, the Estradas were characterized by their fair skin and prominent features. Among them, four brothers stood out; two of them moved near Guadalajara, facing the issues posed by the region's bandits.

This family legacy, intertwined with the history of courageous ancestors, reflects not only the inherited strength and determination but also a deep connection to the land and cultural roots that define us. Through these narratives, we glimpse the essence of a family that, over generations, has contributed to the social and cultural fabric of our region.

The Courage and Strategy of the Estrada Family in the Fight Against Bandits

In the heart of our family history, the prominent figure of the Estrada brothers emerges, including my great-uncle Florencio Estrada, who alongside his brother played a crucial role in defending the region against bandits. These brothers, who chose to settle near the hacienda in a challenging area, implemented ancient and effective tactics to maintain peace and order.

My grandmother Chita recalled how these brave Estradas trained their Great Dane dogs for protection and combat, and how expertly handling the saber was an integral part of their preparation. These practices, witnessed by my grandmother in her childhood, demonstrated the skill and prowess they possessed in the art of personal defense and military tactics.

Two of the Estrada brothers, according to the accounts, settled in the hacienda and later found their eternal rest in the village cemetery of Taterosco. This place became a point of reflection and prayer for my mother and me during our travels, recognizing and honoring the bravery and sacrifice of our relatives.

The Estrada family, along with the community of La Capilla, faced significant challenges, tirelessly battling the bands of bandits that ravaged the region. Their commitment to not only safety but also the well-being of the community positioned them as key figures in the history of our town.

This chapter of our family history is a testimony to the courage, determination, and fighting spirit that characterized the Estradas and undoubtedly left an indelible mark on the collective memory of our community.

The Courage and Resilience of Demetrio Estrada

The story of my great-grandfather, Demetrio Estrada, is a tale of courage and tenacity. His active participation in defending his community against bandits is a testament to his brave and committed character. The anecdote of the bullet he carried near his spine throughout his life is a testament to his resilience and strength, qualities that defined his existence.

Demetrio, wounded in a confrontation with bandits, demonstrated his cunning and survival skills by hiding among the reeds of a pond, avoiding capture or further injury. Although the bullet was never removed, his unbreakable spirit allowed him to continue his life without diminishing his energy or commitment to his family and community.

The house he built in La Capilla, still standing and preserved in its magnificent original structure, is a symbol of his legacy and the place he held in the heart of his town. With its imposing portals, this house reflects not only the physical greatness of its construction but also the greatness of Demetrio's spirit and his family.

Demetrio Estrada, with his courage and ability to overcome adversity, became an emblematic figure in the history of our family and the community. His life is a source of inspiration and a reminder of the value of resilience and determination in the face of challenges.

Enriching the Story of the Life of Don Florencio Estrada and His Son Justo

The story of my great-grandfather, Don Florencio Estrada, and his son, Justo, is a tale of courage, leadership, and adventurous spirit. Don Florencio, known for his firmness and respect in the community, served as Delegate in La Capilla for two terms. Under his leadership, the town enjoyed a period of peace and order, demonstrating his ability to maintain harmony and security in the region.

The house he built with iron beams, brought from Mexico City via Guanajuato, is a symbol of his tenacity and vision. These beams, transported on ox-drawn carts, reflect not only a logistical feat for the time but also Don Florencio's determination to build a solid and enduring home.

His son, Justo Estrada, inherited the entrepreneurial and adventurous spirit of his father. The story of Don Florencio traveling to Colima, a small state southwest of Jalisco, illustrates the fearless nature of the Estrada family. Although the reasons for this journey are not certain, they were likely related to business or simply exploration and discovery, characteristic traits of the family.

Don Florencio Estrada's union with a woman from the Gómez family of Presa de Gómez is an example of how families in the region interwove, creating networks of kinship and mutual support that strengthened the community. These family stories, full of anecdotes and memories, not only narrate the lives of individuals but also weave the rich social and cultural history of Los Altos de Jalisco.

The lives of Don Florencio Estrada and his son Justo in La Capilla and San Antonio, near the foothills of Cerro Gordo, are marked by episodes of courage and joy. A story my grandmother used to tell highlights Don Florencio's daring and courage. On a trip with his son Justo, young and inexperienced in confrontations, they were caught in an ambush. Don Florencio, with his proverbial strength, encouraged his son amid crossfire, giving him an opportunity to demonstrate his bravery. This experience was not only a rite of passage for Justo but also a testimony to Don Florencio's cunning and resilience.

As Justo matured, he became a man of youthful and pragmatic spirit. His relationship with his horse, which he had trained with such skill that it responded to gestures and words, is an example of the special connection Justo had with animals. His horse was so intelligent that it could perform remarkable actions like greeting at Justo's signal demonstrating a blend of ingenuity and good humor that characterized Justo.

The coexistence in La Capilla and San Antonio was a blend of tradition, culture, and family solidarity. Don Florencio and Justo's stories, with their adventures and their closeness to the community, paint a vivid picture of life in these places. Courage, loyalty, and joy were part of everyday life. These narratives not only recount personal events but also illustrate the resilient and joyful character of the Estrada family and their contribution to the communal spirit of the region.

The Refinement of the Story of Rancho La Cebadilla and Juanacasco

La Cebadilla, an emblematic corner to the north of Rancho El Centro, housed the Cacillas family, distinct from the Casillas of Terrero. This region, characterized by its people of prominent stature and robust physical constitution, was also home to the Markes. The presence of these families reflects the diversity and cultural richness of the region.

Not far from there, in El Cuatro, another branch of the Gonzales family settled. It seems that the surname Gonzales has deep roots in northern Spain, specifically in Castilla La Vieja and the mountainous region of Santander, there is evidence of an important historical and genealogical connection with the Castilla region in Spain.

To the south of El Cuatro, about ten kilometers away, lies Juanacasco. This place has witnessed the breeding of brave cattle, gaining notable fame in the region. Juanacasco is not only known for its cattle-raising activity but also as a place filled with stories and traditions that reflect rural life and the customs of its inhabitants. The interaction between families, the land, and their traditions forms a cultural mosaic that enriches the history of this part of Mexico, showcasing the strength and vitality of the communities that have made these ranches their home.

Juanacasco, a historic and prominent ranch, has been a symbol of the bull breeding tradition in Mexico. This ranch, known for breeding pure-blooded and fierce cattle, has also been the stage for memorable rodeos, contributing to the emergence and strengthening of "charrería" as an organized and unique sport in Mexico, recognized nationally by the National Federation of Charro Associations. The legacy of Juanacasco is intimately linked to the Franco family, particularly Don Miguel Franco the Great, my great-great-grandfather, whose anecdotes and achievements have been passed down through generations in my family. My grandparents, Don Antonio Martín del Campo Franco, a grandson of Don Miguel, and Doña María de Jesús Estrada, have shared countless stories about life in Juanacasco and its influence on the region.

In the early 19th century, Juanacasco stood out for its high-quality brave cattle breeding, a legacy that extended until the end of that century. It is said that the cattle were brought from unknown places, and a breeding ground was established on a nearby hill, known as El Cerro Carnicero, due to the nature of raising fierce cattle. This ranch not only became a pillar of cattle culture but also a gathering center for events and celebrations that defined the cultural identity of the region.

The Refinement of the Story of Franco's Bull Breeding in Juanacasco

The history of the Franco family's bull breeding in Juanacasco is a narrative filled with anecdotes and lived experiences, passed down through generations. My grandparents used to share fascinating stories from this era, emphasizing the caution needed while traversing the pastures of El Cerro, especially due to the fierceness of even the youngest calves.

An anecdote my grandmother Chita used to recount with emotion involved her encounters with these seemingly harmless calves. In an instant, what appeared to be a peaceful encounter would transform into a dangerous situation, forcing her to run to avoid being charged. My grandfather, with his skill and experience, would intervene to control the situation, but these episodes left my grandmother with a mixture of fear and admiration for my grandfather's bravery and skill.

These stories not only reflect daily life on the ranch but also the generational change and contrast with modern life, where the challenge is no longer fierce bulls but traffic on the streets.

The Francos, originally from Mirandilla, expanded their cattle breeding legacy by creating several ranches in the late 18th century. These lands extended from Juanacasco to part of Cerro Carnicero, covering a significant area dedicated to cattle breeding. This territorial expansion not only strengthened the family's economic position but also solidified their reputation as prominent cattle ranchers in the region.

The Refinement of the Story of Rancho Juanacasco and Don Miguel Franco

Rancho Juanacasco, under the careful management of Don Miguel Franco, my great-great-grandfather, became a symbol of bull breeding at the end of the 18th century. This territory, stretching from Cerro Gordo to Camino Real, encompassed a vast expanse of fertile land, ideal for the development of the estate and cattle care.

Don Miguel, known for his skill and passion for bullfighting, inherited not only Juanacasco but also a significant portion of land and the renowned bull breeding. This inheritance conferred upon him not only a prestigious position in Tepatitlán and Guadalajara but also the responsibility to maintain the tradition and quality of bull breeding.

In addition to the fierce cattle, Don Miguel owned large herds of gentle cattle, characterized by their spotted white and red skin. Although not known for their dairy production, these cattle provided rich, thick milk, ideal for making a unique artisanal cheese, typical of the Altos de Jalisco. The large and robust horns of these animals were a distinctive feature, used in various ranch tasks.

The legacy of Don Miguel Franco in Juanacasco is reflected not only in the success of his cattle breeding but also in the preservation of the customs and traditions of the region, making him an iconic figure in the history of cattle breeding in Jalisco.

The Refinement of the Story of Rancho Maravillas - Los Villaseñor

Rancho Maravillas, a place whose name reflects the beauty and uniqueness of its surroundings and inhabitants, is known for the warmth and friendliness of its residents. The Villaseñor family, of Castilian ancestry, were the founders of this ranch, located to the west of Rancho Los Sauces, very close to the foothills of Cerro Gordo and on the route to Juanacasco.

The Villaseñor family, part of the Castilian lineage that settled in the region, significantly contributed to the development of Maravillas. This ranch, immersed in a peaceful and socially cohesive environment, reflects the spirit of community and collaboration that is characteristic of the area. The proximity to the Francos, another prominent family in the region, indicates the interconnectedness and mutual support among the families that have formed the social fabric of this corner of Jalisco.

Maravillas is not only a place for gathering and coexistence but also a testimony to the cultural richness and Castilian heritage that persist in its traditions and in the daily lives of its inhabitants. This unique blend of history, culture, and community makes Maravillas a truly special place in the heart of Jalisco.

The Refinement of the Story of Rancho El Cinco - Los Domínguez

Rancho El Cinco, located in the prosperous region of Los Altos de Jalisco, is a place known for its proximity to the historic Camino Real and as the birthplace of the Domínguez family. Situated south of Rancho Los Sauces, right at the beginning of the foothills of Cerro Gordo, this ranch shares the rich history and tradition of the area.

My most vivid memory of El Cinco dates to my childhood when my mother took me to visit this special place. Although in those times, the Camino Real was no longer a frequently traveled route, it retained its charm and historical significance. I remember the large stones scattered along the path and the lush ash trees that cast their shade over the reddish soil, features that make this place a picturesque and unique landscape.

The Domínguez family, residents of Rancho El Cinco, has maintained a close and friendly relationship with the inhabitants of Rancho Los Sauces and the surrounding areas. This ranch, through generations, has been a testament to the spirit of the Mexican rural community, where hospitality and human warmth are deeply ingrained values.

El Cinco is not only a physical place but also a symbol of the roots and identity of the region, reflecting the history and traditions that have been passed down from generation to generation, creating a rich and diverse cultural legacy.

The Refinement of the Story of the Descendants of Castilian Families and Rancho El Cinco

Rancho El Cinco, a legacy of the great Castilian families, is home to the Domínguez family, known for their nobility and simplicity. The Domínguez family, with imposing physical stature and generous hearts, remains an integral part of the community in this corner of Mexico.

I vividly recall a pond at El Cinco that I used to visit as a child, especially during the rainy season. Despite warnings about the danger of swimming in it, the allure of its waters was always irresistible. A local tale narrated the tragic story of a mule loaded with gold that submerged in that pond and never resurfaced, adding a veil of mystery and adventure to the place.

Regarding the 47 Castilian families that settled in the region, there are many surnames and ranches that could be mentioned. Over time, some of these families chose to establish residences in the towns near their ranches, seeking comfort and access to education for their families. An example of this is the Orozco family, who, like many others, lived in two worlds: the rural one of their ranches and the more urban one of the nearby towns.

These families, with their stories and traditions, have woven a rich tapestry of culture and heritage in the region, representing the resilient and entrepreneurial spirit of the descendants of those first Castilian settlers.

The Refinement of the Narrative about "El Palenque" and Other Ranches

El Palenque, located on the eastern slope of Cerro Gordo, is a ranch known for its natural beauty. I distinctly remember a visit there where we encountered several rattlesnakes. We captured them and, after removing their skin, grilled their meat, which turned out to be surprisingly tasty. The skill and bravery of the inhabitants of El Palenque in the face of such natural challenges are a testament to their connection to and respect for the land they inhabit.

Near my town, to the north and adjacent to Rancho El Centro de los Estrada, are the ranches La Paleta and El Montecillo. These are close to Presa de Gómez, an area known for its lush nature and rural traditions. El Lavadero de Don Salvador Castellanos is famous for its Triángulo paddock, a space used for exciting horse races that attract enthusiasts from across the region.

On the other hand, El Saltillo, a ranch located east of La Capilla, holds countless anecdotes that reflect the rich history and culture of the area. Although I don't exactly remember who owned it, my visits to El Saltillo were always filled with memorable experiences and fascinating stories that enrich the tapestry of our family and regional heritage. These places, with their histories and people, are an integral part of the identity and legacy of the descendants of those original 47 Castilian families.

The Jiménez: Prominent and Traditional Inhabitants of Los Altos de Jalisco

In the rich tapestry of families that make up the region of Los Altos de Jalisco, the Jiménez family holds a special place. This family, settled on a ranch near La Capilla whose name I don't remember now, is known for their distinctive Arab features, unique in the region. However, their integration with the Castellanos in Spain is evident, as they share a deep Christian faith and fervent Catholicism. The Jiménez family has stood out for their entrepreneurial spirit and friendly character, being recognized in the community not only for their hard work but also for their skills in trade. Don Andrés Jiménez is an iconic figure in the locality. Known as a passionate "parejero," he has organized and won numerous horse races, demonstrating his ability to select and train the best specimens in the area. Additionally, his interest in cockfighting is well-known; he has a breeding ground where he prepares his roosters to compete in the cockpits during the annual festivities held in towns and cities.

Alongside the Jiménez family, other families like the Vargas have also left their mark on the region, contributing their culture, traditions, and effort to the development and richness of Los Altos de Jalisco. Each surname, each family, contributes its unique essence to this vibrant and diverse community.

The History and Development of Surnames in the Region of Los Altos de Jalisco and Valle de Guadalupe

In the rich and diverse history of Los Altos de Jalisco and Valle de Guadalupe, surnames like Lopes, Morales, Gallegos, Casillas, Gutierrez, Franco, Martín, Lozano, Muñoz, and Arias play a crucial role in the development and formation of the region's identity. Each of these surnames carries a unique history, with roots extending to various parts of Spain, including regions like Galicia in the northwest. The Gutierrez surname, for example, has been notable in the research and preservation of the roots and foundation of my town. I want to highlight my great-great-grandfather Francisco de Aceves. Although I don't have exact data on his birthdate, it is plausible that he, being still young, was one of those who traveled from Castilla in 1772 alongside his parents. His settlement in Estancia de Mirandilla could have been a significant step in the formation and consolidation of the Aceves family in the region.

These surnames not only represent family lineages but also stories of migration, adaptation, and contributions to the economic, cultural, and social development of Los Altos de Jalisco and Valle de Guadalupe. Each family has left an indelible mark, contributing to the rich tapestry of the history of this Mexican region.

Revision and Improvement of the Text about Don Francisco de Aceves

Don Francisco de Aceves, a pioneer in Mirandilla, is a key figure in the region's history. Although the Francos were the first to settle there, their stay was ephemeral as they soon moved south, near Cerro Gordo, acquiring vast expanses of land to establish some of the most important cattle ranches in the area, including bull breeding.

The Aceves family, on the other hand, remained in Estancia de Mirandilla. Francisco, a son of this family, grew up in the vast and beautiful valleys of the region, which flourished splendidly during the rainy season, resembling enormous gardens with lush green and dense grass, ideal for cattle.

Being young, Francisco had to take on important responsibilities on the estate, including the care of cattle and the supervision of the lands. It is presumed that he had a good horse, essential for moving around the extensive grounds and visiting neighboring ranches. Estancia de Mirandilla was a strategic point on the route, where travelers and stagecoaches traveling between Mexico and Zacatecas would often stop to rest.

As the years passed, Francisco emerged as a leader in his community, maintaining and improving Estancia de Mirandilla, a place that not only served as a mandatory stop for travelers but also became a vital center for the development and prosperity of the region.

Revision and Improvement of the Text about the Birth and Youth of Don Antonio de Aceves

Don Antonio de Aceves was born in 1757, into the Aceves family, which had settled in Mirandilla. He was the son of Francisco de Aceves and a distinguished lady from the Casillas family, established in El Terrero, an area near Mirandilla, in a westward direction. His parents were married on an unspecified date, but surely when both were of legal age.

Young Antonio was baptized in honor of his mother, Doña Antonia Casillas, reflecting the deep affection and respect his father felt for her. He grew up as an energetic and lively child, with the typical characteristics of a European youth of the time. Under the careful guidance of his parents, Antonio developed in an environment where the values of good Christianity and fervent Catholic devotion were emphasized.

He was often taken to attend Mass in Tepatitlán or possibly in San Miguel el Alto, the nearest town. These visits also served to stock up on provisions and for Antonio to become familiar with the surroundings and neighboring communities. He learned to ride with skill and cunning, an essential skill in those times, especially in a region where the horse was not only a means of transportation but also a symbol of status and skill.

In his youth, Antonio de Aceves moved to Presa de Gómez to work with one of the Gómez family, a prominent family in the region. This experience was crucial for his personal and professional development, providing him with the opportunity to learn and grow in an environment different from his family home in Mirandilla.

Revision and Improvement of the Text about Don Antonio in Presa de Gómez and His Marriage

After settling in Presa de Gómez, Don Antonio began to work diligently on the lands of the Gómez family, known for their skill and success in agriculture. During this time, he had the opportunity to meet a young lady from the same family, affectionately called Lolita, a woman who presumably stood out for her beauty and stature, typical characteristics of the region.

The relationship between Antonio and Lolita flourished, culminating in a marriage that was seen as ideal for the time. Over time, the couple earned the respect and affection of the community, becoming known as Don Antonio and Doña Lola. This marriage was blessed with children: three daughters and a son, whom they named Agustín.

Don Antonio continued his work with even greater dedication and responsibility, now not only supporting his in-laws but also his own family. However, an unexpected event would mark a significant turning point in his life. One day, a large shipment of gold from the mines of Zacatecas, guarded by soldiers of the Viceroyalty, was on its way to its destination. This event would prove to be a turning point in Don Antonio's life, completely altering his trajectory and fortune.

Revision and Improvement of the Text about the Foundation of La Capilla and El Amo Aceves

In those times of uncertainty and audacity, Don Antonio, who would later be known as "El Amo Aceves," had a fortuitous encounter that would change his destiny forever.

It is told in the story that a shipment of gold, pursued by bandits and destined elsewhere, was hidden near the Estancia to safeguard it. Those responsible for its custody never returned, leaving the treasure forgotten.

One fateful day, as Don Antonio was traveling in his ox-drawn cart from Mirandilla to Presa de Gómez, near Estancia, one of the wheels sank into the ground. This mishap turned out to be a disguised blessing, as it was right there that he discovered the abandoned gold. This discovery radically transformed his life, making him immensely rich and powerful, earning him the moniker "El Amo Aceves."

With his newfound wealth, he bought extensive lands, becoming one of the most prominent landowners in the region. However, notoriety did not come without risks. Bands of bandits, aware of his wealth, began to pursue him with the intention of robbing him.

On one occasion, while riding through his domains, where my town, La Capilla, is located today, he was ambushed by a gang of outlaws. In that critical moment, Don Antonio, an excellent rider, skillfully evaded them among the underbrush and bushes. In his desperate escape, he invoked the protection of the Virgin of Guadalupe, asking for her intercession to save him from his pursuers.

Don Antonio Aceves: Brave Castilian and Devotee of the Dark Virgin Guadalupana

Don Antonio Aceves, possessed of the innate bravery of a noble Castilian, faced great danger one day. Pursued by a band of bandits, he found himself in a desperate situation. Trusting in his equestrian skill and divine protection, he invoked the Dark Virgin Guadalupana to guide him in his escape. Despite being outnumbered, his skill and divine intervention allowed him to escape unscathed, baffling his pursuers who were astonished to lose sight of him.

Grateful for the miraculous escape, Don Antonio promised the Virgin of Guadalupe to build a chapel in her honor, in the place where he felt the danger had passed. The exact year of this event is not known, nor how long it took to fulfill the promise, but it is believed to have been around 1810, after the death of Doña Dolores Gómez.

After this event, Don Antonio married again, this time to a maternal relative named María Casillas. Possibly, it was during this period that he decided to fulfill his promise to the Virgin. In 1823, he went to his lands, where my town is now located, with the firm purpose of building the promised chapel. First, he erected a large house to oversee the construction up close. Once established with his family, he proceeded to build the chapel in honor of the Virgin of Guadalupe, thus fulfilling his vow of gratitude and devotion.

La Capilla and the Emergence of a Town

In 1823, after the construction of the chapel dedicated to the Virgin of Guadalupe, Don Antonio Aceves, known as "El Amo Aceves," along with his family and close associates, began to give life to the town that surrounded this sacred place. His sons-in-law Navarro, originally from Rancho La Tinaja, and his son-in-law De la Torre, from Rancho San Jorge, joined in this effort, accompanied by his son Agustín. Together, they managed the vast lands and numerous livestock of Don Antonio.

The construction of the chapel was received with enthusiasm by the ranchers from the surrounding areas. Before its existence, inhabitants had to travel long distances to attend Mass in places like Tepatitlán, Arandas, or San Miguel el Alto. Motivated by Don Antonio's initiative, these ranchers began to build their homes around the chapel, forming orderly streets and a spacious square.

In this emerging settlement, lacking a nearby river, several ponds were created to supply water to the community. One of the most notable was "El Tajo," a reflection of the effort and community unity inspired by the miracle attributed to the Dark Virgin Guadalupana and Don Antonio Aceves's vision. This town, rooted in faith and cooperation, began to flourish, becoming a testament to the power of belief and collective work.

The development of La Capilla, driven by Don Antonio Aceves, known as "El Amo Aceves," marked a new era for the region. After the construction of the chapel dedicated to the Virgin of Guadalupe in 1823, numerous families, including the Gonzales, Castellanos, Gómez, Barba, and Orozco, began to settle in the area, especially after 1860. La Capilla became a hub of activity and growth, attracting more families over time.

"El Amo Aceves" used the gold he had found to acquire extensive lands around the chapel. These extended beyond the Royal Road, which crossed the slope of Cerro Gordo, and reached almost to Presa de Gómez. Furthermore, his properties covered large areas both to the east and west of the town.

Among his most significant acquisitions, Don Antonio bought a piece of land from the Guarro family, using pure gold as payment.

This site, measuring two square leagues, was located near where the Orozco family later settled, southeast of La Capilla. In this area, the Guarro family had established a hacienda called "La Trasquila," named after their vast flock of sheep, whose wool was sheared annually. Over time, the name "La Trasquila" became popular due to the importance of this economic activity in the region.

Through the vision and effort of Don Antonio Aceves, La Capilla and its surroundings flourished, becoming a prosperous center of agricultural and livestock activity, rooted in the rich cultural heritage of its founders.

The story of Don Antonio de Aceves, a key figure in the founding of La Capilla, is a tale of determination and resilience. By the time he founded the chapel in 1823, Don Antonio, at the age of about 66, had already lived a life full of changes and challenges. After the death of his first wife, Doña Dolores Gómez, and subsequently his second wife, Doña María Casillas del Terrero, Don Antonio quickly found solace and companionship in Doña María Gregoria de la Cámara, a daughter of a captain.

At the time of the founding of La Capilla, Don Antonio had already formed a new family with Doña Gregoria, with whom it is said he had several children. This stage of his life was marked by stability and family consolidation, fundamental aspects for the development of the new community. Along with his son Agustín, his three daughters, and three sons-in-law, including one from the De la Torre family and two sons of Luciano Navarro, Don Antonio embarked on the task of building not only a physical structure in honor of the Virgin of Guadalupe but also a united and prosperous community. The story of Don Antonio de Aceves is a testimony to his tenacity and ability to overcome personal adversities, transforming his vision into a tangible reality that would endure over time. His legacy, evidenced in the founding of La Capilla, remains a pillar in the history and identity of his community.

Don Luciano Navarro and His Connection to Don Antonio de Aceves

Don Luciano Navarro, a prominent descendant in my family history, played a crucial role in uniting two prominent families. He married María, one of the daughters of Don Antonio de Aceves and Doña Dolores Gómez, thus strengthening the ties between both families. From this union, two male children were born, Felipe and Simón, and one daughter.

Another daughter of Don Antonio and Doña Dolores, whose name is not specified in the narration, found a partner in a young man with the last name De la Torre, originally from Rancho San Jorge, near San Miguel El Alto. From this marriage, María del Refugio was born, affectionately known as Doña Mariquita, who in turn married her cousin Felipe Navarro, also a grandson of Don Antonio.

Don Agustín Aceves, the only son of Don Antonio, had a daughter named María Concepción (Conchita) Aceves. Although it is not detailed whom she married, it is mentioned that Conchita married Simón Navarro, the brother of my great-grandfather Felipe and also a cousin of Conchita, reflecting the customs of the time that favored marriages among close relatives.

These family unions, although they may be considered unusual today, were common in that era and played an important role in consolidating ties between prominent families in the region. The story of Don Luciano Navarro and his relationship with the Aceves family is an example of how family dynamics and strategic marriages influenced the formation of community and power networks in the society of that time.

The Fusion of the Families of Don Luciano Navarro and Don Antonio de Aceves

The story of the union between the families of Don Luciano Navarro and Don Antonio de Aceves is a tale of deep and complex family connections. This union, marked by the marriage between first cousins, had a significant impact on the subsequent generations.

The Consequences of Marriages among Relatives

The practice of marrying close relatives, although common in those times, brought certain challenges. A notable example is the offspring of Don Simón Navarro and Conchita Aceves, where a prevalence incidence of deafness and several natural abortions were observed, probably because of their consanguineous relationship. From their union, only one daughter thrived, Matilde Navarro Aceves, who would become the mother of my grandmother, Doña Jesusita Estrada Navarro.

The House in San Antonio and the Foundation of the Chapel

My great-grandfather Simón Navarro, brother of Felipe Navarro, built a large house near the Royal Road and the slope of Cerro Gordo around 1860. This house became a significant home for the family and a landmark in the region.

Family Diversification and Legacy

On the other hand, the marriage of Felipe Navarro to Doña Mariquita de la Torre did not present the same complications, possibly due to less consanguinity. This marriage, between members of different lineages, brought new diversity to the family. The history of these two prominent families, the Navarros and the Aceves, reflects the customs and marital practices of the time. Despite the challenges and complexities, these marriages wove a network of relationships and legacies that have endured over time, shaping an important chapter in family history and in the history of the region.

The Evolution of the Chapel and the Town of Guadalupe

The history of Don Felipe Navarro and his brother, Simón, unfolds in the context of a growing town, originating around the chapel founded by their grandfather, Don Antonio Aceves, in honor of the Virgin of Guadalupe. Originally known as Guadalupe, the town eventually adopted the name Capilla de Guadalupe.

Growth and Development under Don Antonio's Guidance

Under the guidance of their grandfather, Don Felipe and Simón grew and thrived in this prosperous environment. The family, benefiting economically from their vast lands and cattle, played a crucial role in the organization and expansion of the town. As the community grew, more people from nearby ranches came to settle, contributing to the orderly development of the place.

Don Felipe: A Beloved Grandson

Don Felipe, being the eldest of the brothers and greatly cherished by his grandfather, assumed an important role in managing the family's lands and cattle. Although Don Antonio had other descendants with his last wife, Doña Gregoria de la Cámara, Felipe stood out as the most trusted and competent grandson, especially after his marriage.

Family Consolidation and Legacy

The union of Don Felipe with his wife, along with his brother Simón, further strengthened the family's position in the community. Their ability to efficiently manage family resources and their commitment to the well-being of the town helped solidify the legacy of their grandfather Don Antonio, ensuring the progress and prosperity of Capilla de Guadalupe. The story of these brothers represents not only an important chapter in the family chronicle but also a testament to the entrepreneurial spirit and community vision that characterized this generation.

The Departure of Amo Aceves and His Legacy

The death of Amo Aceves, Don Antonio, marked a turning point in family and town history. Before his passing, around 1834 and 1835, he ensured to leave a well-structured will, distributing his wealth among his heirs. He specifically granted a considerable portion of his gold to his grandsons, Don Felipe and Don Simón Navarro, recognizing in Don Felipe, his favorite grandson, the capability and leadership needed to continue his legacy.

Don Felipe Navarro: Continuing Amo Aceves' Vision

Already married, Don Felipe embarked on the construction of a large estate south of the original small chapel, with the purpose of demolishing it and erecting a larger temple in its place. This decision not only reflected his commitment to the family legacy but also his devotion and respect for the beliefs and traditions instilled by his grandfather.

The estate, built on previously unoccupied land, became a focal point for the community, especially during the annual festivals, where bullfights were held using the fierce bulls from Don Miguel Franco, located on Cerro Carnicero. These events, in addition to showcasing the region's cultural heritage, also strengthened community and family bonds.

CHAPTER 10

The Legacy of Don Miguel Franco and the Bullfighting Tradition

Don Miguel Franco, the great-grandfather of the narrator and a prominent figure in bull breeding, played a crucial role in establishing these bullfighting traditions. His cattle not only provided a source of entertainment and celebration for the community but also contributed to the local economy and the maintenance of regional culture.

The story of Don Felipe and Don Miguel embodies determination, entrepreneurship, and cultural depth that characterize this family, leaving an indelible legacy in Capilla de Guadalupe and its surroundings.

The Majestic Residence of Don Felipe Navarro

The grand house erected by my great-great-grandfather, Don Felipe Navarro, in our beloved town, was a construction that commanded respect and admiration. I vividly remember its spacious hallway and the vast courtyard, adorned with a variety of herbs and flowers cared for by my grandmother María. Among them, several banana trees stood out, offering sweet and juicy fruits.

The house was designed with at least four bedrooms, and in the eastern corner, there was an even larger hallway, where horses and carts were housed. One of these bedrooms, especially spacious, was where I used to sleep when visiting my grandmother. The robust adobe walls, some double-thick, supported a second floor that added grandeur to the whole. I remember counting to 34 wooden beams in the ceiling, a testament to the meticulousness and quality with which it was constructed.

The House as a Bastion against Bandits

The house was not only a home but also a bastion of security. Equipped with gun ports on each side of the door, these openings allowed for effective defense against bandits and rustlers who plagued the region in those times. These defensive elements were essential, especially considering that Don Felipe was the treasurer of the community and the guardian of significant sums of money earmarked for the construction of the new temple.

Don Felipe: A Pillar of the Community and His Legacy

Don Felipe's role in the community went beyond being a mere resource manager. He was seen as the custodian of the trust and well-being of the town, a responsibility inherited from his grandfather, Amo Aceves. His leadership and dedication not only ensured the economic prosperity of the locality but also reinforced cohesion and a sense of community among its residents.

This house, with its deep roots and history intertwined with that of the town, remains a symbol of my family's legacy and resilience, and a constant reminder of the crucial role Don Felipe played in the history and development of our beloved Capilla de Guadalupe.

The Bandits' Siege and Don Felipe's Cunning Defense

As the construction of the temple progressed around 1860, my great-great-grandfather Don Felipe Navarro's figure solidified as a cornerstone of the community. He was not only the reliable and dynamic treasurer but also the guardian of a significant gold legacy, inherited from his grandfather, Amo Aceves. His wealth and prominent role in funding the temple made him a target for bandits, especially those lurking on the other side of the Río Verde.

The Ambush and the Brave Community Response

The threat from bandits was real and constant. My grandmother, Doña Mariquita de la Torre, wife of Don Felipe, recounted to me how the bandits meticulously planned an attack on our town. Employing a distraction tactic, a part of their gang staged an assault, leading the town's defenders into a rapid mobilization. The bandits, in an act of deception, feigned fear and retreat, causing the defenders to pursue them.

Don Felipe's Heroism in Defense of the Town

At this critical moment, Don Felipe's bravery and leadership shone brightly. Understanding that the town was left unprotected during the pursuit, he organized a small group to safeguard the town, anticipating the true attack. This decision was crucial, as the bandits, seeing their initial plan thwarted, launched a full-scale assault on the undefended town.

The Battle and Sacrifice for the Community

The battle that ensued was fierce and desperate. Don Felipe, along with his small but resolute group, faced the bandits with a combination of cunning and valor. Despite the numerical disadvantage, the determination and courage of the town's defenders prevailed, safeguarding the integrity and possessions of the community.

The Legacy of Don Felipe: Beyond Material Wealth

The successful defense of the town against the bandit attack not only preserved the safety and prosperity of its residents but also cemented Don Felipe's reputation as a local hero. His bravery and leadership in times of crisis left an indelible mark on the collective memory of the town, reaffirming his legacy as much more than that of a wealthy man; Don Felipe Navarro was a true guardian and protector of his people.

Don Felipe and Doña Mariquita's Forethought and Strength

Don Felipe, anticipating the possibility of deception, decided not to join the pursuit, and remained in his large house, a stronghold of safety in these tumultuous times. Alongside him, his wife Doña Mariquita, a trusted servant, and their twin children took refuge in one of the most fortified rooms in the dwelling, which I recall clearly from my childhood. That room, with sturdy walls and a single exceptionally strong wooden door, became their refuge and fortress.

The Assault on the House and Heroic Defense

Upon realizing that Don Felipe had not fallen into their trap, the bandits directed their attack towards his residence. With determination and courage, Don Felipe and his armed and prepared wife defended their home. The door, though strong, was the only vulnerable point. The noise of the blows and the fervor of the struggle echoed in the air as Don Felipe and his family bravely resisted the siege.

The Situation of the Other Children and the Outcome of the Conflict

Meanwhile, the fate of Don Felipe's other children, who were outside the fortified room, remained uncertain. Tension and danger filled every corner of the house. The family narrative, passed down through generations, recalls this episode as a moment of extraordinary tension and bravery, where Don Felipe and Doña

Mariquita stood as pillars of resistance and courage against the greed and violence of the bandits.

The Courage and Resistance Legacy of Don Felipe

This episode, etched in the family's memory, highlights not only the heroic figure of Don Felipe but also that of his wife Doña Mariquita. Together, they faced one of the most difficult trials in the history of our town. Their struggle and resistance were not just acts of personal bravery but also symbols of the steadfastness and unbreakable spirit of our family and our community.

The Bandits' Siege and Don Felipe's Defense

During a tense siege, Don Felipe Navarro displayed valor and cunning worthy of his Castilian lineage. Sheltered in his home alongside his brave wife, Doña Mariquita, and other family members, he confronted a group of bandits seeking to seize his fortune.

The Impregnable Strength of the House

The room they sought refuge in became an impregnable fortress. The door, with wood so thick it seemed impenetrable, resisted the assailants' assaults. Meanwhile, from within, Don Felipe and his family made use of shotguns and powder pistols, typical weapons of the time, defending themselves with bravery. The triangular holes of the skylights acted as gunports, allowing them to repel attacks without exposing themselves to danger.

The Family's Strategy and Resistance

Doña Mariquita and her sister played a crucial role, reloading the weapons to maintain resistance. As the hours passed, the frustrated bandits, unable to penetrate the solid defense, began planning an alternative attack.

The Fate of the Children During the Siege

Meanwhile, the younger children of Don Felipe, who had not managed to enter the fortified room, hid in trojes—large containers where seeds were stored. In these improvised hideouts, they waited, gripped by fear and uncertainty, while their parents bravely fought off the assailants.

The Courage Legacy of Don Felipe

This episode in the life of Don Felipe Navarro, a moment of desperation and courage, has been engraved in the family's memory as a testament to strength and valor in the face of adversity. The heroic defense of his home and family against the bandits is remembered as an exceptional act of bravery, a legacy that endures through time.

The Heroism of Don Felipe and the Family's Escape During the Bandit Attack

Amidst the chaos and bravery displayed by Don Felipe Navarro, his family struggled to survive. The house, with its extensive size and orchard, offered multiple hiding spots. While Don Felipe valiantly resisted the attacks from inside, his children found refuge in various places.

The Ingenious Hideout in the Trojes

The younger children, including my great-grandmother Teodora, hid in the house of some relatives. Others, displaying early courage, fled to CEDAZO, now Los DOLORES, to seek help. Meanwhile, in the trojes, where bales of chili and bundles of corn leaves were stored, some of the children ingeniously hid among the bundles, avoiding detection by the assailants.

The Protection of a Child and the Cunning of a Worker

Amid the turmoil, one of the house's workers, responsible for caring for a young boy named Vicentito, Don Felipe's son, showed extraordinary presence of mind. When questioned by the bandits, she firmly asserted that the child was hers, thus saving the boy's life and fleeing the scene with him in her arms.

Don Felipe's Unyielding Resistance

Despite the ongoing siege, Don Felipe continued to defend his home with exceptional tenacity and courage. From his fortified position, he repelled the attacks with great skill, efficiently using the skylights to fire at the bandits. This tireless resistance ultimately led the assailants to abandon their attempt to break into the house, demonstrating Don Felipe's strength and courage, a true hero in defending his family and home.

The Tragedy and Heroism in the Defense of Don Felipe's House

In an act of desperation, the bandits, unable to break down the door, decided to set fire to Don Felipe's house. The smoke, mixed with the pungency of chili, became unbearable. In a final attempt to save the twins, Don Felipe took refuge under the bed's mattress. Unfortunately, the three of them suffocated and died in this heroic act.

Doña Mariquita, his wife, and her sister fell unconscious in the middle of the room. When the bandits entered and found them, they thought they were feigning and brought embers closer, but they did not react, saving themselves because they were unconscious.

The Miraculous Rescue of the Youth from CEDAZO

Meanwhile, a miracle was unfolding. The youth who had fled to seek help at CEDAZO, now Los DOLORES, returned with a multitude of people from the area. Melitón, Albino, and Miguel, the brave children of Don Felipe and Doña Mariquita, led the inhabitants of CEDAZO in a desperate race back to the house. Upon seeing the situation, the BARBA family, esteemed neighbors of the family, did not hesitate to gather all available horses, mules, and donkeys to form a large herd and quickly head to the site of the attack.

In this dramatic scenario, the story recounts the bravery and sacrifice of Don Felipe, a man who defended his home and family to the last breath, and the solidarity of the community that came together to face adversity and danger. These events deeply marked the family and the town, leaving a lasting legacy of courage and unity in their history.

Don Felipe Navarro's Heroic End

In an act of desperation and courage, the CEDAZO volunteers, armed and riding an imposing herd of animals, launched a rescue mission. Their thunderous arrival, with shots fired into the air and the sound of cavalry, made the bandits believe they were facing an army. Surprised, they fled the town, leaving behind Don Felipe's house.

Unfortunately, for Don Felipe Navarro and the children, it was already too late. Despite efforts to revive them, nothing could be done. Don Felipe's bravery was etched into everyone's memory as that of a great hero.

Amidst the chaos, Don Felipe had attempted to reveal to his wife, Doña Mariquita, the hiding place of the gold, thinking of the future of his family if he did not survive. However, in an act of love and loyalty, she refused to listen, not wanting to know the secret if it meant losing him.

The tragedy plunged the town of Guadalupe into deep sadness. Don Felipe, recognized as a pillar of the community, left an irreplaceable void. His death not only meant the loss of a good and just man but also marked the end of an era in the town's history.

Doña Mariquita's Resilience After the Loss

After the devastating loss of Don Felipe and his children, mourning shrouded the community of Guadalupe. The construction of the Temple, a project initiated with so much enthusiasm and dedication by Don Felipe, temporarily halted amidst collective sorrow. The remains of Don Felipe and his children were buried in the local cemetery, near the tomb of his grandfather, Don Antonio de Aceves, and other deceased family members.

However, over time, Doña Mariquita de La Torre, widow of Don Felipe, found the motivation to move forward in her faith and inner strength. Despite the pain, she understood that there were unfinished responsibilities and a legacy to continue. With renewed spirit and determination, she took on the task of completing the construction of the Temple, a commitment not only to her late husband but also to her community.

Doña Mariquita, aware of the legacy and wealth left by her husband, likely knew the location of a significant portion of the gold Don Felipe had accumulated. This resource was vital to resume and complete the construction of the Temple, fulfilling the promise made by her husband and her grandfather. In this act of bravery and dedication, Doña Mariquita demonstrated not only her strength but also her unwavering commitment to the traditions and well-being of her community.

The Emblematic Figure of Doña Mariquita

My grandmother, my father's mother, used to tell stories about her grandmother, Doña Mariquita, a woman of remarkable presence and character. Of medium height, fair skin, and eyes of an almost greenish hue, Doña Mariquita possessed a generous and kind heart but was also known for her firmness and determined character, especially when it came to correcting something that was not right. Despite her firmness, Doña Mariquita was extremely affectionate and attentive to her children. As they grew and started their own families, she provided them with unconditional support, offering them land and livestock as a display of her love and generosity. Among her children, my uncle Vicente, the youngest after the twins who tragically passed away, remained unmarried and lived with his mother in the large family house, providing her with companionship and care.

Doña Mariquita's other children, Melitón, Miguel, and Albino, though they had already formed their own households, never left their mother alone. They visited Doña Mariquita daily to ensure she lacked nothing. On the other hand, her son Juan, referred to by my grandmother as Uncle Juan, led a more reserved and discreet life. It is unknown whether he ever married and started his own family because, in his youth, deeply marked by certain family events, he decided to distance himself from home.

This narrative about Doña Mariquita and her children illustrates the complexity of family life in those times, marked by strong bonds of love, respect, and by decisions that defined the course of each family member.

CHAPTER 11

Uncle Juan, The Avenger

The story of Uncle Juan is one of bravery and determination, marked by tragedy and a desire for justice. After the death of his father and his two younger brothers at the hands of bandits, Uncle Juan developed a deep resentment towards those who had caused so much pain to his family. My grandmother María Gonzales used to tell me that Uncle Juan, a young man of medium stature, slim, with light brown hair and a serious demeanor, was an excellent rider. He had a magnificent horse and enjoyed riding to neighboring towns, especially to Tepatitlán.

However, I believe that behind these excursions lay a deeper purpose: Uncle Juan was searching for clues about the bandits responsible for his father's death. One day, as my grandmother told me, Uncle Juan prepared his horse, saddled it, and armed himself with a pistol and a rifle, both equipped with elegant holsters. At that time, rifles and pistols of high quality were already available.

Before leaving, Uncle Juan bid farewell to his mother and asked for her blessing, following the beautiful Christian customs of the region, which demonstrate deep respect and love for parents. This scene reflects the strength and determines character of Uncle Juan, a young man marked by tragedy but guided by honor and the pursuit of justice.

The Disappearance and Fate of Uncle Juan

In this stage of the story, we encounter a mixture of concern and determination on the part of Doña Mariquita, Uncle Juan's mother. Her son had been missing for an extended period, raising fears and speculations about his whereabouts and well-being. Aware that something unusual was happening, Doña Mariquita, along with her children, decided to embark on a journey to Tepatitlán to gather information about Juan, trusting that God would protect them in this quest.

Upon reaching Tepatitlán, where some relatives lived, they received conflicting news about Juan. On one hand, the good news was that Juan was alive, but on the other hand, respectable individuals had seen Juan involved in bandit activities. Doña Mariquita, a shrewd and perceptive woman, quickly sensed that her son was on a personal mission of revenge, seeking the murderers of his father. With a mix of concern and resignation, she expressed her wish that God would watch over her son on his perilous path.

After receiving this news, Doña Mariquita and her family returned to the Chapel, facing the harsh reality that Juan, driven by pain and a thirst for justice, had taken a dangerous and possibly irreversible path. This part of the story reflects the complexity of family feelings and conflicts in a time when justice and revenge often intertwined.

The Return of Uncle Juan and the Rejection of Ill-Gotten Gold

In this chapter, a dramatic turn in the story of Uncle Juan is revealed, as he returns to the Chapel of Guadalupe after two years of absence. Upon his return, he has an emotional reunion with his mother, Doña Mariquita, marked by hugs and tears. Despite his usually stoic nature, even Doña Mariquita cannot help but shed tears at the return of her son.

Uncle Juan, in an apparent gesture of remorse or perhaps trying to make amends for his past actions, presents his mother with two bags filled with gold coins. However, this gesture is met with moral steadfastness on the part of Doña Mariquita. While she recognizes her son's good intentions, she rejects the gold, aware of its illicit origin and her son's criminal activities.

This moment is crucial in the narrative as it reflects the complexity of Uncle Juan's character and the unquestionable integrity of Doña Mariquita. She understands that accepting that gold would be condoning and benefiting from his immoral actions, a stance she is not willing to adopt, regardless of the circumstances. This episode underscores the importance of principles and values, even in the face of hardships and the temptations.

The Tragic End of Uncle Juan and the Integrity of Doña Mariquita

In this chapter, the outcome of Uncle Juan's tragic journey is revealed. Despite his attempt to convince his mother, Doña Mariquita, that the gold he offered had been honestly earned through gambling, she remains steadfast in her decision to reject it. Her integrity and moral convictions do not allow her to accept something she suspects comes from illegal activities.

Uncle Juan, unable to settle into a quiet life and immune to any attempts at redemption, decides to leave the Chapel of Guadalupe once again, plunging himself into adventure and danger. This decision leads to a tragic end. After some time, Doña Mariquita receives the devastating news: her son has been killed by the police in Tepatitlán.

This event highlights the complexity of Uncle Juan, a character whose path of adventures and challenges to the law ultimately leads to a fatal destiny. The narrative also emphasizes the strength and moral resolve of Doña Mariquita, who even amid the pain of losing her son, maintains her dignity and principles.

The episode reveals the difficult decisions and harsh realities of life in those times, where law and order often clashed with a life of adventure and challenges to the norm, represented by characters like Uncle Juan. His death, though tragic, is a representation of the consequences of a lifestyle marked by risky and often dangerous choices.

Uncle Juan and the First Cemetery of the Chapel of Guadalupe

This chapter narrates the tragic end of Uncle Juan, Don Felipe's son, whose life ended at the hands of the police. His death, shrouded in mysteries and undisclosed secrets, leaves his relatives and the town with a sense of desolation. Uncle Juan, who had sought justice for his father's death, took with him to the grave the secrets of his actions during his time with the bandits, including whether he managed to find and punish those responsible for his father's murder.

After his death, Uncle Juan's brothers transported him in an ox-drawn cart and buried him in the same cemetery where his father, Don Felipe, lay. This cemetery, the first in the Chapel of Guadalupe, became the final resting place not only for Don Felipe but also for other prominent members and founders of the town, such as Don Antonio de Aceves, the patriarch of the family.

Facing the loss of her husband and son, Doña Mariquita decided to build a temple in the cemetery, in memory of those who had played a crucial role in the foundation and development of the Chapel of Guadalupe. This temple would serve not only as a place of prayer and reflection but also as a monument to the resilience and courage of those who helped shape the town's identity.

Doña Mariquita Builds a Temple in the Cemetery

In this chapter, we witness the determination and dedication of Doña Mariquita to erect a temple in the cemetery of the Chapel of Guadalupe. Her purpose was not only to honor the memory of her deceased loved ones but also to create a lasting symbol of the community's history and legacy.

As the town rapidly grew and its population increased, Doña Mariquita made the decision to build another cemetery farther south of the chapel. Simultaneously, the construction of the new temple began. This architectural project had solid foundations and sturdy walls made of brick and mud, featuring an aesthetically pleasing nave adorned with attractive arches. The temple, designed to be spacious and elegant, would encompass all existing graves, becoming a place of great significance and beauty for the community.

Among the last to be buried in this sacred place was Mama Teodora, my great-grandmother, the mother of my grandmother María. Mama Teodora's story is significant, as she and her sisters survived the bandits' attack by taking refuge in another house. Additionally, Mama Teodora, married to my great-grandfather Elogio González, is remembered as a person of great virtue and kindness, considered a true saint by many in the community.

This chapter not only narrates the construction of the temple and the new cemetery but also highlights the figure of Mama Teodora, showing how each member of the community contributed, in one way or another, to the rich history and heritage of the Chapel of Guadalupe. Through their actions and legacies, characters like Doña Mariquita and Mama Teodora have left an indelible mark on the collective memory of the town.

The Story of Doña Teodora and Don Eulogio González

The story of Doña Teodora and Don Eulogio González delves into the roots of distinguished Castilian heritage in the Chapel. Don Eulogio González, the father of my grandmother María, was a man known for his demeanor and erudition. Tall, slim, with dark hair and a distinctive beard, he reflected the elegance and style of the time, blending Spanish traditionalism with the distinctive touch of a "chinaco."

His love for elegant attire earned him the nickname "El Platiado" because he adorned his suits and even his horse's saddle with silver details. Moreover, he was known for his passion for horses, always riding high-quality specimens.

The marriage of Don Eulogio to Mama Teodora was one of harmony and mutual respect, in line with the principles and values of the time. Three daughters were born from their union: Valentina, Refugio (nicknamed "Cuca"), and my grandmother María. Unfortunately, the family did not expand beyond these three daughters due to a series of misfortunes that Mama Teodora faced.

This narrative not only highlights the personal characteristics and life of Don Eulogio but also paints a vivid portrait of family and community life in the Chapel of Guadalupe. The story of Doña Teodora and Don Eulogio is a window into the daily life, customs, and culture of a town marked by its rich Castilian heritage.

In 1955, a shadow of sorrow hung over the family, marked by Doña Teodora's illness. Afflicted by relentless cancer, doctors found themselves powerless against its progression, offering only resignation as a remedy. Don Eulogio, overwhelmed by the situation and his inability to care for his wife as he wished, found solace and support in Doña Mariquita, his mother-in-law.

Doña Teodora was moved to her mother-in-law's house, accompanied by her three daughters, where she spent her last days. My grandmother recalled how her mother, in the advanced stage of the illness, crawled on the floor, unable to walk, immersed in progressive and constant pain. However, Doña Teodora faced her suffering with unwavering faith, offering her pain to God and finding comfort in comparing her sufferings to those endured by Jesus Christ.

This stage of her life was lived with deep resignation and devotion, turning her suffering into an act of faith and sacrifice. Doña Teodora became a symbol of strength and piety, remembered by all as a saint in life.

Finally, when her time came, Doña Teodora left this world. She was buried with all the funeral honors in the cemetery that Doña Mariquita had begun to build, leaving a legacy of spiritual resilience and unconditional love for her family and faith. The story of Doña Teodora is not only a tale of courage in the face of adversity but also a testimony to the power of faith and love in the darkest moments.

In this chapter, the story focuses on Don Eulogio González, who, after the death of his wife Doña Teodora, experiences a significant change in his life. Doña Teodora was one of the last people to be buried in the new temple, a work initiated by Doña Mariquita. This site became an emblem of the community, marking the end of an era and the beginning of another.

After Doña Teodora's funeral, her daughters stayed with her grandmother, Doña Mariquita. They grew up and got married under her care, leaving Don Eulogio alone. Despite owning extensive lands and properties, Don Eulogio began to lead a dissolute life. He immersed himself in the world of gambling, a common passion in the Los Altos region. His fondness for cockfights, horse races, and bullfights became the center of his life. Although he never succumbed to alcohol, his neglect of business and inherited properties was noticeable.

This change in Don Eulogio's lifestyle reflects a shift in his character and priorities. The story illustrates how grief and loneliness can sometimes lead people down unexpected paths. The narrative of Don Eulogio González is a tale of transformation and adaptation to life's circumstances, showing how even the strongest and most respected personalities can change over time.

This chapter narrates the story of Don Eulogio González, who, after facing a series of adversities, finds a new purpose in life. After selling his properties for a considerable sum of gold and silver, Don Eulogio fell into the misfortune of gambling, losing a large amount of money in a bet against Don José María Franco. This loss meant the acquisition of the "Lagunillas" estate near Tepatitlán for Franco, a property of notable importance in the region.

The story of Don Eulogio is one of ups and downs, where fortune and adversity intertwine. After his devastating loss in gambling, Don Eulogio found himself in desolation, practically in ruin. However, his education and resilience drove him to seek a new direction in life. In an unexpected turn of events, he moved to Rancho de Tres Palos to work as a schoolteacher with the Acencio family, known for their kindness and nobility. This change of course in Don Eulogio's life reflects a message of hope and overcoming. Despite difficulties and past mistakes, there is always an opportunity for redemption and finding a new purpose. The story of Don Eulogio González serves as a reminder of the human capacity to recover and adapt, even in the most challenging circumstances.

Biography of the Father

The story of Don Eulogio González and his wife, Doña Teodora Navarro, my great-grandparents, is a tale of resilience and overcoming. After Doña Teodora's tragic illness, her life ended in the hands of her mother-in-law, Doña Mariquita, who cared for her until her last breath. This experience profoundly transformed Don Eulogio, who, after losing much of his fortune in gambling, dedicated himself to teaching at a school in Rancho de Tres Palos, owned by the Acencio family. This change of occupation served as therapy for him and brought him great satisfaction.

The marriages of Doña Mariquita's three granddaughters marked a new chapter in the family's history. My aunt Cuca married a member of the wealthy González family, known as "Los Gorditos," from Rancho de la Loma. Her sister Valentina married Don Asunción Acencio, likely belonging to the Acencio family of Tres Palos. Don Asunción was known for his seriousness and dedication to teaching, remembered for his rigor and effectiveness in the field of education. This family narrative reflects not only the ups and downs of life but also the ability to adapt and find new paths in the face of adversity. Don Eulogio González's story, in particular, highlights the importance of resilience and the transformative power of engaging in new activities, such as teaching, to overcome difficult moments.

Doña Mariquita and the Divine Destiny of Her Marriage

The story of my grandmother's marriage, the last of Doña Mariquita's daughters to marry, is particularly unique and extensive, and I consider it guided by divine will and the blessing of the Virgin of Guadalupe. During those times, as the temple was being built and the parish was managed, Doña Mariquita, thanks to her abundance of gold and the enthusiastic support of the entire community of La Capilla, made progress on both temples' construction.

At that time, a priest known as the Señor Cura de la Mora, originally from Arandas, stood out for his kindness and deep commitment to Doña Mariquita's ideas and projects, fervently supporting the construction of both temples. In the main temple, dedicated to the Virgin of Guadalupe, the works had significantly progressed. The building was complete both inside and out, and it already had a finished tower, although there was still much to do to reach its current state. I am talking about around the years 1889 or 1890. At that moment, the need for specialized personnel to continue the temple construction project became evident, an event that would mark a turning point in my grandmother's life and in our family's history.

The Arrival of My Grandfather Tacho in La Capilla

During those times, La Capilla required specialized skills for its construction, such as stonemasonry from San Miguel el Alto. Furthermore, the presence of skilled stonemasons to carve and decorate the temple, especially its interior, became indispensable. It was in this context that my grandfather Anastasio, affectionately known as Tacho and a resident of San Miguel, entered the scene. A carpenter by profession and recommended by the Sr. Cura of San Miguel, he was sent to La Capilla to collaborate on the project under the supervision of the Sr. Cura de la Mora. At that time, around the 1870s, my grandfather Tacho was about 22 or 23 years old.

Upon his arrival in La Capilla, my grandfather Tacho met my great-great-grandmother, Doña Mariquita, who was in charge of the temple works. Since he did not have a place to stay, and it was common to provide accommodation to workers while they settled in, Doña Mariquita offered him a space in her extensive house. She arranged a place for him in a second courtyard, a separate area from the main residence. While other workers stayed in different places, my grandfather Tacho remained in that space for quite some time, marking the beginning of a significant stage in both his life and our family's history.

Meeting and Romance of María and Tacho

The story of how my grandmother María and my grandfather Tacho met and fell in love is a narrative of love at first sight, marked by social and cultural differences. My grandmother María, from a wealthy family, stood out for her beauty, fair complexion, and dark hair, attributes inherited from her father. On the other hand, my grandfather Tacho, of humble origins, had a darker, almost indigenous appearance. Nevertheless, his attractiveness could not be denied, something that obviously captivated my grandmother María.

They, aware of the looks and expectations of their surroundings, kept their relationship a secret. However, love finds its way, and as a result, my grandmother María became pregnant. This fact surprised and worried Doña Mariquita, known for her strict nature and who had placed her trust in my grandfather Tacho. Upon hearing the news, Tacho, feeling overwhelmed and fearful of the consequences, fled back to San Miguel.

Doña Mariquita, upon realizing her granddaughter's pregnancy, reacted with determined fury. Immediately, she took steps to locate Tacho, driven both by the protection of her granddaughter and the need to confront the situation that had arisen between the two young lovers.

The Marriage of Tachito and María Isabel González

In the tapestry of my grandparents' lives, the marriage between "Tachito" and María Isabel González stands out as a vivid portrait of love and commitment. Doña Mariquita, upon learning that my grandfather was in San Miguel, decided to take matters into her own hands. She mounted her horse, a skill in which she excelled, and accompanied by her children, set off with determination to San Miguel.

Upon arrival, surprise was evident on my grandfather Tachito's face. Doña Mariquita, with her characteristic firmness, confronted him and urged him to assume his responsibility. "You thought I wouldn't find you," she said sternly but with a hint of understanding in her voice. Tachito, although initially fearful, felt a profound relief in understanding that Doña Mariquita's intention was to unite him in marriage with María Isabel, his beloved.

Without delays or ostentatious celebrations, they returned to La Capilla, where they married. Doña Mariquita, always generous and practical, offered them a house surrounded by a nearby fruit orchard, providing them with an idyllic refuge to start their new life together. They lived there until the birth of their daughter, marking the beginning of a new stage filled with love and hope.

This marriage not only symbolized the union of two hearts but also the fusion of two worlds, demonstrating that true love transcends social and economic barriers. Approved.

My Indigenous Heritage

On this occasion, let's delve into the intriguing story of the controversy surrounding my grandfather Tachito's surname and its transformation. When Don Anastacio Mexía Cortés arrived in La Capilla in 1889, his surname remained intact. However, later, the surname underwent an interesting change, a controversy that, while perhaps not of great significance from my perspective, is worthy of exploration.

Don Tachito, as we affectionately used to call him, was born in 1867, during the time of Benito Juárez, in San Miguel el Alto, Jalisco. His education was solid, partly thanks to his relationship with a priest, his mother's brother, which facilitated his access to formal education and music in San Miguel's band, linked to the local parish.

Once he had completed his formal education, and due to the early loss of his father, Don Tachito found himself compelled to learn carpentry as a means of livelihood. Later, as I mentioned earlier, he arrived in La Capilla, where he crossed paths with destiny that would lead him to marry María Isabel González Navarro, simply known as María. When their first child was born, he was baptized with the name Anastacio Mexía, referring to his original surname. This change of surname, though it may seem insignificant from my perspective, raises interesting questions about identity and heritage. Throughout our family history, diversity and cultural richness have interwoven to shape our identity as descendants of indigenous peoples and mestizos of Mexico.

Silviano Mejía and the Family Link

Silviano Mejía, later known as Silviano Gutiérrez, is a significant character in our family history. His story intertwines with the birth of an aunt who was baptized as Soledad Gutiérrez. This aunt played a crucial role in the lives of our entire family, becoming the guardian angel of each one of us. In San Francisco, California, I had the opportunity to gather a valuable amount of information about our indigenous ancestry through conversations with her. My grandfather, just as with me, shared many of these stories with my aunt "Chole," as we affectionately used to call her.

Chole, being the second of the siblings, received the surname Gutiérrez upon baptism. Gathering all the information I could collect, I will begin with the story of my father, who married my great-grandmother, Martina Cortés. He met Martina after making several trips between Guadalajara and San Miguel. During these trips, he, and a partner, who was also a relative, managed a transportation business that used a group of mules.

At this stage, Martina lived in San Miguel el Alto and shared her home with her brother, who was a priest and was linked to the local parish. The arrival of my father and his partner in San Miguel marked the beginning of a new stage in their lives. This priest uncle, although barely remembered by my grandfather Tacho, played a fundamental role in the family when, after the death of Abundio, they all temporarily moved to live with him.

The family history continues, full of intrigue and connections that link each generation to its past and heritage.

The History of Surnames and Abundio's Legacy

As my grandfather Tacho grew up, he discovered an interesting detail about his father's arrival in San Miguel. On his first arrival in this locality, his father used the surname "Gutiérrez." However, when his children were born, he baptized some with the surname Gutiérrez and others with Mejía. Even my grandfather was baptized with the surname Mejía. This change of surnames is related to an important historical event.

In 1866, Abundio, my great-grandfather, left Mexico City and joined General Mejía, who was leading a rebellion against the regime. Later, in 1867, Benito Juárez regained control of Mexico City, and Maximilian and his two generals, Miramón and Mejía, were executed on Cerro de las Campanas. Both generals had indigenous Nahua ancestry, which represents a significant part of my heritage. My aunt

Chole, my father's sister, and Abundio's granddaughter, told me that Tacho had recounted that his father Abundio participated in this revolution alongside his uncle, General Mejía.

Additionally, Tacho mentioned that his family came from the town of Jamay, Jalisco, which is near Lake Chapala, the largest lake in Mexico, also extending into the state of Michoacán. In Jamay, before the arrival of the Spaniards during the conquest, the indigenous people were of the same ethnicity as the Aztecs. This was true not only for Jamay but also for all of Jalisco, highlighting the historical importance of the region.

This revelation about the history of our surnames and Abundio's participation in the revolution connects us more deeply to our indigenous roots and the heritage we carry in our DNA.

The Odyssey of Abundio and His Surname Change

Returning to the story of my great-grandfather Abundio and his departure from his uncle's army, General Mejía, I can explain why he arrived in San Miguel under the name Abundio Gutiérrez. Abundio found himself in a complicated situation as the Juaristas, followers of Benito Juárez, gained more and more supporters, and he increasingly aligned himself with their ranks.

At some point around 1866, Abundio decided to leave Mexico City, sensing that Juárez was about to regain control in the capital. This marked a point of no return, as the Juaristas offered an amnesty to Generals Miramón and Mejía, urging them to join their forces due to their Mexican nationality. However, both generals decided to remain loyal to Maximilian of Austria's Empire.

The fate of Maximilian, Miramón, and Mejía was sealed in 1867 when they were captured by Juarista forces. They were executed on Cerro de las Campanas in a tragic episode of Mexican history. Abundio Gutiérrez, my great-grandfather, made a crucial decision to leave

Mexico City and seek refuge in San Miguel, carrying the surname Gutiérrez with him, thereby concealing his previous involvement in the conflict. This chapter in Abundio's life illustrates the complexity and unexpected twists that characterized this tumultuous period in Mexican history. His story, as part of our family heritage, is a testimony to the courage and determination passed down from generation to generation.

Maximilian and Decision-Making

The story of Maximilian and his brief reign in Mexico was a complex and controversial episode in the country's history. Although many Mexicans had indigenous ancestry, some opposed joining the Juarez ranks not because they disagreed with the idea of an empire, but out of respect for Emperor Maximilian himself. Maximilian earned the affection and trust of many people due to his kind character and willingness to listen and trust his advisors.

Often, when problems arose, he would say, "Don't worry, we'll handle this smoothly." He could often be found counting butterflies around the Chapultepec Palace, oblivious to the political struggles and tensions affecting the country. However, Maximilian was unaware of the harsh reality faced by workers on the estates of wealthy landowners.

The Arrival of Benito Juarez

The arrival of Benito Juarez marked a crucial point in Mexican history and in Maximilian's life as emperor. Although some might consider his offer of amnesty to Miramón and my father's uncle, Thomas, General Mejía, as a betrayal of Mexico, it is important to understand the context of the situation. At that time, even within the Mexican army itself, young cadets from the Military College were trained to be loyal to Mexico and their superiors, even to death if necessary.

The conservative Mexican army had placed these young cadets to protect the emperor and his highness. Therefore, it would not be considered a betrayal of Mexico if Miramón and Mejía had decided to join Benito Juarez's liberation army. However, it is crucial to remember that, in that context, if Miramón and Mejía had joined Juarez, they would not have been able to live in peace due to the distrust and remorse they would have felt.

Indigenous people, by their nature, tend to be loyal to the death, and this loyalty would have created a great emotional conflict for them. Additionally, considering that Juarez intended to execute them, their decision to remain loyal to the empire is understandable from their perspective. History shows us how loyalties and decisions in times of conflict can be complicated and ambiguous, and how context and circumstances can influence people's actions.

Abundio's Renaissance in Jamay

Abundio, my great-grandfather, made a brave decision to join Benito Juarez's army in those turbulent times. However, as the war ended and with the execution of Miramón and Mejía on Cerro de las Campanas in 1867 by Juarez's order, Thomas's life took a radical turn. He decided to return to Jamay, his hometown, marking the beginning of a new stage in his life. From there, he embarked on a journey to Guadalajara in search of a relative involved in the transportation business with a group of mules.

Sharing his experience and the reasons that led him back, his relative understood his situation and invited him to join the transportation business operating in the eastern towns, where they already had an established clientele in San Miguel el Alto. This business proved to be a lucrative source of income, providing Abundio with the rest he needed after years of struggles and conflicts in wars, as well as living in constant hiding and changing his identity.

It was during this period that Abundio met my great-grandmother, and together they began building their family in San Miguel. They had three daughters and two sons, one of whom would be my grandfather. Despite the passage of time and the adversities they faced, Abundio held faint memories of his father but was determined to chart a new path for his family.

Abundio's Legacy and His Place in History

The history of my great-grandfather is marked by his courageous participation in the war, even though his father died when he was young. Although he barely retained memories of his father, he knew that his father liked to play the guitar and was a talented troubadour. Furthermore, my father Tacho shared with me that his grandfather

Abundio had actively participated in the Revolution, supporting General Mejía.

I never heard from my grandfather Tacho that General Mejía was his uncle, but my aunt Chole, his daughter, was the one who shared that information. Abundio, my great-grandfather, lived through tumultuous times that left a mark on his spirit. He witnessed numerous deaths in the conflicts and carried with him the scars of the wounds he suffered, as well as the weight of the lives he had taken in the conflict. This experience deeply marked him, and according to my grandfather, it was one of the reasons why he passed away at a young age, leaving his three daughters and two sons orphaned.

One of his daughters got married and moved to Chihuahua, where, according to my grandfather, she also passed away after living for more than a hundred years. Another sister got married and settled in Irapuato, Guanajuato, where she had children who carried the Bobadilla Gutierrez surname from their mother. According to them, they conducted genealogical research that led them to Jamay, Jalisco, to trace the origin of their surname since some of them bore it as Gutierrez and others as Mejía. These investigations sparked their interest in learning about their family roots.

The Controversy in the Surname and the Strength of Heritage

A curious controversy arose in our family regarding the surname. After exhaustive research, it was discovered that the true surname was Gutierrez, leading my grandfather to change his surname to Gutierrez. This change extended to my uncle Silviano, the youngest of the siblings. The other family members were baptized as Gutierrez, totaling thirteen people along with my grandmother Maria and my grandfather Tacho. Despite the initial doubt, we at least affirmed one surname in the descent of my father Abundio.

My grandfather's brother also chose to change his surname and moved to Aguascalientes, where he lived a long life, surpassing seventy years. He left behind a daughter whom I know as Aunt Elvira and another sister who resides in Mexico City. My grandfather Tacho, who left us in 1963 at the impressive age of 96, was a devout admirer of the Virgin of Guadalupe.

He never failed to perform music for the traditional "mañanitas" celebrated every December 12 in the early morning in honor of the Virgin. His devotion to her was unwavering, and often it seemed to me that his likeness resembled Juan Diego, the Aztec indigenous man who lived in 1531 and to whom the Virgin appeared. My grandfather radiated an essence deeply rooted in his Nahua heritage.

Tacho's Unwavering Devotion and the Origin of Surnames

My grandfather, don TACHITO, was a man deeply marked by his Nahua heritage, a race with roots in the very AZTECS. His devotion to the Virgin of Guadalupe, whom he affectionately called "my MORENITA," was undeniable. Surprisingly, the Virgin of Guadalupe responded to his love in a touching way. On December 17, at 5 in the morning in 1963, precisely when he used to sing the "mañanitas" to the Virgin, my grandfather don TACHITO departed from this world. It was a beautiful gift that the MORENITA GUADALUPANA granted him on that special day. After sharing this beautiful story, I am ready to address the final aspects of this controversial history. In reality, when the Spaniards arrived in Mexico, the indigenous people did not have surnames. It was the friars who, through catechism and baptism, assigned surnames to the natives.

These surnames were generally taken from the baptismal godfather, explaining the diversity of surnames in our family. We could have carried any surname, like Mexia or another, but what truly matters is the essence of everyone. In the end, we are the product of our heritage, and regardless of the surname, what truly matters is our uniqueness and how we live our lives. Thus, concludes this fascinating and dubious controversy, but above all, I affirm that we are a family proud of our indigenous roots.

The Importance of Identity and Tacho's Resilience

Sometimes, some people find reasons to bother others, but personally, these issues do not affect me. It's not about losing an arm or a leg, but how they see us and label us. I was baptized as Gutierrez, and I am proud of it. If it had been Mexia, it would have been fine too, as I like both surnames equally. My grandfather, don TACHITO, was an extraordinary person. He was humble, simple, and never attached importance to wealth.

Although my grandmother inherited a large house and land, my grandfather was not a farmer or cattle rancher, and she did not know how to manage those resources either. Gradually, my grandfather began sharing those lands with his relatives without asking for anything in return. He sustained himself with his carpentry and never asked his wife for anything.

In conclusion, I believe that God sent my grandfather Tacho to strengthen both our physical heritage and our CASTILIAN identity. Throughout generations, some of our ancestors practiced a custom that may seem strange today: marriage between first cousins. This contributed to the appearance of deaf people in our town and its surroundings. Furthermore, some of them developed additional disabilities, such as blindness, as is the case with a cousin of my mother named MATILDE ACEVES, who is still with us. Her story is a testimony to the strength and resilience of our family over time.

Tacho's Legacy and the Union of Two Races

The history of my family is marked by the union of two worlds and the creation of a new identity, the "MESTIZO," a race we are proud of in Mexico. On one side is my mother, Matilde Navarro Aceves, whose sad yet inspiring story is a testimony to the consequences of the union between first cousins in past generations. She was born deaf and mute, and over time, she lost her sight due to this blood connection. In contrast, on my father's side, a miraculous turn occurred when my grandfather TACHITO came into the life of my grandmother Matilde.

Despite the social and economic differences between them, their union was destined to be. God had a special purpose in this union, and that's how my great-grandfather ABUNDIO, part of the true indigenous and Mexican heritage, united two strong races and gave rise to mestizaje, which is a source of pride for all of us in Mexico. My great-grandfather ABUNDIO left a legacy of love for the Virgin of Guadalupe, which he shared with my father ANTONIO de ACEVES. Both adored her with all their hearts and demonstrated this love by building a temple in her honor in our town. This symbiotic union, both physical and spiritual, strengthened our family. With this, I conclude this part of our history.

The Legacy of Simon Navarro Aceves

Talking about the figure of my great-great-grandfather, Simon Navarro Aceves, is delving into an important part of our family history. I had already mentioned Simon as the brother of Felipe Navarro, both grandsons of the illustrious Don Luciano Navarro Aceves and his wife, Doña Dolores Gómez. This branch of the family, in addition to its indigenous origin, has deep Castilian roots.

Simon Navarro played a significant role in acquiring an extensive piece of land that was bequeathed to him by his respected grandfather, Don Luciano Aceves. Interestingly, this coincided in time with the construction of his brother Felipe's majestic house, located next to the little chapel in our town.

The land obtained by Simon was vast and strategically located near the royal road and at the foot of the imposing Cerro Gordo. What initially was a parcel of land eventually turned into a castle, a fortress that defended his heritage and was notable, among other things, for a tower with 125 steps adorning one of its corners.

It's worth noting that Simon Navarro Aceves also married his cousin, Doña Conchita Aceves, a union that, while it may seem unusual in our days, was a more common practice in that era.

This episode in the history of our family demonstrates how the legacy of Simon Navarro Aceves, his tenacity, and vision, contributed to shaping our lineage and our heritage.

CHAPTER 12

National Charros at La Capilla

The history of the Aceves family continues to surprise us with fascinating episodes. In this chapter, I want to talk about a prominent figure: Don Agustín de Aceves, the son of the respected AMO ACEVES. Don Agustín, true to his lineage, desired to be close to his family in the imposing house that had been built in a strategic location in the town.

At that time, his brother Felipe had already erected a grand residence, notable for its size and splendor. Felipe had meticulously planned his home, even constructing a large bullring that would be ready to host bullfights when the opportunity arose. Additionally, he owned a considerable amount of cattle, which facilitated the organization of magnificent branding ceremonies and provided opportunities for charro sports practice. It's not surprising that talented riders emerged from there, making a name for themselves in the world of charros.

Over the years, the new owners of the property, the Franco family, have not only upheld the tradition but also elevated it to new heights. With palpable pride, they have accomplished numerous feats, including achieving the title of National Champions on several occasions, an achievement that fills the entire Mexican nation with pride, especially our beloved chapel.

Now, returning to San Antonio, during the time of Don Simón Navarro, significant improvements were made to the property. Additional rooms were built around the main house, with elegant porches that added a distinctive charm. Furthermore, in one of the rooms, there is a date engraved on the ceiling, reminding us of the 1860s, a significant period in the history of the property.

As if that weren't enough, Don Simón Navarro also added additional stables to accommodate the numerous horses that were a part of his life and his horsemen who worked tirelessly on the estate. This chapter highlights the historical richness of our family and its legacy in Mexican charro tradition.

Bandit Attack on the Great House of San Antonio

The majestic residence still retained its imposing structure, and the Royal Road that traversed the region was in full swing, frequented by numerous travelers and merchants, but also by bandits who threatened to steal cattle.

According to my grandmother's memories, there was a time when these outlaws decided to launch a bold assault on San Antonio, attempting to breach the property. However, thanks to security measures and the loyalty of the workers who held Don Simón Navarro in high esteem, the bandits encountered staunch resistance. Although the bandits believed Don Simón had a considerable amount of gold, they were taken aback by the strength of the castle, which stood at

one corner of the property, protected by loopholes that hindered their advance and kept them at bay even from a distance.

At this critical moment, neighbors came to the aid of San Antonio. Some of the Galbán and Torres families, of Castilian lineage, who had established their homes in the region for over a century, bravely joined the defense. Furthermore, notice was sent to the nephews Albino, Miguel, and Melito, who arrived swiftly to join the cause. The memory of the bandits having killed their uncle Felipe was not easily forgotten, and they were determined to prevent the same fate from befalling their uncle Simón.

Finally, when the bandits realized the determination and resilience they were up against, they chose to retreat. This episode of bravery and unity in the defense of San Antonio is etched in history, reminding us of the importance of protecting what we value and love.

In those days when San Antonio held the title of Champions, and the threat of bandits seemed to have subsided, a new reality loomed over the region. Armies of soldiers and revolutionaries were constantly moving through the area. The Juaristas were striving to defeat Emperor Maximiliano's government and were facing off against the wealthy landowners who oppressed the working peasants. However, in San Antonio, the same tension was not felt, as the landowners treated their workers as family members, contributing to the harmony in the community.

In those years, around 1865, large contingents of French soldiers under the command of Napoleon III were also sighted. These soldiers intended to establish a monarchy in Mexico and passed through San Antonio in significant numbers on their way to Guadalajara. My grandmother, Chita, recalled that every time these groups crossed paths with a revolutionary faction or government forces, they would take one or two cattle for sustenance on their journey. However, when they reached San Antonio, the astute Papa Simón, a skilled political man and conversationalist, managed to persuade them and offer them what they needed, including pigs and sheep. Thus, he established friendships and, on occasion, obtained promises of protection if needed.

My grandmother, Chita, and María de Jesús Estrada, as she used to call her, watched these events closely, knowing that Papa Simón's ability to deal with circumstances and maintain peace in San Antonio was invaluable in times of uncertainty and conflict.

My grandfather Simón, although he did not remember his grandfather Simon in detail, felt profound sadness when he passed away shortly after the death of his beloved wife, Conchita. Their love was palpable, and the loss of Conchita deeply affected Simón, hastening his own departure.

After Conchita's passing, Simón longed for companionship and, in a gesture of love and family connection, invited his daughter Matilde and son-in-law Demetrio Estrada to live in the family home in San Antonio. He wanted to avoid loneliness and, at the same time, witness the birth of his three granddaughters: María, Trina, and Jesús Estrada Navarro. My grandmother, María, was one of these three daughters, as I mentioned in the chapter about the Estradas from the center.

However, Simón's life with his granddaughters was brief, as he passed away when they were still young and growing up. Matilde, being the only daughter, inherited her father Simón Navarro's considerable estate. She lived a happy life with her husband Demetrio and their daughters on the San Antonio ranch until tragedy struck. Matilde died due to complications during childbirth, leaving behind her three daughters, who were still very young, ranging from ten to twelve years old, approximately.

Demetrio took on a pivotal role as a devoted father and stayed in San Antonio for a while, caring for his daughters and trying to provide them with a stable life despite the adversity.

Chapter 13

Quirino Navarro: The Legend of a Brave Revolutionary

In my grandmother Trina's heart, there persists a story that has remained in her memory since her childhood in San Antonio. This narrative revolves around her cousin, Quirino Navarro, whose presence left an indelible mark on the community.

Quirino, a tall and robust man, stood out for his bravery and determination. With a height of over six feet, blue eyes, and blond hair, he was an imposing figure. Despite the age difference, Trina and Quirino forged a deep friendship that led them to become compadres.

What stood out most about Quirino was his deep and resonant voice, which captivated everyone who heard it. He was a true Castilian in every sense, and his involvement in the revolution only solidified his reputation as a fearless man.

Despite the battles and dangers, he faced in the revolutionary ranks, Quirino emerged unscathed, earning the respect and admiration of all. His courage was such that a song was even created in his honor, immortalizing him as a hero who knew no fear. His bravery was tested during the Cristero Revolution, where he once again demonstrated his skill and determination.

The story of Quirino Navarro, this brave revolutionary, is a legend that will endure over time, reminding us of the strength of the human spirit and the importance of fighting for what we believe in.

Quirino Navarro: A Bold Defender in Revolutionary

In the tumultuous year of 1926, marked by the presidency of Plutarco Elías Calles, Quirino Navarro found himself serving as a

Commander in Tepatitlán. Without warning, the Cristeros besieged the city, putting Quirino and his comrades in imminent danger.

The accounts of those who witnessed this event alongside him reveal the harsh reality they faced. The Cristeros, mostly young men without a solid organization, fired shots without a clear objective. Quirino, however, displayed astonishing composure amid chaos, bravely defending his position. The situation became even more challenging when the Cristeros began firing from outside the building. To shield themselves from the bullets that pierced through doors and windows, they had to improvise with adobe and bricks.

Quirino held his ground until the government army finally arrived and lifted the siege. This episode of courage and determination led to the composition of a song in his honor, which became a popular anthem for a long time. It is important to note that Quirino, despite his role in the government, shared the Christian beliefs of the Cristeros. He learned to be a man of faith in San Antonio, influenced by his uncle, my great-grandfather Simón Navarro, who welcomed him since his childhood. In this house, like in many others, they prayed daily and cultivated a deep spirituality.

The story of Quirino Navarro is a testimony of courage in turbulent times of revolution, a reminder of how faith and determination can stand firm even amid chaos.

Quirino Navarro: Faith and Courage in Times of Change

As we step into Chapter 13 of this chronicle, we encounter a unique character: Don Quirino Navarro. While his official role was linked to the government of those times, his inner essence revealed his true nature as a fervent Christian.

Don Quirino was not simply a servant of the atheist and communist government of the era; he was a man who lived his faith in private. His apparent loyalty to the government was more of a survival strategy, as, as we well know, in those turbulent times, professing the Christian faith could be dangerous.

A particularly significant event illustrates his commitment to faith and courage. Every year, on the Feast of the Lord of Mercy, April 30th, an impressive pilgrimage took place, gathering thousands of faithful. Two days prior, on April 28th and 29th, the image of the Lord of Mercy was taken out of the Sanctuary, and a grand procession through the streets commenced.

However, in one year, the government, aware of this celebration, plotted a sinister plan to attack the pilgrimage and destroy the image of the Christ of the Lord of Mercy. Don Quirino, who was working at the Municipality of Tepatitlán at that time, became aware of this evil plan. In an act of bravery and faith, he chose to keep it secret to avoid endangering his own life or his Christian faith.

Acting discreetly, he saved many people from certain massacres. His decision to keep the information silent was an act of genuine heroism, a testament to his firm religious conviction and deep love for his fellow men.

Don Quirino always acknowledged his kinship with us, and even though his role in the government may have distanced him from his faith, he never ceased to be a courageous defender of his Christian beliefs in times of change and challenge. His story reminds us that faith and courage can coexist in a person's heart, even in the darkest moments of history.

Don Quirino: Amid Revolutions and Family Anecdotes

From the paternal perspective, my grandmother recounted experiences that hold the intrigue of a forgotten time.

My grandmother nostalgically remembered that in the era when my uncle Vicente Navarro resided in the magnificent mansion my father Felipe built, everyone had departed for eternity. Not even the shadow of his mother, Mariquita, remained. However, Don Quirino, after his involvement in the Revolution, had roamed various places and occasionally made stops at the House of the Chapel. His purpose was to inquire about his nephew Vicente, but upon detecting the search, Vicente would hide. Vicente also concealed his valuable steed, the object of Don Quirino's desire, who longed to appropriate it unsuccessfully.

My grandmother narrated how Don Quirino would inquire about his uncle Vicente under the pretext of greeting him, but his true intention was to obtain the coveted horse. However, his efforts always proved futile. In the community, his uncle Vicente had an excellent reputation, and his horse was considered an unbreakable treasure.

Leaving behind the enigmatic stories of Don Quirino, we resume the chronicle of my great-grandfather Demetrio Estrada alongside his three marriageable daughters. Demetrio chose to change his residence to the grand mansion he had built on a complete plot of 42x42 meters in San Antonio. This property exchange took place with the Franco family, who also lived in the locality and were close friends of the Estrada family. Through this exchange of properties, the life of the Estrada family continues its course in the fascinating history of San Antonio.

In the Pages of San Antonio's History: The Residence of Don Demetrio Estrada

In the picturesque setting of San Antonio, Don Demetrio Estrada, endowed with refined architectural taste, embarked on the construction of a splendid mansion on a plot he exchanged with the Franco family. This exchange resulted in the creation of a majestic residence that still stands as a tangible testament to his good taste.

After the meticulous completion of his grand work, Don Demetrio decided to move in with his three daughters, who were already of marriageable age. The first to seal her union was his daughter Trina, whose marriage united her with a relative named José Guadalupe Aceves.

This union bore fruit in the form of four sons and three daughters, with the youngest being baptized with the name Matilde, in honor of her grandmother. However, life presented challenges to this last daughter, who was born with hearing and speech limitations and lost her sight approximately two decades ago.

Despite these adversities, her resilient spirit, and her ability to communicate in unique ways are a touching testimony to her inner strength.

Another daughter, María, chose not to marry. While the reasons for her choice remain a mystery, she stood out for her beauty and her interest in acquiring knowledge, amassing a collection of books that, in their diversity, offered fascinating stories and wisdom.

In this tale of life in San Antonio, Don Demetrio Estrada's house becomes a hub of intertwined stories, where every corner holds memories, and every inhabitant contributes to the rich tapestry of this unique community.

A Legacy of Solvency and Valor in San Antonio

In the vast tapestry of San Antonio's history, the imposing figure of my father, Demetrio Estrada, stands out. His presence left an indelible mark, marked by his skill in pharmacy and later, his prominent role as a municipal delegate.

The last union that sealed my father's life was with my grandmother, Chita, also known as Doña Jesucita. She married Antonio Martín del Campo Franco, thus intertwining her lineage with the distinguished

Martín del Campo de Mirandilla and the renowned Franco families, known for their generosity and nobility throughout the region.

Upon settling in La Capilla, my father took on the role of municipal delegate, firmly confronting the troublemakers who dared to threaten the peace of the town. His courage and determination became the guardians of tranquility, successfully maintaining peace in the town for two consecutive terms.

As the years passed and two of his daughters married, only my aunt María remained to take care of my father. However, feeling lonely, he decided to embark on a new chapter of his life. He married a lady he met in Arandas, about 25 kilometers southeast of La Capilla.

According to my grandmother Chita's memoirs, this new union brought my father years of happiness. However, the fleeting joy was overshadowed by the early loss of his young wife, like the fleeting splendor of fine roosters in the arena of life.

The Legacy of a Magnificent Husband

The departure of my father, Demetrio Estrada, left behind an echo of magnificence as a husband, both in his first marriage to my great-grandmother Matilde and in his second union. His legacy shines as an indelible memory of an exemplary husband and an extraordinary father.

After his passing, the dilemma of dividing the two substantial inheritances arose: that of my father Demetrio and that of my mother Matilde. Both came from the legacy left by their fathers, which included the extensive San Antonio ranch, the impressive house, and vast stretches of land. Although the division was meant to be equal in three parts, no disputes arose. However, the only issue was the lack of cooperation from Papa Demetrio's sons-in-law, neither Don Guadalupe nor Papa Antonio showed willingness to work on their share. Even my aunt María, who remained unmarried, chose not to participate in the process.

Ultimately, they decided to sell the property, and the Francos, close friends who had an almost fraternal relationship with Papa Demetrio, became the buyers. The sale included the majestic house that Demetrio had built with sacrifice. Don Juanillo Franco and his family, people of great worth, became the new custodians of this legacy. The transaction took place without disputes, respecting the bond of friendship between the two families.

Don Juanillo Franco once shared that for years, the two families helped each other like brothers. The sale of San Antonio marked the closing of a chapter, but the legacy of magnificence and friendship endured in the memories of those who once called that land their home.

The Assault of Bandits and New Directions

A chapter of San Antonio's history was colored with intrigue and valor when the threat of bandits loomed over the community's tranquility. The audacity of these wrongdoers was evident as they attempted to steal the Franco family's cattle, distinguished residents of the region.

As soon as Papa Demetrio Estrada, a faithful resident of San Antonio, learned of these criminal acts, he set out in pursuit. Tracking skillfully, he reached the bandits in the vicinity of Arandas. The accuracy of the information suggests that Don José María Franco, Juanillo's father, still resided in the area.

The account omits the details of the confrontation, but Papa Demetrio's firm resolve and José María Franco's skill in recovering the cattle are perceived as key elements. Although the exact circumstances of the confrontation remain in the shadows, the victory over the bandits added another feat to San Antonio's history.

Continuing with the course of inheritances, Aunt Trina and her husband, Don Guadalupe Aceves, used their share to acquire a nearby hacienda by the Verde River, known as "El Comal," in the lands of Yahualica. On the other hand, luck did not favor my mother, Chita, who married a son of Don Jerónimo Martín del Campo, a prosperous rancher.

Don Jerónimo Martín del Campo belonged to a distinguished family of Castilian roots that settled in the region in 1718. His lineage, composed of several solvent and upright families, has endured in the place, contributing to the growth and strength of the community.

With the conclusion of this chapter, new narratives are unveiled, exploring the journey of these families and the legacy they have forged in the lands of San Antonio.

Roots in Mirandilla and the Encounter of Two Souls

The family saga continues its course, now weaving its threads in Mirandilla, the land that welcomed the growth of my grandfather Jerónimo Martín del Campo. Rooted in the land, Jerónimo, along with his brothers, thrived as cattle ranchers and farmers, expanding the borders of their possessions.

With an imposing presence, Jerónimo stood out among his brothers for his stature and chestnut hair. His physical and chivalrous demeanor was manifested in his elegant attire, a characteristic shared with his brothers, who never missed any celebrations, especially the exciting bullfights. It was at one of these events where destiny introduced him to the woman who would change his life: Doña Dolores.

Framed by the fairness of her complexion, blonde hair, and blue eyes, Dolores exuded beauty and youth. This meeting at a bullfight, featuring bulls from Don Miguel Franco's ranch, Dolores's father, marked the beginning of a love story that culminated in an elegant marriage and a memorable celebration, worthy of the time.

The romance between Jerónimo and Dolores was sealed with their move to Mirandilla, where they started their family. Four sons, Rafael, Salomé, Silviano, and Antonio, along with four daughters, laid the roots of this new generation. Among them was my grandfather Antonio, who, during these pages, will be revealed as a significant figure in our family history. This chapter invites us to explore the experiences of this family in Mirandilla, where each child, like a branch of a sturdy tree, will contribute to the blossoming of new stories and legacies.

Roots That Branch in Different Lands

In the fertile soil of Mirandilla, my uncles and aunts came into the world, growing as vigorous shoots within the family. Comfort and work in the fields marked their days, forging deep bonds with the land that saw them grow.

Uncle Rafael and Uncle Silviano chose to follow different paths. The former embarked on the road to Guadalajara, establishing himself as a successful merchant with a prosperous clothing factory that led him on the path to wealth. However, his journey came to an early end, a victim of the exhaustion that comes with excessive success.

On the other hand, Uncle Salomé acquired a ranch, named "Popotes," to the west of Tepatitlán. Although I had barely the chance to meet him, his presence adds another branch to our family tree, extending to new lands.

My grandfather Antonio, the only one to marry in La Capilla, led a different life. During his youth, he showed inclinations towards a leisurely life, preferring to attend cockfights in nearby towns. This pastime, more than a hobby, became an intrinsic part of his life, to the point of learning how to tie the rooster's spurs.

Although distant from fieldwork, Antonio found occasional sustenance in cockfights, despite the risks and losses it also entailed. Thus, Antonio, my grandfather, found his own path in life, marked by his own choices and experiences.

A Bittersweet Marital Dance

The love between my grandparents, Tono, and Mama Chita, was a romantic waltz that led them to the sacred commitment of marriage. Captivated by each other, they sealed their union, unaware of the shadows that loomed over their destinies.

Mama Chita, unaware of Tono's gambling vice, or perhaps choosing to ignore it, immersed herself in this whirlwind of emotions. They say love is blind, and with this veil, she did not perceive the addiction that would soon affect their lives. The fruit of this union, their first child, was named "Miguel" in honor of the family patriarch, Don Miguel Franco.

Despite the inheritance that Tono received after his father's departure, his aversion to work led him to spend seasons gambling, enjoying fleeting pleasures. They ventured to Juanacatlán, where Mama Chita briefly shared her life with her mother-in-law Dolores, gaining valuable insights into Don Miguel Franco and the brave bull breeding that characterized him.

The return to La Capilla marked an unexpected turn. Mama Chita's inheritance, entrusted to Tono, quickly disappeared, like the crowing of a rooster at dawn. The marital relationship, although marked by love, also witnessed the dance of an uncompromising temperament. Despite the difficulties, Tono, with his peaceful temperament, chose not to replicate the disagreements woven by his wife's relentless will.

Following the Traces of Adversity

The marriage of my father, Toño, and Mama Chita, witnessed the arrival of their children and the flourishing of a lineage destined to withstand the blows of destiny.

After a while, life led Mama Chita into destitution. Taking refuge in Juanacatlán with her mother Dolores, who was still alive at that time, she immersed herself in cockfighting and a liking for games of chance. Although she did not completely surrender to these pursuits, her passion for roosters prevailed, fortunately without falling into the clutches of drunkenness.

With Dolores's passing, Juanacatlán lost its splendor, and the bull cattle was transferred by one of Don Miguel Franco's sons, Dolores's brother. The inheritance that belonged to my grandfather Toño after his mother-in-law's death barely sufficed to sustain him. With this meager capital, he returned to Mama Chita and their rapidly growing children.

However, this prosperity was short-lived. Mama Chita, affected by her temper, succumbed to illness without communicating her suffering. In silence, she endured adversity, without treating or revealing her anguish. Despite the difficulties, she found herself abandoned, depending on the charity of others to survive and face the upbringing of her four children: Miguel, María, Trina, and my mother.

Facing Destiny with Dignity

The marriage of my father, Toño, and Mama Chita, brought with it the arrival of their children, forming a family that, although marked by adversity, never lost hope.

Tragedy struck when Mama Chita's mental health was affected, plunging her into a painful reality. Her brothers, Uncle Rafael and

Uncle Silviano, who lived in Guadalajara, learned of the situation and called her. So, Mama Chita departed for the city, where Uncle Silviano, owner of a house on Valda Street, generously welcomed her.

During her stay in Guadalajara, life smiled at them like a divine gift. The revolution, which displaced many families from towns and ranches to cities, soon arrived. My uncle Miguel, young and enterprising, found employment thanks to a cousin named Ángel Franco, who would later become the owner of the famous Casa Franco in the city center.

Meanwhile, my mother devoted herself to studying sewing, and my youngest aunt, Carmen, prepared to become a teacher. Recognizing the talent of my aunt María, the government sent her to San José de Gracia to teach at a civilian school. There, she married Lorenzo Angulo, a respectable politician.

This chapter of our family history highlights the strength and dignity with which they faced the vicissitudes of destiny.

The Legacy of Uncle Miguel and the Journey of Uncle Lorenzo

The history of our family is enriched by the experiences of extraordinary figures, such as Uncle Miguel, whose legacy lives on in our memories. His departure left a void, but his memory inspires us as an exemplary husband and an exceptional father.

Although Uncle Miguel considered a life in the seminary in his youth, destiny led him to San José, where he crossed paths with Aunt Carmen. The connection they shared transcended words, manifesting in a pure and sincere love that touched the hearts of those who witnessed it.

Uncle Lorenzo, with an entrepreneurial vision, established a prosperous grocery store in the heart of the city, near the Temple of the Comiche, on Obregón Street. There, he dedicated his life to the business, writing a chapter rich in experiences and achievements that endured over time.

Returning to the core of Papa Toño's family, my mother lived with Mama Chita in Uncle Silviano's house. Uncle Miguel, seeking opportunities, emigrated to the United States with the intention of working and sending money to Mama Chita. However, time darkened the prospect of his return, and when Mama Chita returned to La Capilla, she faced the harsh reality of economic hardship.

When he finally returned, Uncle Miguel brought with him an illness that confined him to La Capilla. The financial situation became precarious for Mama Chita, and in that context, my father followed her to Guadalajara. It was then that they made the brave decision to marry, marking a challenging chapter in Mama Chita's life, who took on the responsibility of raising her family amid economic adversities.

My Two Brothers, with Me in Between

The Meaningful Union of My Parents

Marriage, a sacred bond that joins two souls on a shared path, also came to our family in remarkable ways. My aunt María, after establishing her life in Guadalajara, found love in Gustavo Uribe Santana, a member of a distinguished family from Autlán de la Grana. This uncle, Gustavo, earned the respect and affection of everyone, just like my aunt María.

In contrast, my mother was the only one who chose a member of our community in La Capilla as her life partner. My father, a third cousin of Mama Chita, carried the Navarro surname, a direct descendant of Amo Aceves and Don Luciano Navarro. This marital union transcended, uniting two Castilian families in a strong and profound bond.

It was as if the Morenita Guadalupana, with her indigenous blood and unwavering love, had orchestrated this encounter to unite two races with physical strength and a shared devotion to faith. Thus, the union of my parents, José Gutiérrez González and my mother, del Refugio Martín del Campo Estrada, was forged. I, as their child, am the fruit of this manifestation of love, and I deeply proud of a being part of this history, as well as my eternal love for Our Lady of Guadalupe, who has guided our steps with her blessing.

With this, I conclude the retelling of the history of my great-great-grandparents, great-grandparents, grandparents, and parents, thus completing a portrait of our family roots.

Now, as promised in the previous chapter about Rancho Juanacasco, I would like to share everything I have learned about my great-great-grandfather, Don Miguel Franco el Grande.

CHAPTER 14

Don Miguel Franco el Grande and His Equestrian Legacy

Don Miguel Franco el Grande, as everyone in the region used to call him, was my great-great-grandfather, and I am deeply proud of him. He was a true gentleman and a real expert in the art of horsemanship. He was tall, strong as a bull, with blonde hair and blue eyes that radiated gallantry and an enviable personality.

He always rode his majestic bay horse with skill and elegance, as if they were one. No cattle or rebellious colt could escape him when he decided to capture them, handling the rope with mastery, demonstrating his skill as an experienced cattleman. Sometimes, he even outperformed his own ranch hands, giving them a lesson when trying to catch a foal or perform a "mangana."

In addition, he had exceptional control over his dark bay horse, communicating with it through the reins in an astonishing way. He trained them so well that his mount obeyed him even with the slightest gesture, anticipating his intentions. Don Miguel Franco el Grande was a true legendary rider, as my grandparents described him to me.

Don Miguel Franco el Grande's Equestrian Mastery and the Legacy of Criollo Cattle

My father, Mr. Martín del Campo Franco, Don Miguel's grandson, and my grandmother, María de Jesús Estrada, known as Mamá Chita, lived in Juanacasco with their mother-in-law, Doña Dolores Franco, Don Miguel el Grande's daughter. Everything I've been told about my grandparents; I have stored in my memory.

As I mentioned earlier, Don Miguel had outstanding roping skills for catching any kind of animal that needed to be branded, from colts to mares, mules, and even donkeys. These festivities were real celebrations, where music was never lacking, brought in from other localities. Deer were sacrificed, and a delicious barbacoa was prepared in a hole dug in the ground. The pit was heated with firewood, and the meat was wrapped in agave leaves, allowing it to cook for about eight hours. Pigs were also sacrificed, sometimes two, to prepare tender and tasty carnitas. Carnitas were served in clay pots, accompanied by handmade tortillas wrapped in cloth to keep them warm. There was always a special sauce, either spicy or mild, according to individual preferences.

To accompany these delights, pulque was enjoyed, served in large jugs to avoid getting stuck in the throat while eating carnitas. After the meal, when satisfaction and camaraderie had been established, music and dancing took over. These festivities were memorable moments filled with great joy and fraternity.

Don Atenógenes, the Master Pulquero, and the Harvest of Agave

The day after the branding festivities, it was time to enjoy the mastery of Don Atenógenes, the ultimate pulque maker. His skill lay in giving pulque the right fermentation time, resulting in a drink that could be either smooth or robust, depending on individual taste. In the days leading up to the event, he would begin extracting aguamiel from the maguey plants and let it ferment in clay pots with two fresh jugs. After three or four days, the pulque was ready to be tasted.

In Juanacasco, maguey plants were abundant, and Don Atenógenes had an orchard full of mature maguey plants. He always kept several maguey plant capados, meaning he had to wait seven or eight years for the maguey to grow large enough and develop its aguamiel. Capar un maguey meant cutting the "kiote" or stalk that grew in its center. If allowed to grow, this stock could reach heights of up to five or six meters, affecting aguamiel production. Therefore, it was essential to cut it in time.

The capado process involved creating a round hole in the center of the maguey, with a diameter of approximately 30 centimeters, tailored to the size of the maguey. This hole allowed the collection of aguamiel, which, once fermented, would become the exquisite pulque that Don Atenógenes prepared with such care for the delight of everyone present at these festivities.

The Extraction of Aguamiel and the Treasures of the Maguey

In this undertaking, the maguey plants took center stage and were treated with special care. First, an incision of approximately 30 centimeters in diameter and about seven centimeters in depth was made in them, which was then covered with an improvised lid to prevent any animal from accessing the aguamiel. There, the maguey plants "cried" for a period of 24 hours, producing up to five liters or more of aguamiel each day. Once the extraction was complete, a gentle scrape was given to the maguey plants to allow them to free comfortably.

Don Atenógenes, the master pulque maker, collected all the aguamiel and poured it into large pots, where it rested to become pulque. If someone wanted to taste the aguamiel in its sweetest and most substantial state, they had the option to do so, as it was a delight on its own.

Some people choose to transform aguamiel into maguey honey by cooking it until it becomes thick and acquires a dark brown color, similar to bee honey but with a unique and delicious flavor. It is important to mention that the maguey plant resembles a plant known as "mezcalillo," but the latter is smaller with narrower leaves. Mezcalillo is the plant used to produce tequila and mezcal and also requires several years of growth before being harvested. In the Altos region, blue mezcalillo is especially appreciated for its quality.

This concludes my account of Don Atenógenes, the master pulque maker, and his expertise in aguamiel extraction and the transformation of maguey into pulque and honey, a treasure of the land that enriches the festivities of Juanacasco.

Don Miguel Aceves Galindo and the Branding Festivities

Don Miguel Aceves Galindo, the master pulque maker who added joy to the heirs of Juanacasco with his famous pulque, was a prominent figure in these festivities. Continuing with the description of the branding events, they were also used to castrate steers and raise oxen for fieldwork. Colts that were to be castrated also went through this process.

However, I cannot forget to mention that from these renowned branding events emerged the best charro and rope floreo performer, who became famous throughout Mexico. I am talking about Don Miguel Aceves Galindo, who also descended from Castilian people and was related to most of us in the region. Don Miguel had unparalleled skill in rope floreo, a skill he learned and perfected in the famous branding events I mentioned in Juanacasco and Rancho de San Antonio, primarily.

Continuing with the narrative about Don Miguel Franco el Grande and his extensive ranch in Juanacasco, his house was located next to the Camino Real. Travelers constantly passed along this road from Guadalajara to Mexico City and vice versa. Juanacasco was right in the middle of this road, between La Capilla to the east and Tepatitlán to the west. My grandfather Antonio used to tell me more about this.

It is said that Grandfather Miguel Franco had a house in Tepatitlán. When he visited this city, he took the opportunity to dress in his finest attire, especially when bullfights with his own cattle were held. At such times, he stood out like all the landowners in the region. Despite his firm character, he had a generous heart and was never considered a malicious person.

The foremen and their workers deeply respected him and loved him as if he were a father. He treated his employees as if they were members of his own family. This fair and kind treatment of workers was a common characteristic among landowners in the Altos de Jalisco. Thanks to this relationship of respect and affection, there was never any revolutionary uprising caused by mistreatment from landowners.

At that time, Mexico was dealing with several issues, including the conflict with Benito Juárez and the French under Napoleon III, who attempted to impose a monarchy in Mexico by appointing Maximilian, the brother of the Emperor of Austria, as emperor in 1864.

This situation arose after Napoleon III sent 30,000 troops to Mexico and was defeated in Puebla by General Zaragoza in 1862, precisely on May 5th. Juárez had been organizing the Reformist Army since 1858, running for president against the Conservatives, who had the influence of the Catholic Church.

Juárez suspended payments that Mexico owed to its foreign creditors, further worsening the country's political and economic situation at that time. Even England and Spain joined the threat by landing in Veracruz. However, both England and Spain abandoned the enterprise when they realized that France's intentions were more political than financial. It was then that French troops, under the command of Napoleon III, arrived on the shores of Veracruz with their army and marched toward Mexico City.

Things didn't go as France had planned, and the French army was defeated with great joy by the Mexicans on May 5, 1862. It was in this context that Benito Juárez entered Mexico City and was appointed interim president.

However, Napoleon III was not satisfied, and in 1864, he landed in Mexico with 30,000 soldiers, once again occupying Mexico City. With the collaboration of the Conservative Government, Napoleon imposed Maximilian of Austria as Emperor to rule Mexico.

In this part of my narrative, I want to mention that my family had distant ties to Generals Miramón and Mexía, who were prominent military figures on the Conservative side at that time. Although these family connections were very distant in my family tree, it is interesting to note that both had 100% indigenous ancestry.

This connection had been mentioned before, but now I want to revisit the story of my great-grandfather Don Miguel el Grande in Juanacasco, where he constantly observed the passing of Conservative and Reform armies, as well as diligences and caravans that incessantly crossed the road.

The Legacy of Don Miguel Franco El Grande: Passion and Mystery in Juanacasco

In those days, the life of my great-great-grandfather Don Miguel Franco El Grande unfolded peacefully in Juanacasco. He was a regular observer of the constant caravans and travelers passing along the road, always ready to exchange news and anecdotes with those who crossed his path.

However, Don Miguel's true passion lay in his brave cattle, a treasure he cherished with pride. My grandparents, especially my grandfather Antonio Martín del Campo, Don Miguel's great-grandson, used to share that this cattle were the family's jewel.

But there was more to the story that intrigued the family. My grandmother Chita, the wife of my grandfather Toño, was passionate about bullfights. She knew the rules and the art of bullfighting perfectly and avidly followed the bullfights through the radio, getting extremely excited with each bullfighting maneuver. She didn't tolerate interruptions during broadcasts, and her enthusiasm was contagious.

The passion for bullfighting was passed down from generation to generation in our family. My grandmother Chita, in turn, had inherited this fervor from her mother-in-law, Doña Dolores Franco, the daughter of Don Miguel El Grande. My mother Dolores shared everything she knew about her father and his brave cattle, further strengthening the bond between the two women.

However, an enigma surrounded Don Miguel's brave cattle. The precise details of its origin and how it became part of our family were never known. This mystery, which added a touch of intrigue to our family history, remains unresolved to this day.

My great-great-grandfather Don Miguel Franco El Grande's brave cattle extended majestically in the lands north of Juanacasco, specifically in Cerro Carnicero. This vast expanse of land was dedicated to bull breeding, and the stories I heard from my grandparents indicated that he owned hundreds of specimens. Don Miguel dedicated constant time and effort to ensure that his cattle were cared for meticulously, knowing that this was crucial for breeding the best fighting bulls.

Don Miguel was a true expert in all aspects of bull breeding and always paid attention to details. His knowledge encompassed all aspects of caring for these animals, but despite his skill, he rarely participated in bullfights himself. However, from time to time, he immersed himself in the bullfighting spirit and took part in the famous branding festivities. There, he delighted people with his riding skills and occasionally let his horse get involved in rounding up, although this was not his strong point.

Don Miguel's story reminded me of one of the first bullfights held in America, in Lima, Peru, in 1540. Francisco Pizarro, mounted on his horse, stood out as a rejoneador by killing the second bull in the bullfight.

It was a historical bullfighting memory that somehow connected with the passion that my great-great-grandfather felt for these events. Bullfights with his cattle were exciting and adventurous events held in nearby towns, from Arandas and San Miguel to Tepatitlán, and even on special occasions, they reached Guadalajara. It was a time filled with fascinating and thrilling stories in the life of Don Miguel Franco El Grande, a true lover of bullfighting.

The Splendor of Bullfights in Tepatitlán

In the past, the transportation of bulls for bullfights was done by land, a process that required the animals to be driven to their destination on foot. In an era before modern means of transportation existed, bulls were guided through streets and royal roads to reach their destination. This method was arduous and required a lot of effort, but it was the only way to transport them.

My great-great-grandfather, Don Miguel, always had exceptional breed cattle in his possession, which meant that he constantly received orders for bulls for bullfighting festivals. I can imagine the bustle and excitement that erupted in Tepatitlán during the annual celebration of the Señor de la Misericordia. Every year, crowds of people gathered in the city center, coming from all over, filling the streets to the point where it was difficult to walk.

Men and women mingled in the square, spinning in opposite directions. Men tried to win the hearts of ladies by giving them carnations and gardenias. After all the revelry and movement, the local band played, providing a brief break before the fireworks began. Powder castles were ignited, launching strings of colorful rockets that painted the sky and filled hearts with joy. The highlight of these celebrations came on April 30th, when the Señor de la Misericordia was celebrated in his sanctuary. This event was accompanied by a grand bullfight that concluded the celebrations with an exciting and tradition-filled spectacle. It was a moment of splendor and excitement in Tepatitlán, where bullfights were the soul of the festivity.

Bullfights in Tepatitlán were a unique and dazzling spectacle that brought together the best bullfighters from Mexico and sometimes even from Spain. Bullfighting unfolded in its full glory, and the bullring, though spacious, quickly filled up on the most anticipated day, April 30th. If one had not purchased a ticket in advance, it was certain that they would not be able to witness the bullfight.

The excitement was palpable, and people were eager to get their ticket, even if it was just for a seat in the sun, as there were three categories of seats: sun, shade, and box seats, with the latter being the most expensive. When I was young, around the age of 15, we moved to Tepatitlán, and I had the opportunity to attend several of these bullfights. The bullfighting festivities were still celebrated with the same passion and quality as when my great-great-grandfather, Don Miguel El Grande, was present.

Don Miguel always had his special box reserved, as it was the moment when he presented his impressive breed of fighting bulls. He took pride in his bulls, some of which weighed up to 600 kilograms. These imposing animals sometimes managed to leap over the bullring barriers like arrows, bringing excitement to the audience enjoying the bull's action inside the ring. Often, applause and cheers from the audience accompanied these bullfighting feats, creating a vibrant and thrilling atmosphere that made bullfights in Tepatitlán truly unforgettable.

The art of bullfighting displayed its splendor at every moment in the bullring. The picadors, brave defenders of the ring, faced the bulls with determination, sometimes having to pierce them repeatedly to control their momentum and allow the bullfighters to perform with skill and get the most out of these powerful animals. On some occasions, the bullfighter took his time with the muleta, as the bulls possessed boundless energy, reminiscent of the renowned "Miura" bulls.

In my mind, I can visualize Don Miguel, seated in his box with elegance and gallantry, accompanied by his family. I imagine Mama Dolores, who would later become my grandfather Antonio's mother, standing out for her feminine beauty, blond hair, tall stature, and blue eyes, a characteristic that was common in the Franco family.

In the bullring, when Don Miguel and his family entered, the local band played an emotive melody, whether it was a pasodoble or a march. When the time for the bullfighting came, the judge, with great elegance, was ready to give orders to the band, which announced the start of the celebration with a trumpet fanfare. Everyone stood up and stopped as the first bullfighter, brave and determined, positioned himself in the center of the ring to face the bull, marking the beginning of an exciting and thrilling bullfighting afternoon.

If any bullfighter wanted to challenge further and take greater risks, he would stand with his cape, waiting for the bull before it burst out like an arrow, snorting and exhaling smoke. The bull, with its coat of short and Defiant Look, Charging with Force like a Whirlwind

The bull would charge with force like a whirlwind, while the bullfighter faced it bravely, using his cape to calm it and extract its courage. Occasionally, the bull would leap over the bullring barrier in a spectacular jump, requiring caution to prevent it from reaching anyone in the audience.

Thus, the joy of the bullfight continued until they finished dealing with the fourth bull. Everyone retired satisfied, each to their own home, awaiting the last day of celebration in the main square.

On that night, the music band would resonate again, people would walk around the square, and the bullfighters prepared to face the final challenges. But this time, the spotlight would be on the fireworks, with thunderous rockets and castles of lights illuminating the night sky.

At dawn, those who suffered the consequences of the celebration were none other than the street sweepers, responsible for cleaning the square and its surroundings, which were covered in confetti, colorful streamers, and other remnants that resembled mattresses. This sight, which I witnessed as a child, was repeated in all the nearby towns during the annual festivities, announced in advance in the streets and accompanied by exciting bullfights that kept the intrepid spirit of tradition alive.

The bullfight parades were a spectacle full of excitement and tradition. With the sound of one or two drums and their bullfight banner, they marched through the streets of the town. At night, lanterns were lit, and a town crier, equipped with a fairground horn, energetically announced the distribution of bulls that would take place in the square.

Thus, they traversed almost the entire town, carrying with them the contagious rhythm of the drums and stopping at every corner to announce the four bulls that would be part of the event, all coming from Don Miguel Franco's cattle.

I remember having the opportunity to witness this beautiful tradition. In Tepatitlán, there was a relative of the Franco family named Juan González Franco, known as Don Juan Largo, perhaps due to his height and build.

He inherited an extensive ranch called El Aguacate, near Cerro Gordo, and shared the passion for brave bulls that had been passed down by his father and grandparents. Don Juan González Franco may have had a close relationship with my father, Miguel Franco El Grande.

What struck me the most was that Don Juan Largo had also inherited the drums used to announce the bullfight, and he conducted them in the same way they did in the past. I remember seeing him when I went to witness a bullfight in Tepatitlán, organizing the parade with the drums with incredible enthusiasm and passion. This memory makes me reflect on the deeply rooted tradition and heritage that the Franco family shared with other bullfighting enthusiasts in the region.

The Odyssey of Taking the Bulls to Guadalajara

I want to share more details about Don Miguel Franco, my great-great-grandfather, and the challenges he faced when taking cattle to Guadalajara when receiving a special order. This was a journey of about 90 to 95 kilometers from Juanacatlán to Guadalajara, and it usually took at least two days, sometimes more, to travel the Royal

Road. During this journey, they faced numerous seemingly endless problems.

The bullring where they brought the brave bulls was in the heart of the city of Guadalajara, near the Temple of San Juan de Dios and next to the hospice. Don Miguel had to meticulously coordinate the preparation of the brave bulls before taking them to the city.

One of the fundamental tasks was to gather the cabestros, which were docile cattle, to accompany the brave bulls during the journey. This was done to prevent the brave bulls from suddenly charging at anyone. This precaution was essential as everyone's safety was a priority.

Early in the morning, the caporales, with their expertise, selected five of the best bulls for the bullfight. Although bullfights were usually held with four bulls, they always brought one or two additional ones as a precaution in case of any unforeseen circumstances.

The process of taking the bulls to Guadalajara was a true odyssey, full of challenges and obstacles that Don Miguel Franco and his team faced with determination and a passion for bullfighting. This journey was not only a logistical challenge but also a demonstration of the Franco family's commitment to the bullfighting tradition and their dedication to providing exciting bullfights in Guadalajara.

The Bulls' Journey: From Juanacatlán to Guadalajara

Let me recount in detail the fascinating journey that Don Miguel Franco, my great-great-grandfather, and his team undertook to take the bulls from Juanacatlán to the city of Guadalajara. This odyssey began with the selection and gathering of cabestros, docile cattle that would accompany the brave bulls during the journey.

The bulls were left in the corrals near the Casa Grande de Juanacatlán the night before the trip. At dawn, they set out early with the cabestros along the Royal Road toward Guadalajara.

However, an hour before departure, a group of men on horseback would ride ahead on the road.

Since the Royal Road was frequented by stagecoaches, muleteers, and travelers on horseback, extra precautions were taken to avoid any accidents that might occur if a bull separated and posed a danger to people or other animals on the road.

Despite having a considerable number of cabestros, meticulous care was necessary due to the cunning nature of the brave bulls. The journey to Guadalajara was a challenging and demanding task, but the team was motivated by the excitement of taking the cattle to Guadalajara's bullring, where Don Miguel Franco's bulls would be the center of attention in an exciting bullfight. They arrived in Guadalajara tired but satisfied, knowing that they had cared for the cattle with great dedication and knowledge.

In Guadalajara, they prepared in advance for a week to announce to bullfight enthusiasts that Don Miguel Franco would present his brave cattle in the bullring. Each bull was personally known to those who had seen them grow from their earliest age, and they knew which ones possessed more lineage and bravery. This commitment and passion were evident in every step of this incredible journey.

In Guadalajara, the atmosphere of the bullfights was nearly identical, but there, they began by pasting posters with glue on every corner, announcing the participation of the famous bullfighters of those times, including picadores and banderilleros. There was no shortage of announcements stating, "FOUR BULLS FROM THE GREAT CATTLE OF DON MIGUEL FRANCO EL GRANDE WILL FIGHT." Thus, the day of the bullfight approached, and the square filled to the brim, as in those times, there was more enthusiasm for bullfighting festivities than now.

Don Miguel, as always, had his special box as the owner of the brave cattle to be fought. This box was close to the judge's, a figure of great importance in the event. Without the judge's presence and decisions, nothing could happen. He was the one who gave the orders to start the show and had the final say in rewarding the bullfighters according to their performance, granting them one or two ears, and sometimes, if the performance was exceptional, two ears and the tail, always respecting the audience's opinion.

Don Miguel, whom we affectionately called "Papa Miguel," was always ready in his box long before the festivities began, with his imposing presence and unique style. He wore his round hat, not too large, and his thick chinaco-style jacket, completing his outfit with an elegant suit.

In those times, my father wore a very elegant suit, a blend of Chinaco and Spanish styles, distinctive of that era. He used to be accompanied in his box, sometimes by his children, and other times even by my great-grandmother, his daughter, who had to look very beautiful. As I mentioned before, he resembled his father a lot, with blond hair, blue eyes, and rosy cheeks, typical characteristics of the Franco lineage.

Outside the bullring, there was also great excitement. As people entered, you could find all kinds of vendors taking advantage of the opportunity to sell their products: fruits, fresh drinks, corn, tamales, and much more.

The competition was such that prices were a true negotiation. And of course, there were ticket scalpers outside the ticket booth, who, especially when the arena was full, raised their prices to exploit the demand.

Scalpers would often buy a bunch of tickets in advance and then sell them at higher prices, especially if they saw that the bullfight promised to be good. With Don Miguel El Grande's cattle, the event was better guaranteed due to the quality of the livestock. This made for a great "Taurine Festival." Sellers ensured their sales, and as people entered, the music band had been playing all kinds of pasodobles and Spanish-style marches for a while, even inspiring some to dance.

Listening to the music band with their exciting pasodobles, one couldn't help but feel pumped with excitement, almost like a peacock. The anticipation grew even more knowing that the elegant parade would soon begin. At the front of the parade, a horse that danced to the rhythm of the pasodoble played by the band would usually appear. This spectacle began right when the reveille ordered by the judge sounded.

The rider, wearing a Napoleon-style hat, a cape, and a sword that almost covered the entire horse, saluted with the sword in hand, raising it to the level of the jaw. Behind him, the parade lined up in two rows: first the picadores mounted on their one-eyed horses - one eye was covered so they wouldn't see the bull coming - and protected with cushions. Then came the banderilleros, the subordinates, and finally, the bullfighters, parading with unique elegance.

The bullfighters' suits, made of a special fabric to make the bull's horn slip, were adorned with chiseled brilliance and dazzling colors. The capes, equally beautiful, were held and wrapped around the bent arm as they walked with their characteristic step towards the ring's platforms and barriers, where they hung their capes on the fence. It was a moment of great solemnity and beauty, anticipating the excitement and courage that would be experienced in the bullfight.

The bullfighters, greeting the standing audience, finished their parade and sat down, giving way to the resumption of the music that signaled the entry of the first bull. When everything was ready, the judge signaled to start the bullfight. The judge gave the signal to the band, which announced the entry of the first bull. The music abruptly stopped, and the trumpeter, with a special touch, announced the opening of the gates.

The bull, already enraged from being pricked with a small sword as a banderilla to incite its courage, came out snorting. It reached the ring's fence in an instant, and sometimes even jumped over the fence, while the bullfighters watched attentively. Some bullfighters, in a display of bravery, would sometimes position themselves in the center of the square with the cape ready to face the bull, making the audience anticipate what might happen.

I have witnessed several acts of bravery like these. I remember one occasion when a bull, like a hurricane, charged at the bullfighter. Although it didn't gore him, the impact was such that the bullfighter was left limping. He was quickly assisted by the subordinates, and, showing great courage, he withdrew with the help of his colleagues. On another occasion, a bullfighter, with great bravery, performed an almost perfect faena. Although he didn't manage to kill the bull with the first thrust, requiring a second one, the skill and art displayed were memorable. These moments, filled with tension and excitement, define the essence of the bullfight, a spectacle of valor, tradition, and deeply rooted art in the culture of Guadalajara.

My experiences and memories in bullfights are deep and varied. I learned by attending many bullfights, getting to know almost all the rules and moves. I was fortunate to see legendary bullfighters like Carlos Arruza, Armillita, and had the incredible opportunity to see Manolete in Guadalajara. I also remember Capetillo, a brave bullfighter and a complete charro, who also made several movies, proving to be a fabulous artist in everything he did.

I have a deep respect and admiration for Capetillo, a true pride of Mexico, although I feel that he has not yet received the recognition he deserves. Although I am fascinated by bulls and enjoy watching them, I must admit that I do not have the 'suicidal' blood necessary to be a bullfighter.

Returning to the story of my great-great-grandfather

Don Miguel, who watched from his box the performances of his good cattle and skilled bullfighters, explained to them the procedure with each bull. First, the bullfighters would tire the bull a bit with several capes. Then, the judge gave the order, and when the special trumpet sound played, they called for a change. Two or three pairs of banderillas were placed, exhausting the bull considerably. Then they called for another change for the picadores, followed by the entrance of the two great horses.

This sequence of events, full of ritual and skill, captures the essence of bullfights in Guadalajara. It reflects not only the skill and courage of the bullfighter but also the strength and indomitable spirit of the bull, making each bullfight a show of deep emotions and cultural tradition.

Honor and Tradition: The Legend of Don Miguel in Bullfights

When the crucial moment of the bullfight arrived, the bullfighter, ready to deliver the final thrust, bent his knee to advance and execute the perfect strike. If luck was on his side and he managed to kill the bull with the first thrust, and had also performed an impressive faena, the audience responded with thunderous applause. The level of applause from the audience was the criterion the judge used to decide whether to award one or two ears to the bullfighter. And if the faena was exceptional, the tip of the bull's tail, the tail, was cut, and it was also given to the bullfighter. The bullfighter would then take a lap around the arena, with the audience standing and applauding, women throwing carnations, and men their hats, as a sign of recognition for the magnificent performance. In those moments, Don Miguel El Grande shone, as he too stood up to applaud, showing his pride for the fine lineage of cattle he had provided. I imagine that Papa Miguel must have felt like a peacock, just like those sitting with him in his box.

What more can I say about my great-great-grandfather? I am very proud of him, and I would have loved to have met him in person, as well as my great-grandmother Dolores Franco, his daughter. Perhaps, if God permits, we will meet at the end of our journey. When Don Miguel passed away, he was buried in the cemetery of Tepatitlán, where his very beautiful tomb still stands as a reminder of his legacy and our rich family history.

Legacy of Don Miguel Franco: History of a Taurine Dynasty

Don Miguel Franco's tomb, an iconic figure in the world of bullfighting, resembles a small chapel with its railing door, dating back to around 1890. Near his grave lies another Miguel Franco, possibly a descendant of Mama Dolores. The next time I visit Tepatitlán, I intend to investigate more about these family connections.

With great pleasure, I have shared everything I know about my great-great-grandfather Miguel Franco El Grande, renowned as a great cattle rancher and expert in all matters related to extensive ranches and the breeding of brave cattle. He maintained an excellent reputation until his death, leaving this legacy to his children and descendants. Not long ago, that same cattle ended up in the hands of the famous Mexican comedian Cantinflas, who bought it from my father's second cousin, María González, widow of Franco. She was the daughter of Don Francisco González, my grandmother María González's double first cousin on my father's side. María married José María Francés, a descendant of my great-great-grandfather Miguel Franco El Grande. Don José María maintained his cattle ranch on a ranch near La Capilla, my hometown, called "El Burrol." Unfortunately, due to an accident, Don José María passed away, but his legacy and his bulls in the "Aprobadas" ranches persisted for a long time, thus preserving the history and pride of an exceptional bullfighting dynasty.

Heritage of Valor: The Saga of Franco's Bulls

The story of my great-great-grandfather Don Miguel Franco El Grande and his legacy in the world of bullfighting is one of bravery and tradition. The bulls from the Franco ranch, known in the bullrings for their bravery and nobility in the fight, maintained their prestige until an unfortunate accident precipitated the decision to sell the ranch. It was then that Cantinflas, recognizing the quality and renown of these bulls' lineage, offered to buy it.

This real narrative culminates with the sale of the ranch to Cantinflas, a significant chapter in our family's bullfighting history, marking the end of an era but preserving the legacy of a lineage of exceptional bulls. This is where the true story of my great-great-grandfather, a character whose name and heritage remain in the memory of all those who value the tradition of bullfights, comes to an end.

Now, I am about to tell another interesting story, just before reaching my birth. Although I am yet to get to that part, I can assure you that I have some very interesting things to share, especially because when I was a child, I was quite mischievous.

CHAPTER 15

Era of Change: Mexico between Revolutions and the Birth of my Parents

My parents were born in the year 1912, a crucial period in Mexican history marked by the beginning of a new government after Porfirio Díaz's departure to France. This era of transition is essential to understand the context in which they grew up. Porfirio Díaz, who went into exile in 1911, was a general under the command of Ignacio Zaragoza, who played a decisive role in the famous Battle of Puebla on May 5, 1862, when the Mexican army defeated the French forces.

Time of Change: Porfirio Díaz and the Start of the Mexican Revolution

In the context of Mexican history, Porfirio Díaz's government represents a period of contradictions. Díaz, a true mestizo, kept Mexico under a dictatorship that lasted for more than 30 years. Despite improving the country in certain aspects, his government was also characterized by growing popular discontent due to his failure to fulfill his obligations to the Mexican people. Eventually, this led Díaz to leave the country and go into exile in France in 1911.

This situation is ironic considering that Porfirio Díaz was one of the generals who in 1862, during the Battle of May 5th, fought to expel the French from Mexico. Despite the hostility towards the French during the battle, Díaz found asylum in France years later, highlighting the changing nature of politics.

Since 1910, Mexico was already immersed in the Constitutional Revolution, which aimed to create new laws and fulfill the Plan of

San Luis Potosí. Francisco I. Madero, a character considered the apostle of the Revolution, emerged as a president committed to change but faced opposition from Victoriano Huerta, a general with authoritarian tendencies. Huerta, leading a coup, assassinated Madero in 1913 and took the presidency.

During this period, figures like Francisco Villa in Chihuahua, invited by Governor Abram González, and Emiliano Zapata in the south, rose in arms supporting Madero and opposing Huerta. These events marked the beginning of a turbulent period in Mexico, full of struggles and transformations that would eventually shape the modern nation.

Revolutionary Times: Madero's Legacy and the Struggle of Villa and Zapata

Following the assassination of Francisco I. Madero in 1913, the Mexican Revolution took a new direction. Despite losing the support of the United States, the revolutionary efforts of Pancho Villa and Emiliano Zapata succeeded in ousting Victoriano Huerta from power. In 1914, Venustiano Carranza assumed the presidency, remaining in office until 1920.

During this period, Villa and Zapata continued their revolutionary struggle. Villa achieved significant victories in battles such as those in Zacatecas, Torreón, and a major triumph in Ciudad Juárez in 1915. The latter victory was so notable that even Mexico's General Álvaro Obregón and the United States' General John J. Pershing, known as "Blackjack," personally congratulated him, capturing this moment in a historic photograph that I have.

Villa, in an agreement with General Pershing, hoped that the United States would sell him arms and ammunition. However, the material received had little gunpowder and proved ineffective in combat, leading to a frustrated Villa taking drastic measures. In 1916, he attacked the town of Columbus in New Mexico, causing the deaths of around 18 people and casualties on both sides. This incident infuriated President Woodrow Wilson of the United States, who ordered General Pershing to pursue Villa. These events reflect the complexity and violence of a period defined by the struggle for power, justice, and sovereignty in Mexico.

Challenges and Changes: The Era of Villa, Carranza, and the Cristero Revolution

The history of the Mexican Revolution is a chronicle of cunning and power. Pancho Villa, with the tacit support of the Mexican government, proved to be a formidable strategist. In one of the most emblematic battles, in Celaya, Guanajuato, Villa faced off against General Álvaro Obregón. Despite losing an arm due to Villa's cannon fire, Obregón managed to defeat the revolutionary leader, forcing him to retreat to Chihuahua. After the assassination of Victoriano Huerta, Venustiano Carranza ascended to the presidency. During his term, he ordered the assassination of Emiliano Zapata, an act that deeply marked the course of the revolution. Subsequently, Álvaro Obregón took power in 1920, and, in a twist of fate, Carranza was assassinated. Obregón held the presidency until 1924, although he attempted re-election but lost to Plutarco Elías Calles.

Calles, nicknamed "Satan," assumed the presidency amid considerable turbulence. His government was characterized by attempts to align Mexico with the communist ideals of Russia, which included the introduction of atheistic communism, the closure of churches, the prohibition of religious worship, and the persecution of priests and religious figures. Communist symbolism was promoted in government educational materials, unleashing a fierce response from Catholic Christians.

This tension culminated in the Cristero Revolution, a rebellion of faithful Catholics against Calles' anticlerical policies, marking his government until 1928. This bloody and conflict-filled period laid the groundwork for the creation of the Institutional Revolutionary Party (PRI) in 1928, a political entity that would play a crucial role in Mexico's political history in the decades to come.

Resistance and Faith: The Story of My Parents in the Cristero Revolution

In the year 1929, amid a Mexico convulsed by politics and ideological struggle, my parents grew up and lived their early years. Their childhood and youth unfolded in the heart of the Cristero uprising, particularly in the Highlands of Jalisco, a region known for its staunch resistance and bravery.

The Cristeros, as they were known, fought with an indomitable spirit and unwavering Christian faith. Despite the efforts of Plutarco Elías Calles, who attempted to transform Mexico into a communist nation, he never succeeded. It was unthinkable to eliminate or even weaken the Catholic faith, which at that time constituted 90% of the Mexican population. Even within the government itself, there were many Catholics who, anonymously, secretly cooperated to counter Calles' anticlerical policies.

What Calles failed to grasp was the determination and courage of the people of the Highlands of Jalisco, descendants of Spaniards, willing to defend their beliefs and faith to the death if necessary. In this Cristero Revolution, it was once again demonstrated that divine presence was on their side, as it had been during the ancient conflicts between Moors and Christians in Spain. This struggle, marked by the heroism and sacrifice of many martyrs, ultimately culminated in a significant triumph. It showed that divine grace cannot easily be uprooted by a government attempting to suppress a deeply rooted and pure faith. The story of my parents, their upbringing and development in this context, is a testament to resistance, faith, and the power of conviction in times of adversity.

Liborio and Castro: Cuba's Transformation

The history of Cuba, particularly during the era of Fidel Castro, is a narrative of change and disillusionment. Fidel Castro, upon assuming power by overthrowing Fulgencio Batista, initially promised to improve the nation. However, his alignment with Russia and communism only worsened the situation, plunging the Cuban people into a deep economic crisis. The only beneficiaries were those who joined the communist regime and Castro, enjoying privileges while the rest of the country suffered.

The symbol of pre-Castro Cuba, Liborio, represents the hope and solace of the poor, especially the guajiros, the sugarcane cutters. Before Castro came to power, Liborio was a figure promising a better future, even under Batista's troublesome government. However, with Fidel taking power, Liborio's promise to make things better faded away.

Castro, under the banner of nationalism, exploited the guajiros, forcing them to work in grueling conditions without adequate compensation. This led Liborio, the consoler of the poor, to retreat under a tree in despair, symbolizing the loss of hope for the Cuban people.

Despite this, the narrative suggests that Liborio has not completely given up, and his spirit may resurface in the struggle for the guajiros and the underprivileged in Cuba. This story reflects the struggle and resistance of the Cuban people amid dramatic political and social changes.

Chapter 16

Reflections on Existence and Faith

In my reflection on life and eternity, I thank God for the ability to overcome adversity, as we have done in Mexico. It is incomprehensible to me how some people do not recognize the existence of an eternal life. From our birth, God grants us eternity and reasoning, inseparable elements of the soul. Whether we accept it or not, we cannot detach ourselves from either eternity or our own soul.

God chose the human being, out of the 23 million animal species discovered by scientists, as the only rational being. We are the only ones capable of laughing, reasoning, and acknowledging the existence of God. Even those with limited intelligence or immersed in ignorance, deep within their being, know that something superior exists.

God manifests in everything around us: in plants, fruits, trees, and in all animals. Every living being grows and develops for a reason, utilizing what is necessary for its members, which move by a command of the brain and are nourished by cells in perfect coordination. All of this is part of a divine design, united with spirit and soul.

We are a breath of God Himself, created with His great love to enjoy this world and, subsequently, the other, where true eternity lies. Although some may be skeptical or indifferent to these truths, the essence of our existence and God's presence in everything around us are undeniable, offering us purpose and a deeper connection to the universe and life itself.

Between Light and Darkness: Reflections on Human Destiny

In life, each individual faces a crossroads between good and evil, between actions that nourish the soul with goodness or empty it with wickedness. It is a constant choice that defines our existence and shapes our conscience. At the end of our days, each of us must face the path we deserve: one of two inevitable destinations, light or darkness, glory or punishment, heaven or hell.

But even on the threshold of eternity, hope is never lost. God, in His infinite goodness and mercy, is willing to forgive even the repentant who turn to Him in the last minute of their earthly life. That sincere act of repentance can save a soul from eternal suffering, a suffering that, unlike any temporary punishment, never ends.

Eternity, often misunderstood by the human mind, is a concept that transcends our understanding of time. A million years, or even a billion, is insignificant compared to eternity. In eternity, there is no end, no hope of conclusion, only endless continuity.

These reflections on God and human nature do not seek to delve into the dogmas of any religion but to share what I have learned and observed about these topics. They serve as a reminder that our stay in this world is temporary, a kind of vacation that is sometimes brief and sometimes a bit longer. Let us always remember that our actions and decisions here have a lasting impact, extending far beyond our earthly existence.

CHAPTER 17

The Cristeros and My Parents: Witnesses of the Revolution

My parents were born in 1912, in a Mexico shaken by political and social changes. This period coincided with the beginning of the Constitutional Revolution initiated in 1910, which led to Francisco I. Madero assuming the presidency after defeating Porfirio Díaz in the elections. Díaz's exile to France in 1911 and the subsequent assassination of Madero in 1913 profoundly marked my parents' childhood.

They grew up hearing stories of the bloody revolutionary conflicts and how presidents who took power in Mexico were frequently assassinated. These tales were common in the region of the Highlands of Jalisco, where they lived. My parents spent their early years in the large house inherited from my grandmother María, in the Chapel of Guadalupe. My mother also grew up in the same area, and for a time in Juanacatlán, where she moved with her mother Dolores Franco and my grandfather Antonio.

In the Highlands of Jalisco, the revolution was a constant topic. The government armies and those of Villa, among others, frequently passed by the Royal Road, near where my parents lived. Although there were no specific reasons to protest in that region, the atmosphere of change and political turmoil was palpable and left an indelible mark on my parents' memory, shaping their character and understanding of the world in those formative years.

The Challenge of Calles and the Cristero Struggle: Family Account

When Plutarco Elías Calles assumed the presidency of Mexico, it marked the beginning of a challenging era in my region and many states in the central part of the country. His attempt to align Mexico with Russia and turn it into a communist nation generated a deep crisis. Calles's first order was to close churches and prohibit religious worship. This event deeply marked our family's history and that of many others.

Of all the stories I have heard about this time, the most important ones come from my aunt Chole, whom we affectionately called that, and who spent much of her life in South San Francisco, California. I legally came to the United States in 1965, joining other family members who were already living there, including my aunt Chole and my uncle José Navarro, both originally from the Chapel and who became our guardian angels in the United States, supporting us in every way. My aunt Chole and my uncle José got married in the Chapel just a year or two before the Cristero Revolution began.

They witnessed the tumultuous events of that time and, like many others, sought a better future in the United States. Their accounts of the problems faced during the Cristero Revolution and the reasons they emigrated to the United States are an essential part of our family legacy, narrating the struggle and resistance in a time of change and adversity.

Resistance and Exile: The Story of the Navarros in the Cristero Revolution

The arrival of the Cristero Revolution transformed the lives of my uncle José and my aunt Chole, who were a happy couple and had their first child, Reynaldo Navarro. José, a dedicated carpenter, became involved in the revolt when he was named a promoter of the protest against Calles's government. However, betrayal and persecution did not take long to appear, forcing them to flee to the United States, thus saving themselves from certain death.

For over 60 years, they lived in South San Francisco, where I spent many years with them. It was in their home where I heard stories about the Cristeros and the government armies, who tirelessly pursued the rebels. The first major protest against Calles originated in Tepatitlán when the town and the surrounding peasants united against the government, besieging the municipal presidency building where Quirino Navarro, then the municipal president, was located.

When the army, which now had vehicles to travel on the old Royal dirt roads, was sent from Guadalajara to break the siege on Quirino Navarro, they had a decisive encounter in nearby pastures known as the Plan de Arenas. These events and family stories paint a vivid picture of the struggle and sacrifice during the Cristero Revolution, a time of resistance and faith that deeply marked my family and many others in Mexico.

The Cristeros' fight, marked by bravery and sacrifice, began with a tragic and symbolic episode. At that time, about 1,500 to 2,000 young people from the Mexican Catholic Youth Action (ACJM) gathered, playing and riding their horses, firing shots into the air without taking the gravity of the situation seriously. They saw the army approaching in their trucks in a row but paid no attention to it.

The army, upon arrival, stopped and prepared their machine guns. What followed was a stampede, but very few managed to escape, resulting in a massacre. This tragedy awakened the conscience of many; the situation was no longer a game. With the fall of the first martyrs for the faith, the Cristeros began to organize seriously.

One of the brave individuals who emerged from this struggle was Victoriano Ramírez, known as "El Catorce," named so after a memorable confrontation. A soldier from the army, nicknamed "Sardo," tried to search him for weapons. In self-defense, Ramírez killed Sardo and fled, being pursued by a platoon of fourteen soldiers. They cornered him in a field near San Miguel el Alto, but he valiantly defended himself, taking refuge among some rocks.

This episode became a symbol of Cristero resistance, demonstrating the determination and courage of those who fought for their faith and beliefs, even in the most extreme adversity. The story of the ACJM youth and heroes like Victoriano Ramírez is a reminder of the indomitable spirit that characterized the Cristeros and their struggle in Mexican history.

El Catorce and the Cristero Legend

Victoriano Ramírez, known as "El Catorce," became a legendary figure during the Cristero Revolution. Possessing extraordinary visual acuity and incredible marksmanship, he earned his nickname after a confrontation in which he eliminated fourteen enemy soldiers. This feat led him to join the Cristeros, later becoming one of their bravest leaders.

Another prominent character was Victoriano Martín, a native of Mirandilla. Known for being feared by government soldiers, his reputation was similar to that of General Fierro, who served under Pancho Villa. Martín found great satisfaction in fighting government troops. Unlike General Fierro, who was killed by federal forces, Victoriano Martín survived the Cristero Revolution, moving to the border and dying of natural causes in Tijuana.

My aunt, who lived in the Chapel during this turbulent period, told me how they detected the arrival of federal soldiers. A strong wind would start blowing, and in the dry months from February to May, dust storms would rise so dense that they darkened the sky.

These signs were a warning for the community, who would hurry to hide the young ladies and take precautions. These accounts not only narrate the heroic acts of figures like "El Catorce" and Victoriano Martín but also the everyday experiences of those who lived under the shadow of the Cristero Revolution, deeply marking the region's collective memory.

The Cristero Ambush in the Chapel

During the Cristero Revolution, a decisive confrontation took place near the Chapel. The townspeople, fearing for the safety of women with the arrival of a detachment of approximately 300 federal soldiers, quickly hid them. The Cristeros, familiar with the terrain and skilled in guerrilla tactics, prepared an ambush.

My aunt Chole told me how the Cristeros, upon detecting the army's entry into the Chapel, executed a cunning plan. While the town appeared deserted, and the army positioned itself in the square, the Cristeros, located about five kilometers to the south, initiated their strategy.

A group of about thirty horsemen began firing towards the square from the edge of the town, attracting the army's attention. At the sound of the trumpet, the soldiers, like fierce wolves, pursued the Cristeros, who took refuge on a nearby hill and possibly in some ravines.

My aunt described how only gunshots were heard, followed by a prolonged silence, leaving the town in uncertainty throughout the night. At dawn, when the trumpet sounded again, it was thought to be the army returning, but it was only a soldier, the trumpeter, who survived the ambush.

According to witness accounts, the soldiers fell into the trap when they entered the ravine, where the Cristeros, camouflaged and with exceptional marksmanship, awaited them. Taking advantage of the dry vegetation of September, the Cristeros set fire to the area, creating chaos from which only the trumpeter barely escaped.

This episode, which ended in a decisive victory for the Cristeros, became a symbol of their resistance and skill in the fight for their beliefs, demonstrating their prowess and knowledge of the terrain in their confrontation against a much larger enemy.

In a key episode of the Cristero Revolution, a group of Cristeros managed to exterminate a contingent of 300 federal soldiers, except for a trumpeter. This survivor, brought before the commander (whose name my aunt could not recall at that moment), was sent to Tepatitlán to report the defeat. The commander immediately mounted his horse and set off with the trumpeter towards Tepatitlán, taking the road that connected the Chapel to the Royal Road.

During their journey, distrust between the soldier and the commander grew. Both were armed and alert, suspicious of each other. In a moment of carelessness, the trumpeter was killed, forcing the commander to return alone with the fallen soldier's body. This tense situation reflected the atmosphere of suspicion and fear that prevailed in the Chapel. The townspeople were constantly on alert for the possible arrival of federal forces. The priests, fearing reprisals, offered Mass in private homes.

However, on December 12, the day of the celebration of the Virgin of Guadalupe, the community defied fear and gathered to honor their patroness, regardless of the possible arrival of the army. This act of faith and defiance symbolized the resistance and indomitable spirit of the residents of the Chapel and the Cristeros, who, despite oppression and danger, kept their devotion and traditions alive.

The Celebration of the Virgin of Guadalupe - Conviviality of Soldiers and Cristeros

In a remarkable turn of events during the Cristero Revolution, the celebration on December 12 in honor of the Virgin of Guadalupe became an unexpected moment of coexistence between soldiers and Cristeros. Despite the tension and rivalry, that day, the square came to life with stalls and food stands, prepared to receive people from the surrounding areas.

As the square filled up, a detachment of soldiers on horseback arrived, dismounting as if they sensed the importance of the Guadalupean celebration. Simultaneously, the square also began to fill with sombrero-wearing ranchers, bundled up for the cold but hiding their rifles 30.06 and revolvers 38 special or 38 super under their clothes.

The presence of the ranchers, actually determined Cristeros, soon outnumbered the military detachment. What was notable about this encounter was the attitude of the Cristeros, who, instead of confronting violently, challenged the soldiers to proclaim "¡Viva Cristo Rey!" as a sign of respect for the religious celebration. The soldiers, outnumbered and without clear orders from their captain, joined in the proclamations.

That day, violence gave way to a tacit truce in honor of the Virgin of Guadalupe. Although the Cristeros were ready to defend themselves, the celebration proceeded without incidents, demonstrating that even in times of conflict, faith and traditions could momentarily unite enemies in a fragile but meaningful peace.

El Güero Mónico: Valor and Heroism in the Cristero Revolution

El Güero Mónico, whose true name I do not know, is an emblematic figure of the Cristero Revolution, known for his extraordinary courage and heroic deeds. Along with his brothers and relatives, he participated in numerous confrontations against Calles's government, excelling in each of them. But there is one particular story that highlights his courage and has been immortalized in the collective memory of the Cristeros.

This story dates back to 1926. El Güero Mónico, nicknamed so because of his blond hair and blue eyes, belonged to a family with distinctive features. Although I am not sure if they were of Castilian descent, their physical characteristics and cunning were remarkable. Mónico had his house on a ranch south of Tepatitlán and east of the Chapel of Milpillas, near a prominent hill in the area.

In those times, the government relentlessly pursued priests, and among them, the most sought after was the bishop of Guadalajara. El Güero Mónico, known for his keen eyesight and sagacity, became a key protector of priests and religious figures, defying the government and its efforts to suppress the Catholic faith. His story is a testimony to the unyielding spirit of the Cristeros and their struggle to defend their beliefs and their right to religious freedom.

The Protection of the Bishop: El Güero Mónico's Valor in the Cristero Revolution

El Güero Mónico, a prominent figure in the Cristero struggle, played a crucial role in protecting religious figures, including the bishop pursued by the government. Known for his bravery and skill, Mónico and his family earned the bishop's trust, who, aware of their reputation and that of his brothers, asked them for shelter at their ranch.

El Güero Mónico's response was a resounding "Of course!" And so, the bishop found refuge in his home. However, it didn't take long for the government to discover the bishop's hiding place and send a detachment of soldiers to capture him. This group consisted of Yaqui soldiers, indigenous people from Sonora known for their fierceness in combat.

The Yaquis approached El Güero Mónico's house, which was situated on a hill near a prominent hill. Aware of the risk of advancing uphill towards the house, the soldiers decided to wait and hide at a distance of between two and three kilometers. But El Güero Mónico and his group, already alerted to their presence, prepared for defense.

Armed with rifles 30.06 capable of long-distance shooting, they adjusted their sights to the required range. Mónico and his people's experience and skill in using these weapons were well-known. This confrontation became another example of the ingenuity and courage of the Cristeros, who defended their beliefs and protected their religious leaders against a formidable enemy.

El Güero Mónico's Feat Against the Yaquis in the Cristero Revolution

In a notable episode of the Cristero Revolution, El Güero Mónico and his family demonstrated their skill and bravery when facing a detachment of Yaqui soldiers. The Yaquis, known for their fierceness in combat, approached the ranch where El Güero Mónico had provided refuge to the bishop and others who were being pursued. Upon the soldiers' arrival, El Güero Mónico and his family, with astonishing precision, began to shoot, hitting every target. The effectiveness of their resistance was such that the Yaqui soldiers had to flee, suffering many casualties in the process. The few survivors returned to tell the unfortunate tale of their incursion.

After the confrontation, the bishop and his companions relocated to another place to continue evading the government. From then on, any other Yaqui detachment passing through the area would inquire about "La Monica," avoiding approaching El Güero Mónico's house, already feared for their fame and combat skills.

This feat became one of many carried out by El Güero Mónico and his family during the revolution. Calles's government, confident that it could bring Mexico under communism, made a mistake by underestimating the resistance and Catholic fervor of the Cristeros. In each confrontation, they grew stronger, acquiring weapons, ammunition, and even horses from the same government that sought to suppress them. The revolution was a challenging and prolonged struggle, but the spirit and determination of Cristeros like El Güero Mónico were decisive in their resistance.

Concentration and Change of Strategy in the Cristero Revolution

The Cristero Revolution entered a phase of intensification when the government began implementing a tactic known as "concentration." This strategy involved relocating people from villages and ranches to cities, a measure that proved to be particularly challenging for ranchers and inhabitants of small localities.

In this context, my grandmother Chita made the decision to take my mother, her sisters, and my uncle Miguel, who was around 17 or 18 years old, to a safer place. They chose to move to Guadalajara, where we already had relatives residing. Interestingly, it was in this city that my parents, living close to each other but in different houses, began their courtship at the age of approximately 14 years.

In the abandoned ranches, federal armies conducted constant inspections to ensure that no one was hiding. Those who were found had to carry a "safe-conduct," a special government permit justifying their presence in the area. Without this document, anyone was suspected of being a Cristero and ran the risk of being attacked.

This time was one of great changes and challenges. Forced concentration and constant checks by federal soldiers were strategies aimed at weakening the Cristero resistance, but they also gave rise to stories of love and survival, like that of my parents, who found their way to each other amidst the chaos of war.

Hermits in Times of Revolution: Stories of Resistance and Isolation

In the context of the Cristero Revolution, many families in my region were affected by the "concentration" tactic. Despite the government's efforts to evacuate people from remote ranches and villages, some individuals chose to risk staying in their homes, hiding when federal troops came to inspect. The most secluded corners of the ranches became the target of the federal forces, who discovered that some harbored defiant and reclusive people.

Even airplanes were used to fly over the region, a relatively novel technology at the time, to ensure that ranches and villages were uninhabited. One particular family living on a remote ranch in the municipality of Tepatitlán remained oblivious to the government's orders to evacuate rural areas. This family lived contentedly and in isolation, never visiting nearby towns, Tepatitlán, or the Capilla de Guadalupe. If they needed something, they sent Mercedes, their trusted worker, nicknamed "Meche."

The ranch owner, Vicente, lived there with his entire family, in a self-imposed exile, like true hermits. This story illustrates not only the resistance and isolation of some families during the Cristero Revolution but also the diversity of experiences and decisions that people made in response to the tumultuous political and social changes of the time.

Life on the Ranch During the Cristero Revolution: The Family of Don Vicente

During the time of the Cristero Revolution, a prominent family in my region was that of Don Vicente and his wife, Doña Lupe. They lived on a spacious ranch, likely inherited from the times when the Castilians settled in the area, passing down from generation to generation until it reached Don Vicente.

By the year 1924, when the Cristero Revolution began, Don Vicente and Doña Lupe, both over 40 years old, had a family consisting of their children: Isidro (nicknamed "Chilo"), Tobias, and their three daughters: Concepción (called "Concha"), Dolores ("Lolita"), and Sara ("Sarin"). The ranch was extensive and prosperous, mainly dedicated to farming, with around 15 teams of oxen for planting corn. In addition to the cultivation area, the ranch had extensive pasturelands, totaling approximately 10 caballerías. A caballería, equivalent to about 350 solar squares, and each square was approximately 42 square meters, giving an approximate measurement of 87 hectares per caballería, meaning the ranch covered over 800 hectares.

The house on the ranch, mostly built of adobe, was remarkably large and reflected the family's prosperity. This narrative of life on Don Vicente's ranch and his family not only illustrates a lifestyle during those times but also how the Cristero Revolution affected families in the rural areas of Mexico, marking a significant contrast with the modern life of that era.

Chapter 18

Life on the Hermit Ranch: Self-Sufficiency in Changing Times

In a remote corner of my region, there existed a hermit ranch, whose history was lost in time, so ancient that no one remembered who had built it. Surrounded by centuries-old and lush ash trees, the ranch had enormous granaries to store the seeds from annual harvests and dry corn stalks, essential for feeding the animals.

The house, of impressive dimensions, could be compared to a hacienda and was built with remarkable dedication and attention to detail. It had multiple rooms and bedrooms, as well as a space dedicated to tools and carpentry, serving as a workshop where even complete carriages were constructed.

Activity on the ranch was constant: they had several milking cows and produced cheese for storage, in addition to raising hens, turkeys, and a large number of oxen, mainly used for plowing. They even raised pigs, making use of yellow corn, especially nutritious for fattening, and chickpeas, which were also used to feed the animals. In the vicinity of the ranch, there was a not-so-large hill and a rocky ravine where they cultivated coamiles, a plant that had to be sown manually with a hoe due to the difficulty of the terrain. Cultivating on the hill was preferred for its yield, and although the techniques were traditional, efficiency and self-sufficiency were notable.

This ranch represents rural life during a time of great social and political changes in Mexico. Self-sufficiency, tradition, and ingenuity were essential for the survival and livelihood of the family that inhabited this hermit ranch, reflecting the tenacity and resilience of rural communities during challenging times.

Life on the Ranch: The Family of Don Vicente and Doña Lupe

On Don Vicente and Doña Lupe's ranch, life was a portrait of self-sufficiency and contentment. Located in a region where crops thrived more than in the plains, this ranch was a small world in itself. There, the only need that prompted them to seek outside help was clothing and huaraches, as everything else they had on hand.

During that time, the typical attire for men on the ranch included long white cotton pants and wide-brimmed round hats with high crowns that bent with use. Don Vicente and his family, composed of his wife Doña Lupe and his daughters Lolita, Sara, and Concha, were the only ones who dressed slightly differently. The women always wore long dresses, a custom of the time.

The coexistence on the ranch was harmonious, where employers and workers existed as one big family. There was never a lack of food or mistreatment. Doña Lupe, with her contagious joy, had a special affection for Lolita, the youngest of her daughters, who was the center of attention and happiness in the family. Sara, the middle child, and Concha, the eldest, also played important roles in the family nucleus. Concha, being the oldest, took on additional responsibilities, helping her mother and sisters with daily tasks and personal care.

This portrayal of life on the ranch, with its daily routine filled with joy and family unity, reflects a time when, despite external challenges, rural life maintained its pace and traditions, forging a strong sense of community and belonging.

Hermits in Cristero Times: Life on Don Vicente's Ranch

On Don Vicente's ranch, a haven of ancestral traditions and customs, life unfolded far from the influence of cities and towns. The wives of the workers and their daughters, in a kind of improvised little school, dedicated themselves to teaching children how to read, write, and learn the catechism, keeping alive the teachings of Christianity as they had been passed down from generation to generation.

One notable peculiarity was the way the ranch's inhabitants spoke. They preserved a form of old Castilian, a linguistic relic that clearly distinguished them and led people from cities and towns to say they spoke "like ranchers." Although in modern times this way of speaking has been fading away, it still lingers in some ranches.

During my youth, I myself spent time with ranchers on my father's ranch. I noticed that, after a few weeks without going to town, I would start adopting their way of speaking. This was part of my responsibility in managing the ranch.

The tranquility on Don Vicente's ranch was interrupted when, in the midst of the Cristero era, a group of armed men on horseback arrived looking for Don Vicente. They came galloping, with their large hats, bandoliers full of ammunition, and weapons at the ready, causing everyone on the ranch to seek refuge, especially the women and children. This moment marked the beginning of a challenging period for Don Vicente's family, plunging them into the conflicts and tensions of the Cristero Revolution.

Cristero Challenge on Don Vicente's Ranch

Tension hung in the air at Don Vicente's ranch as a group of armed men approached the main house. Women and children sought refuge, while some men prepared themselves with their rifles, ready to defend if necessary.

Don Vicente, displaying courage and composure, went out to greet them at the front door. Some of his people were already positioned on the roof with their rifles, in case a conflict erupted. With a typical rancher's greeting, Don Vicente welcomed them and asked what they needed, in a cordial yet firm tone.

Upon closer observation of the group, Don Vicente recognized one of them: it was the son of his friend Melquiades Martín, from Mirandilla. Surprised, he asked what he was doing there. The young man, named Victorino, explained that they came as friends and that they were rising up against Calles's government, which was trying to close churches and eradicate the Christian faith, even going as far as killing priests.

Don Vicente, visibly taken aback by not being aware of this news, listened attentively as Victorino expressed his determination not to allow Calles, whom they did not consider the legitimate president of Mexico, to take away their beliefs and religious freedom. This encounter on Don Vicente's ranch reflected the scope and depth of the Cristero conflict, as well as the unity and solidarity among those who resisted the government's anti-clerical policies.

"Viva Cristo Rey"

Hospitality in Times of War: Don Vicente and the Cristeros

Amidst the Cristero conflict, Don Vicente displayed exemplary hospitality by welcoming a group of thirsty and weary men to his ranch. With the sensitivity and generosity that characterized him, he immediately offered to quench their thirst with a pitcher of fresh water from the dining room jars.

Inside the house, as the conversation continued, Don Vicente realized the need to feed so many visitors. Quickly, he instructed Meche, his right-hand woman, to sacrifice a pig and some chickens to prepare a hearty meal for the group. At the same time, he asked Petra to prepare beans and quesadillas, and arranged for tortillas to be made on the tapanco.

Don Vicente, a man of deep Christian faith, expressed his support for the Cristeros, although he regretted not being able to join their cause personally. However, he committed to helping them in whatever way he could. Victor, one of the leaders of the group, thanked them for the hospitality but explained that they couldn't stay in one place for long due to security reasons.

Before the Cristeros departed, Don Vicente offered to provide them with the animals they needed, recognizing that their journey was arduous and that they would require food like gorditas and dried meat for the trip. This act of generosity and solidarity from Don Vicente with the Cristeros in times of war reflects the humanity and mutual support that prevailed even in the most challenging moments of Mexican history.

Time of Scarcity on Don Vicente's Ranch

On Don Vicente's ranch, the generosity towards the Cristeros had a remarkable impact. He provided them with abundant food, including esquite, which is roasted corn on coals, a traditional preparation in the countryside. He also gave them sacks of corn and some coins he had saved to aid their cause. Victoriano, one of the Cristero leaders from Mirandilla, deeply appreciated it, convinced that God would bless Don Vicente for his generosity.

At dawn the next day, after spending the night at the ranch, the Cristeros prepared to leave. Don Vicente and his family, along with all the ranch's inhabitants, gave them a warm farewell, wishing them divine protection on their journey.

After the departure of the Cristeros, the ranch experienced a period of quietude and solitude. The usual buyers of their products, either out of fear or caution, stopped visiting the ranch. Even the pigs, normally sold or transported in carts, remained on the ranch, growing in number and size. More than six months passed without anyone coming to buy the stored corn and beans ready for sale.

This time of isolation and scarcity reflected the difficult situation faced by many rural families during the Cristero Revolution. Despite the abundance of resources on Don Vicente's ranch, the absence of buyers and isolation underscored the economic and social challenges they faced during those turbulent times.

Everyday Life on Don Vicente's Ranch During the Reconcentration

During the period of reconcentration ordered by the government, Don Vicente and his family maintained a quiet and joyful everyday life on their hidden ranch, even though no one came to visit them. Mornings on the ranch began with the bustle of dawn, marked by the competitive crowing of roosters and the awakening of everyone in the house.

Some attended to milking the cows, while others prepared the oxen for plowing, an activity that usually started in late March or early April. Doña Lupe, along with Doña Petra and Conchita, the eldest daughter, would wake up early to prepare breakfast for everyone.

Doña Lupe, always organized, gave instructions to her daughters: she asked Sara to collect the eggs from the nests and check how many the turkeys had laid. She assigned Lolita to bring tomatoes and chili de arbol to Petra for roasting on the comal and making a sauce. Additionally, she reminded Petra to check if she had already set the beans to cook and instructed her to grind the corn on the metates near the hearth.

This description of life on Don Vicente's ranch offers a vivid picture of the daily routine in a rural setting during times of change and challenge. Despite the policy of reconcentration and isolation, the family maintained their spirit and traditions, adapting and continuing with their daily tasks in their rural refuge.

A Day in the Life of the Ranch: Don Vicente and His Family's Routine

On Don Vicente's ranch, each day began with a series of carefully organized tasks to maintain the functioning and harmony of the home. Doña Lupe, with her usual efficiency, coordinated the morning activities. She reminded Lolita to pick up the chocolate bars that Petra had prepared the previous day to make hot chocolate for breakfast. She also instructed Chilo to send someone to take the surplus whey from cheese making to the pigs.

Breakfast on the ranch was a true feast of homemade flavors: freshly milked milk and frothy hot chocolate, spicy chilaquiles with fresh sauce prepared in a Chinese stone mortar and crumbled fresh cheese on top of them. Additionally, they served a dish of pork fried in green sauce, accompanied by hot tortillas made on the clay camalote.

With full stomachs and content hearts, Don Vicente began his rounds on the ranch to ensure everything was in order. Chilo, the eldest son, got ready to accompany his father and assist him in supervision. Meanwhile, Meche stayed at home, as she would later have to go to the nearby hill to collect firewood. Tobias, without specific tasks assigned, was instructed to join the firewood gathering.

This narrative reflects life on the ranch, filled with work, community, and the satisfaction of homemade accomplishments. Each family member and team member played a vital role in sustaining this small agricultural community, a microcosm of efficiency, collaboration, and mutual care.

The Gathering in the Village: A Day of Ingenuity

In the picturesque village of Ermitaños, under the warm Californian sun, an urgent message was conveyed by the matriarch, Doña Lola Tobias, to her devoted companions. "Come with me," she called to Meche, "to help move two donkeys residing in the corral near the bride's house. "Petra, with a quick acceptance, shouted to Doña Lupe, "Where are you, Doña Lupe?" The response echoed, "I'm here in the pasture, where the pond is, surrounded by an abundance of dry manure. Our supply of wood has run out, and in the meantime, Meche needs more fuel for the fire." (The "Raja," dried cattle dung, serves as a quickly burning fuel, similar to firewood).

Don Lola continued with her instructions, "Take Sara and Lolita with you, Petra, to help collect twelve pieces of Raja." In the meantime, a young man was recruited, armed with a basket found in the pantry. He was quickly sent to gather them. "Hurry, his return must be swift.

I intend to prepare Tamales using the leftover pork, and upon his return, they will collect corn leaves to wrap the delights."

These anecdotes not only narrate feats and events but also capture the indomitable spirit and deep devotion of those who fought and lived during the Cristero Revolution.

The Cristeros and Their Conflicts

The Cristero conflict arose during the presidency of Plutarco Elías Calles in Mexico. The most significant issues in my region, the Altos de Jalisco, were concentrated between 1926 and 1929. It was a period marked by "the amnesty that the Mexican government offered to the clergy after the departure of Plutarco Elías Calles, nicknamed 'Satan' because of the devastation that the Cristeros inflicted on the Mexican Army. How could a government, perceived as satanic, confront a predominantly Catholic people?

Calles's caprice to align Mexico with the communist system of Russia caused much mourning in Mexican homes. Masonic lodges began to interfere, creating a president and sheltering themselves in control of ecclesiastical affairs. The Mexican episcopate, seeing its religious freedom threatened, protested vigorously in all relevant circumstances, both at the state and national levels. Archbishop Ruiz y Flores of Mexico and Pascual Díaz of Tabasco confronted President Calles with great energy, responding firmly: "DO WHAT YOU WANT. If you want to take up arms, that is your decision."

Cristeros: Resistance and Faith

The Mexican Episcopate, supported by over two million signatures, went to Congress to present their legitimate protest. However, Congress, affected by nearly blind indifference, ignored the legality of this protest. Exhausted all peaceful means and faced with governmental disdain, peaceful resistance against the authorities of

Plutarco Elías Calles began to emerge. This happened in 1926 when Silvano Barba González was the governor of the state of Jalisco and Quirino Navarro was the mayor of our beloved Tepatitlán.

The Mexican episcopate suspended religious services in many temples across the country, instructing Catholics to observe general mourning and promote opposition organizations to official policies. This was when the Mexican Catholic Youth Association (A.C.J.M.) was born, which became the foundation of the movement. This association had been founded in 1913 by the priest Bernardo Bergoend and the Popular Union of Jalisco, created by a notable citizen of Tepatitlán.

History and Achievement: The Defense of Religious Freedom

Anacleto González Flores and the National League for the Defense of Religious Freedom, along with the Women's Brigades of the Catholic Ladies Committee, led a movement of intelligent and fervent resistance. Several organizations joined to defend the faith that was being attacked by an evil government. Dynamite attacks began, one of which severely affected the A.C.J.M. of Mexico City, and the Mexican flag was replaced with red and black flags in cathedrals and temples. A notable riot took place at the Jesus parish in Guadalajara.

In January 1926, the Archbishop of Mexico, José Mora del Río, wrote a pastoral letter suspending religious services conducted by priests. The federal government faced opposition from state governments, as well as from the chambers of senators and deputies, in addition to labor and peasant unions.

Application of Article 130: With the implementation of Article 130, more than 200 foreign priests were forced to leave the country, including the Apostolic Delegate Monsignor Eugenio Filipei, who had laid the first stone of the Monument to Christ the King on Cerro del Cubilete, near Silao, Guanajuato.

Suspension and Resistance: The Cristero Conflict

On July 31, 1927, a turning point occurred: religious cults were suspended, and the temples were handed over for inventory to the neighborhood boards throughout the Republic. This measure was communicated through a pastoral letter approved by His Holiness Pope Pius XI. From that date until further notice, public worship that required the intervention of a priest was suspended in all the temples of the Republic.

In this context of intransigence and radicalism, what would be known as the Religious Conflict, the Cristero Revolution, or the Civil War began. The Cristeros did not arise on a whim but as a response to the actions of Calles, nicknamed "Satan." State governments, following the federal government's lead, greatly limited the number of authorized priests to officiate religious services in the churches of each Mexican state. The federal forces were composed of two defined groups: the federal soldiers and the agraristas. The federals enjoyed the necessary support, while the Cristeros, despite the adversities, remained steadfast in their struggle for religious freedom and the defense of their beliefs.

Between Battles and Strategies: The Cristero Conflict

The representation and training of the federal forces were outstanding, equipped with advanced weaponry and a vast arsenal. Most importantly, they had the confidence of the Federal Government. Their leaders, who had distinguished military careers, included generals of renowned prestige such as Guillermo Limón, Ignacio Leal, Rodrigo Tischon, Octavio Galindo, Mínguez, López Tafolla, Manuel, and many others prominent in the Altos de Jalisco.

The second group, the agraristas, were viewed with disdain even by their federal comrades and often used as cannon fodder. A clear example was General Saturnino Cedillo, the leader of San Luis Potosí and close to the infamous Plutarco Elías Calles. Under his command, around 6,000 agraristas, although some sources suggest there were many more, were deployed in a crucial operation. General Cedillo positioned himself north of Tepatitlán, on a plateau, two and a half kilometers away.

According to accounts from my elders, from that plateau, the general and his army, along with the vast number of agraristas, looked imposing. That battle was arduous and prolonged, marking a significant episode in the history of the Cristero conflict.

Strategy and Valor: The Cristero Triumph

With cunning and intelligence, the Cristeros set a formidable trap. From Tepatitlán, they made it appear as if they had abandoned the plaza and fled south. A hundred of them, acting as if they were disoriented, dispersed and then, in a tactical move, re-entered from the other side of the city. This maneuver was invisible to General Cedillo and his forces, who from their elevated position could not see the Cristeros' reentry.

Confident, General Cedillo urged his thousands of agraristas, whom he considered cannon fodder, to advance toward their supposed lands. As they rushed down, the agraristas, in their disorder and confusion, resembled a swarm, a chaotic swarm of ants. Not knowing who they were attacking, they entered Tepatitlán, a silent and seemingly deserted city.

In a coordinated move, the Cristeros, hidden in the houses, waited for the precise moment. At the first gunshot, chaos erupted: from windows and rooftops, filled with fighters, even women, they began to shoot at the surprised agraristas. In panic, and not knowing where the shots were coming from, the agraristas began to flee the city in disarray, marking a significant and clever victory for the Cristeros.

Tragedy and Survival: The Battle of Tepa

The result of the confrontation was devastating more than half of the enemy forces were decimated. It is said that blood flowed through the streets of Tepatitlán, affectionately known as Tepa, whose inclination accentuated the macabre flow. In this scenario, General Cedillo was forced to retreat in humiliation, his army diminished, and the survivors wishing for nothing more than to escape from that hell. Deceived by the government with empty promises and inadequate pay, these soldiers faced a brutal reality.

The magnitude of the tragedy in the streets of Tepatitlán was such that it was impossible to bury so many dead. The only solution found was cremation, using the little oil, gasoline, and firewood they could gather. Thus, in a desperate act, they proceeded to burn the bodies, marking this episode as a tragic genocide of the poor Potosino Indians orchestrated by the ruthless General Cedillo, leader of San Luis Potosí.

This attack occurred on April 27, 1927. Subsequently, in June 1924, the Church and the State finally signed a peace agreement, ending this dark chapter in history.

CHAPTER 19

Anacleto González Flores: A Legacy of Valor

This chapter represents one of the saddest of the Cristero Revolution, with countless martyrs whose names are impossible to enumerate. Among them, Anacleto González Flores stands out in a special way. Every time I recall his story, I feel a deep pain in my soul. Anacleto, who I believe was a distant relative on my maternal grandmother's side, was born in Tepatitlán, on Hospital Street number 89, now called Bartolo Hernández.

The son of Don Valentín González and Doña María Flores, Anacleto was the second of twelve siblings, among whom there were three women and nine men. His father was a shawl maker and owned a good loom. From a young age, Anacleto showed a great interest in music, starting to study solfeggio and then learning to play the baritone.

He even became part of the municipal band, where he played every Sunday in the kiosk in the main square. During those serenades, women would stroll around the square, receiving carnations and gardenias from the young men who walked in the opposite direction. The air was filled with confetti and colorful streamers, creating a carpet that lasted throughout the serenade night, a memory that I also cherish.

Anacleto González Flores: A Path of Transformation

Anacleto González Flores, an emblematic figure of the early 20th century, had a typical childhood in elementary school, where he did not excel academically due to his preference for spending time with friends and his inclination for seeking and enjoying fights. This adventurous nature hindered his concentration on studies. However, as he entered adolescence, a significant change began to take shape in his life.

Influenced by a priest, he decided to enter the seminary in Guadalajara. There, his enthusiasm for learning about God was evident, and he soon found himself immersed in an illuminated spiritual path. This transformation was so profound that he began to emanate immense love for the Creator from his soul, spending long hours in the temple and praying the rosary devoutly. As Anacleto matured, he dedicated himself to performing acts of charity in the community, teaching catechism in the neighborhoods, visiting the sick and the invalid. His cheerful and always smiling personality chased away sadness from those around him.

Despite his simplicity and humility, traits of an intelligent human being, he never lost his fondness for beautiful young women and serenades, enjoying the beautiful sound of the Municipal Band. This stage of his life in Tepatitlán was crucial, marking his growth and maturity and preparing him for the challenges and responsibilities he would face in the future.

Anacleto González Flores: A Journey of Wisdom and Leadership

Anacleto González Flores, driven by his insatiable thirst for knowledge, realized that Tepatitlán could no longer satisfy his hunger for culture. Determined to seek a more advanced education, he headed to San Juan de los Lagos, which was then a center of maximum culture.

There, he entered the seminary, where he had the opportunity to learn from magnificent teachers. His enthusiasm and dedication allowed him to quickly polish his skills, especially in oratory, earning the admiration of all. For almost five years in San Juan de los Lagos, Anacleto developed a positive discipline that reflected an incredible change, full of admiration.

He became a winner and a complete lecturer, never losing his characteristic smile and joy. In 1917, he organized a political party he called the NATIONAL CATHOLIC PARTY. In this project, he joined forces with his inseparable friend from the seminary, Miguel Gómez Loza, originally from Pueblito de Paredones (now El Refugio), located west of Tepatitlán.

Miguel was nicknamed "El Chicano" and became Anacleto's inseparable companion. After nearly five years in San Juan de los Lagos, Anacleto decided to move to Guadalajara, leaving behind his ecclesiastical career and embarking on a new chapter in his life, filled with challenges and opportunities.

Anacleto González Flores: Perseverance and Dedication

Anacleto González Flores, in his constant quest for self-improvement, decided to change his academic path to the field of Law at the Free School of Jurisprudence in Jalisco. During this time, he shared accommodation with his friend Miguel Gómez and several colleagues in a house located in the Santa Mónica neighborhood.

The residence, attended by an elderly lady known as Geronima or "Doña Giro," was affectionately dubbed "La Gironda," and its inhabitants, "Los Girondinos." In those days, Anacleto and Miguel, as students of modest means, faced several challenges. Anacleto had to work as a baker to finance his studies and sustenance. In addition, he paid his preparatory and law school tuition by teaching History and Literature at private schools.

Subsequently, with the foundation of the Catholic Action of Mexican Youth (ACJM) in Guadalajara, Anacleto and his La Gironda companions became the soul of this group.

They formed a highly important board, dedicating themselves with great enthusiasm to the organization's development. During this period, "El Gladium" was born, a highly relevant newspaper that became the most sought-after in Guadalajara, causing such a significant impact that Pope Pius XI awarded them the Cross Pro Ecclesia et Pontifice, a recognition of their fervent dedication to the cause. This achievement was a milestone in their lives, marking a legacy of commitment and service.

Anacleto González Flores: A Struggle Against Adversity
Anacleto González Flores, steadfast in his cause to defend the Church, its school, its press, and its doctrine, found himself in the midst of the growing conflict against the Catholic religion in 1926.
His passionate oratory and controversial topics led to him being constantly attacked and surveilled, resulting in multiple visits to jail. Surveillance was so intense that Anacleto could not stay in any known place without the risk of being discovered, always moving strategically to elude his enemies. Despite having many followers, the morning of April 1, 1927, marked a tragic turn in his life. Being watched 24 hours a day, he was violently captured in the Vargas Gómez family's house, located at Mezquitán Street #405 in Guadalajara.
Soldiers surrounded him as if they had encountered a dangerous enemy army. Anacleto was brutally beaten, almost to the point of unconsciousness, in an attempt to force him to reveal the location of the press machinery and the newspaper material. He did not reveal anything despite the severe beating.
In a humiliating act, the soldiers stripped him of his shoes, and according to accounts shared with me, some versions suggest they removed the soles of his feet, although I personally doubt the accuracy of this detail. With this capture, Anacleto was transported

from Mezquitán to the barracks, in a sad episode that highlights his courage and resilience in the face of unimaginable adversity.

Anacleto González Flores: Resistance in Adversity

Anacleto González Flores, after his capture, faced an unimaginable ordeal. Stripped of his shoes and with his feet injured from the arduous journey, he arrived at the Colorado Barracks in deplorable conditions. Soldiers, far from showing compassion, beat and stabbed him with bayonets in a desperate attempt to extract information about the location of the printing press machinery.

A friend I met in Hayward, California, where we worked together at a large tomato canning facility for about five months a year, shared this account with me. During the approximately five months a year we worked there, this friend, who had lived through the Cristero Revolution and served in General Cedillo's army, told me numerous anecdotes about the Cristeros. I vividly remember his words about the day Anacleto was taken to the Colorado Barracks. My friend, then a young man in charge of feeding the horses and rarely leaving the barracks, witnessed how Anacleto, exhausted and wounded, was brought inside. According to his account, Anacleto had to be carried, almost dragged, with the soles of his feet so injured that you could almost see the bones, a heart-wrenching testimony to cruelty and resilience in those dark days.

Anacleto González Flores: Martyrdom and Courage

Anacleto González Flores, facing a cruel fate, displayed exceptional resistance and courage. As my friend Cedillo, who had lived through those dark moments, narrated, Anacleto was relentlessly beaten. Despite immense pain, he seemed insensitive to the blows, a strength that amazed those around him. When they took him to be executed, they attempted to blindfold him, but with inexplicable courage, he tore them off, shouting with a seemingly supernatural strength, "Long live Christ the King!"

Cedillo recounted how the soldiers, despite their apparent hardness, were not inherently evil but were under the command of ruthless superiors, like colonels and captains who seemed like hornless demons spewing fire from their mouths.

The story of Anacleto González Flores is one of suffering and martyrdom, comparable to the calvary of Jesus Christ on his path to death. Without the physical cross, Anacleto, like many Cristero apostles and martyrs, experienced prolonged and atrocious suffering. His story is a testimony of unwavering faith and a legacy of courage that lives on in collective memory.

I have many more anecdotes about the history of the Cristeros, and while this is just a part, it reflects the essence and spirit of those turbulent times and the relentless struggle for faith and freedom.

Attack on the Train: A Decisive Turn in the Revolution

This account narrates one of the most significant episodes of the Cristeros: The Attack on the Colima Train, a key event that influenced the government's decision to sign peace with the clergy in June 1929. The Cristeros, with astonishing ability to always be aware of the government's movements and its armies, carried out this decisive attack. A passenger train loaded with payment for the soldiers, carrying a large amount of silver and gold, had been sent from Mexico City.

Within the government itself, there were dissidents against President Calles, nicknamed "Satan," and many Cristeros who, disguised as government officials, had access to crucial information. As the train approached Colima, the Cristeros were already waiting for it. The strategy they employed was like a lightning-fast, bold, and rapid movement. I remember hearing stories from some of the chapel and Tepa residents who participated in that attack.

They recounted how, on horseback and with bullets whizzing by, they managed to stop the train in an act of precision and courage. Among the Cristero leaders, Victoriano de Mirandilla stood out for his precise marksmanship; he didn't waste bullets, and his skill was comparable to the famous General Fierro of Pancho Villa. This attack was not only a significant strategic blow but also a symbol of the ingenuity and determination of the Cristeros in their fight for justice and their beliefs.

The Awakening of a Nation: The Impact of the Cristero Attack

It was said among the people that before the arrival of the Cristeros, the soldiers would try to change their clothes for civilian attire to avoid being recognized and attacked. Victoriano Martín, one of the Cristero leaders, was celebrated for his bravery and combat skills. It was said that when he ran out of bullets or didn't have time to reload his pistol, he would pull out his dagger and fight tirelessly. In my childhood, I heard the elders talk about how many of them returned with sacks full of coins, even with the pockets of their pants filled after that attack.

This event marked a turning point in 1929, leading the government to sign a peace agreement. With the departure of the president, who was considered a demon, religious worship was resumed, and the churches were reopened. I would like to take a moment to express my admiration for a great writer and historian of Tepatitlán's history, the author of the book, *Marco Histórico de la Parroquia de San Francisco de Tepatitlán*.

This writer, Heriberto Alcalá Cortés, deserves recognition as a master for his dedication to researching life in the Altos de Jalisco. From him, I learned crucial details about the Cristeros, important dates, and information that I was missing to complete this account. His work is a treasure that sheds light on a vital chapter of our history.

Father Tranquilino Ubiarco: A Remembered Martyr

Father Tranquilino Ubiarco is a revered figure in Tepatitlán and the entire Catholic community, a beloved and respected martyr for his deep faith and service. Born in Ciudad Guzmán, Jalisco, south of Guadalajara, he was educated at the Seminary of Guadalajara, where he stayed until his ordination as a priest at the age of 24.

He was ordained by the then Archbishop Francisco Orozco y Jiménez in 1993, and he celebrated his first Mass in his hometown, at the San José parish. His first assignment as a priest was in the small town of Moyahua, Zacatecas, in the Juchipila River basin.

The parishioners of this place deeply appreciated him for his humility, simplicity, and the joy that overflowed in his sermons, reflecting his love for Christ, devotion to the Virgin Mary, and reverence for the Creator. After Moyahua, he was transferred to the Nuestra Señora de la Asunción parish in Lagos de Moreno, Jalisco. However, his stay there was brief, as his destination brought him to Tepatitlán, in the San Francisco de Asís parish. This last stay marked the end of his journey, where his legacy and spirituality left an indelible mark on the community and all those who had the privilege of knowing him.

Father Tranquilino Ubiarco: Valor and Faith in Difficult Times

In Tepatitlán, Father Tranquilino Ubiarco faced constant challenges, as he entered the "lion's den" every day. Surrounded by a hostile environment and closely monitored by the government, he would disguise himself as a laborer or mule driver to secretly celebrate the Holy Sacrifice of the Mass in private homes. In these circumstances, his sister, Timotea, provided invaluable help, always careful not to be caught.

Father Ubiarco maintained his faith and devotion despite the risks, always carrying Jesus in his heart. One day, in September 1928, he decided to travel to Guadalajara, probably for an important reason, as his stay was brief, returning to Tepa the next day. However, upon arriving in Puente Grande, he encountered a checkpoint of soldiers. Thanks to his quick thinking and disguising himself as the driver's assistant on the daily Guadalajara-Tepa route, he managed to avoid being discovered.

At nightfall, back in Tepa, he told the driver that he would get off near the Sanctuary of the Lord of Mercy but without stopping to avoid raising suspicions. Shortly after, his sister Timotea got off with the little luggage they had and returned to where Father Ubiarco was. It was a house lent by Don Celso Baltazar, and in that place, Father Ubiarco would celebrate his last Mass, an act of deep faith in times of adversity and danger.

Last Days of Father Tranquilino Ubiarco: Faith and Martyrdom

On October 3, after celebrating Mass, Father Tranquilino Ubiarco went to the Márquez family's house. The following day, October 4, he visited the house of Dr. Germán Estrada, where he had been invited for a wedding. Dr. Estrada had requested that Father Ubiarco bless and decorate the place. Father's sister, Timotea, along with a reverend sister from the Servants of Jesus the Sacrament, prepared the vestments and other items for the Mass celebration.

However, around 11 o'clock at night, an unexpected visitor brought alarming news. A lady named Medrano, trembling and distressed, informed them that Father Ubiarco had been arrested by the federation. Immediately, they mobilized to speak with the municipal authorities of that time, Arturo Peña, Aurelio Graciano, Francisco

Gutiérrez, and Officer Mendoza, in a desperate attempt to save Father Ubiarco's life.

Unfortunately, all efforts proved futile. In the last hours of October 4, 1928, while Tepatitlán slept, Father Ubiarco was escorted under heavy guard, marking the beginning of his tragic martyrdom. This event is a somber reminder of the struggle and sacrifice that father Ubiarco faced, a martyr whose faith and courage are immortalized in the community's memory.

The Martyrdom of Father Tranquilino Ubiarco: A Heroic End

As they led Father Tranquilino Ubiarco to his final destination, they headed south, advancing along Hidalgo Street until they reached the Alameda, a place surrounded by centuries-old eucalyptus trees that marked the entrance to the dirt road of the time. At the exit of Tepatitlán, near the first eucalyptus trees, the fatal decision was made: to hang the father.

A captain ordered a soldier named Vargas to stretch the rope, but he refused. Faced with his resistance, the captain, without hesitation, ordered another rope to be placed and, in a cruel irony, also hanged the soldier who had disobeyed. Father Ubiarco, facing his end, displayed a serenity and courage reminiscent of the martyrdom of Jesus Christ. It is said that he even sold the rope with which he was hanged, showing an attitude of gratitude to God for granting him the grace to die for his son.

The next day, at dawn, the bodies of the priest and the soldier were found hanged, a heartbreaking sight that deeply moved the Tepatitlán community. The residents of Tepatitlán claimed Father Ubiarco's body and held a wake at the house of Don Tomás Franco on 665, San Martín Street. Subsequently, a funeral procession, accompanied by an immense crowd, carried his remains to the Municipal Cemetery. This tragic story of Father Ubiarco not only reflects the cruelty of those times but also the unwavering faith and heroic spirit of a true martyr.

Father Tranquilino Ubiarco: An Eternal Legacy

Subsequently, the remains of Father Tranquilino Ubiarco were taken to the chapel of the Hospital of the Sacred Heart, where they remained until October 5, 1978, to commemorate the 50th anniversary of his martyrdom. Then, his remains were transferred to the main altar of the parish church. This courageous priest lived and died with exceptional joy and bravery, with his only "crime" being the fulfillment of his sacred ministry. Interestingly, after his death, the eucalyptus tree where he was hanged began to wither, and to this day, it stands as a silent witness to his sacrifice.

This dry tree has become a place for reflection and prayer, where people stop to pay their respects. Around the tree, hundreds of small stones can be seen, placed by those who stop to offer prayers and seek favors, considering Father Ubiarco as a holy martyr. Each stone represents an expression of love and respect for him, a symbol of how his legacy lives on in the hearts of the community and all those who remember and venerate him as a true saint of his time.

"Do you understand, Petra?" Dona Lola asked. Without hesitation, Petra replied, "Of course, Dona Lola."

The Encounter with the Airplane in Ermitaños

As the day progressed, Dona Lola remained busy in the dining area, while Lolita and Sarita joyfully collected dry manure, placing it in a basket. Suddenly, a biplane appeared on the horizon, descending slowly and circling over the tranquil Ermitaños ranch as the day continued. It approached the pasture where Doña Petra and the girls were. Oh my God! They all ran in fear, resembling fleeing deer. They screamed and screamed, never having seen anything like it. They thought it was something devilish, and despair overcame them. Dona Petra got entangled in a Misache (a piece of cloth) with the shawl she had tied to her back and her long hair. Lolita and Sarita, filled with fear, left her behind, screaming in desperation. Like lightning, the two of them arrived back at the house, their hearts nearly leaping out of their chests.

They could barely speak. Doña Lola saw them and asked, "What's wrong? Why are you coming like this?" The lighter and more frightened of the two replied, with her eyes almost popping out of their sockets, "Mom, a devil bird tried to attack us, where is Petra?" She asked Sarita, who also arrived in a daze. Petra, who had stayed behind and was almost stuck in a Huisache (a thick shrub), moaned like a trapped pig. She tried to free herself, but the devil bird, making horrible noises, had her cornered.

"Run, Mom, send someone to save her! The Airplane almost took another turn!" Exclaimed the girls as they watched Petra finally untangle herself, though she had lost most of her hair. In the dense thicket of the Huizache, those who had survived the scare approached trembling, with panic still reflected in their faces. They arrived almost fainting, still murmuring prayers because they believed they were facing a diabolical creature. With caution, Concha approached and heard the commotion coming from the house.

Don Vicente had not yet arrived, but he was approaching quickly on his horse; he had also spotted the airplane. Don Meche and Don Tobias, who had left the donkeys behind, rushed running toward the house. Even Don Meche lost a Guarache (a sandal) in his hurried run and only noticed its absence when he was running. He thought, "I'll go back for my mangoes!" before picking up the devil bird. The first to reach the large house was Don Vicente, who shouted, "Bring holy

water and the holy book to exorcise that Devil's beast!" The airplane continued to circle and passed quickly over the house. Everyone took refuge in the rooms, like frightened mice, and the granaries barely kept them quiet. Not a murmur could be heard. Mrs. Lola began reciting prayers and sprinkling holy water in all directions to...
In Ermitaños, the mysterious sighting of the airplane left everyone perplexed. They began to speculate about its origin. Don Meche mused aloud, "It might be some kind of exotic bird from distant lands, hungry." Don Vicente, in his calm voice, responded, "You may be right, Meche." Then, he addressed Chilo and Tobias, saying, "Go quickly to the granary near the bride's pasture and bring a sack of corn. Meche and I will stay here to observe." When Don Vicente and Meche arrived, the boys were already waiting with the sack of corn held high, while the airplane continued to circle in the sky.
Don Vicente instructed them, "Place the corn on the ground and come hide behind the fence surrounding the well. When the plane leaves here, we won't disturb it." The airplane's pilot, realizing that everyone present was waiting for its landing, chose to continue its flight, leaving those who had waited with curiosity disappointed. Worry overcame them in case the devil bird returned. Finally, night fell over the ranch, and everyone in the place commented and wondered what kind of bird it could be and from what distant lands it might come.
In Ermitaños, the night advanced, and Doña Petra, almost recovered from the shock, busied herself in preparing bitter waters for the oil lamps, making sure not to spill any. Then, everyone retired to sleep, though still troubled by the possible return of the mysterious visitor. Even Don Vicente, in the midst of the midday splendor, seemed to sense something.

The atmosphere was tense, and no one spoke much. Doña Lupe remained by Don Vicente's side, worried but providing comfort, like a companion who shares the burden of the unknown events happening outside the ranch. In the nearby towns and cities, people talked about the strange visit, but it didn't interest them much.

They lived in their own world, peaceful and happy. Don Vicente, a tall man with an imposing figure and fair skin, looked like a Don Quixote of La Mancha, missing only his Sancho Panza. Doña Lupe, of medium height and beautiful appearance, also with fair skin and dark hair, had a simple personality, just like Don Vicente. Although both spoke like the old Spaniards, preserving the richness of their language, they were not influenced by the comments of outsiders who came to buy and sell in the area.

They stood firm in their own world, with a history and culture that Don Atenógenes, who told me this story, knew better than anyone. This story takes me back to the time of Ermitaños, where a man with whom I shared conversations that spanned about 30 years ahead of my time lived. During those conversations, he narrated experiences from our region and events that still linger in my memory.

The ironic thing is that he had no knowledge that one day I would write all the stories he shared with me. Don Vicente, with his wisdom, managed to captivate me in the same way he won over doña Lupe. According to Don Atenógenes, Doña Lupe's parents were people of high lineage and much pretension.

They did not allow anyone to court their daughters. If by chance they crossed paths with young men at the annual celebrations held in the ranches or in the local chapels representing various saints, this was an opportunity to get to know each other. However, they had to meet in secret, whispering conversations through some hole in the wall. If they were ever discovered, they only saw flashes and heard gunshots, which forced them to flee like champions.

I know this because once, a friend and I went to talk to some girls. Shame overcame us because they were beautiful. While we were chatting near some holes in the wall of their bedrooms, the dogs sniffed us out and started throwing bricks and shooting into the air. We ran like athletes, crossing a corral full of fat pigs that were sound asleep.

The Load of Firewood in Ermitaños: An Act of Love and Determination

The night enveloped us, and in the midst of darkness, we found ourselves in a precarious situation. There were so many of us that there was no room to run, and desperation overtook us. We ran over the pigs, practically flying, while the pigs grunted and complained until we finally reached an alley. There, we defended ourselves by throwing stones at the dogs. Amid the chaos, I got lost for a moment. But allow me to return to the story of Don Vicente and how he won over Doña Lupe in those times.

In an era when mistrust was deeply rooted, and parents were extremely selective about their daughters' suitors, the situation was not simple. If the parents didn't like the boyfriend, they resorted to bullets to reject him. However, to avoid this fatal outcome, a clever strategy was devised: delivering a load of firewood outside the bride's house.

If the boyfriend remembered the firewood delivered the next day and brought it to his home, it meant that the parents accepted the marriage proposal. If they didn't want to, the firewood would stay there for two or three days, and the boyfriend had to take extreme measures: kidnapping the bride.

That's how Don Vicente asked for Doña Lupe's hand because the in-laws didn't yield to logical reasons. That same day, they confidently brought the firewood and proceeded to formalize the marriage proposal and plan their future marriage.

I allowed myself to digress a bit from the events of the day following the airplane's arrival, as I mentioned earlier. On another day, Don Vicente, finally approved by the in-laws, took a crucial step in his life. Calmness reigned in the house as the morning advanced, and the sun reached its highest point in the sky. However, the day would take an unexpected turn when one of the workers, who was on the hill, arrived at full speed on his unruly horse.

"Don Vicente!" exclaimed the young man, agitated and worried. "Don Vicente!" Don Vicente, alerted by the urgency in the young man's voice, asked seriously, "What's happening, young man?"

The worker replied breathlessly, "A large column of men is coming, causing a great commotion. They're all wearing the same uniforms, they're federal soldiers. Victoriano Martín warned me that we should be cautious of them. Run, inform everyone to hide their weapons!"

The orders were quickly transmitted, and shortly after, the army, consisting of a large number of uniformed soldiers, arrived at the large house. Before the men dismounted, Don Vicente and his family presented themselves with respect, and Don Vicente stepped forward to give the customary greeting.

"Good afternoon, General," Don Vicente greeted with deference. The officer humbly replied, "I'm not a General, I'm a Captain. Forgive me, Your Grace." Don Vicente, with courtesy, asked, "How can I assist you, Captain?" The captain, surprised by the hospitality, explained his presence. "What are you doing here? You haven't left. Don't you know you're supposed to gather in the city?"

Don Vicente calmly responded, "No, sir, we had no knowledge of this. This is quite an isolated area, and we were unaware of this order." The captain continued speaking and asked, "Didn't you see the plane over there, sir?"

Amidst the surprise and uncertainty, the mysterious airplane hovering over the hermitage left everyone bewildered. Don Vicente, in his usual straightforward tone, expressed his ignorance about what that object in the sky really was. For him and his companions, that plane seemed more like a creature of the devil than a flying machine, and they couldn't hide their astonishment at the situation. The captain, on the other hand, seemed to understand the confusion of the people from the ranch and offered a solution to avoid problems with the federal army. He provided them with a safe-conduct that guaranteed their safety for the next ten days. However, he made it clear that this would be temporary, as he observed that they had many matters to attend to and seemed filled with anxieties and pending tasks.

Don Vicente expressed his gratitude to the captain for his gesture, and after receiving the safe-conduct, the military agent departed. Faced with this unexpected situation, Don Vicente remained thoughtful, feeling the urgency to find a solution for his community. He decided that the first step would be to take a night of rest to reflect and plan his next move.

The next day, he gathered the entire community of the ranch after breakfast and announced that they needed to take concrete actions. He involved Chilo and Tobias in organizing a plan to face the unknown and challenging circumstances. Meanwhile, Meche was tasked with informing others about the meeting they would have the next day to make important decisions. The future of everyone in the hermitage depended on the strategy they could devise in this unusual and challenging situation.

The following morning found Don Vicente, sleep-deprived but determined, reflecting on the situation and seeking a solution for his community. He knew he had to act quickly, but also carefully, to ensure the safety and well-being of all the hermitage's inhabitants.

He gathered the community in a circle and, with heartfelt words, shared his thoughts. He expressed his regret for the upcoming separation but also his commitment not to leave anyone behind. He proposed a plan that would allow them to face the challenges ahead.

Don Vicente acknowledged the importance of animals in their lives and in the community. He decided to get rid of some of his livestock, especially the pigs, and sent Chilo to coordinate this task. He urged them to prepare the necessary carts to transport the thinner animals to Tepatitlán, where they could sell them and obtain resources for their journey.

For another important task, he trusted Meche, a trusted person who had already proven his efficiency in previous trips to Guadalajara. Don Vicente asked him to inform his cousin Atilano about their imminent arrival in the city and to find a suitable house to accommodate everyone. Meche, despite his mature appearance, was a man with great capacity for action and adaptation.

This was a moment of change and farewell in the hermitage, but also the beginning of a new stage full of challenges and opportunities. The community was ready to embark on a new path, relying on Don Vicente's wisdom and leadership to guide them toward a better future.

CHAPTER 20

Meche and Tobias's Legendary Journey

In that corner of the Highlands of Jalisco, the hermitage community prepared for an imminent change. Don Vicente, a tall and lean man of mestizo appearance, stood out in the landscape. Despite his dark skin, thick beard, and large top hat, he could never keep his cotton pants completely white due to the region's typical red soil.

Don Vicente was known for his astonishing physical endurance. It was said that he could run from the ranch to Guadalajara in a single day, covering over 100 kilometers. On his frequent trips, he carried messages and products from the ranch to his cousin, Don Atilano, in the city. He was a man who embodied the tenacity and determination of the people of the Highlands of Jalisco.

Meche, a slim and seemingly mature man, stood out in the community for his efficiency on trips to Guadalajara. He was known for carrying out his assignments quickly and effectively. Don Vicente entrusted him with communicating the impending departure of the entire family to Guadalajara.

Tobias, on the other hand, received the task of gathering a group of people willing to collaborate in the effort to collect and transport the livestock to Tepatitlán, where they could sell it and obtain the necessary resources. Don Vicente owned a large number of livestock, making this task a considerable challenge.

Despite the difficulties and obstacles in their path, Meche and Tobias demonstrated their commitment and determination to carry out the assigned tasks. The hermitage community was ready to face the challenges that lay ahead, relying on the courage and skills of its most outstanding members.

The Challenge of the Journey: Busy Roads and Rebellious Pigs

The journey to Tepatitlán presented itself as a real challenge for the hermitage community. The roads were crowded, and the carts couldn't keep up with transporting everyone. There were moments when they had to leave behind some pigs that were getting tired or simply didn't fit in the carts.

As they advanced toward Tepatitlán, some pigs were inflated and emitted a strong odor that made people cover their noses. The journey became even more complicated due to the numerous pig carcasses that lay on the road, the result of the slaughter carried out in the ranches and the chapel. Many pigs lost their lives on the way, either because of their size or due to the intense prevailing heat, creating a disaster in the concentration of animals.

After two days, Meche returned from Guadalajara with good news from Don Atilano, who assured them he was waiting without any concern. Don Vicente, relieved by the news, sent Meche back to Tepatitlán to supervise the sale of the animals and receive further instructions.

The sale of livestock was carried out quickly, albeit at low prices. Some buyers from Guadalajara took advantage of the affordable prices. In just five days, the entire operation was concluded. Don Vicente, excited and with a hint of nostalgia, generously rewarded each worker, almost with tears in his eyes, aware that they were about to part ways.

Departure and Hope in Times of Revolution

The farewell of the community was filled with emotion and longing. Don Vicente, with serenity, reminded them that they were all in the same situation and that he trusted that God would help them reunite once the revolution passed. He urged them to make their own decisions and take the risks they deemed necessary.

Don Vicente offered to donate all the remaining animals, including the oxen, for their sustenance. He also allowed the horses to roam freely and the use of the trojas' crops for food. Chilo, diligently, found a buyer in Tepatitlán to load ten carts with corn and other essential goods.

The day before the permit expired, everyone prepared for the journey to Guadalajara. They packed two large carts with important belongings, along with horses and donkeys to carry additional cargo. Uncertainty and anxiety accompanied the community on their departure to the bustling city of Guadalajara, not knowing what they would encounter on the way. It was a moment of farewell and hope amidst revolutionary times.

They continued their journey along the Royal Road, passing by the outskirts of Tepatitlán and finally reaching Paredones, now known as El Refugio. There, they took a pause to eat and rest a little, regaining strength as the afternoon progressed. By nightfall, they reached a place called Piedra Amarilla, where they decided to spend the night. Although the large house had no occupants due to the concentration, they made themselves comfortable to rest.

The next morning, they resumed their journey towards Guadalajara. However, they made a mistake and took a path that led them to Tonalá, a suburb of Guadalajara known for its predominantly indigenous population and its reputation for hosting healers and shamans.

Upon arriving in Tonalá, they found a larger town but with a population similar to that of Tateposco. Although they initially experienced some distrust, the local people became friendlier when Don Vicente and his group asked about their location. They observed the abundant local pottery, from jugs to jars and a variety of clay objects.

Doña Lupe suggested that they purchase some pottery, as it could be useful in Guadalajara. They arranged the pieces in the carts and asked for directions to Guadalajara. Faced with the delay, Doña Lupe suggested the possibility of staying to rest there, but Don Vicente decided to move forward, despite the locals' kindness, aware that they still had a long way to go in their challenge to reach Guadalajara.

An Encounter in San Pedro Tlaquepaque

Don Vicente and his group continued their journey, moved away from Tonalá and headed towards San Pedro Tlaquepaque, a town near Guadalajara. On their way, they encountered some sinister-looking healers in Tateposco, which motivated them to continue without delay.

Finally, they reached San Pedro Tlaquepaque, also known as Tlaquepaque, and were fortunate to find a large inn where they could rest and spend the night. Their arrival at this place was a cause for joy, especially for Don Vicente, as he carried a considerable amount of money, and even some gold, hidden in the carts, which provided him with some financial security. However, the most striking novelty for them was the electric lighting that was already present in the area.

Don Vicente's family was completely unaware of the existence of electricity, and it was he who pointed out the strange devices emitting bright light. Intrigued, they tried to understand how these mysterious devices and the networks of cables connecting them worked. Finally, upon reaching the inn, they found refuge and took care of their animals in the pens and stables, while Don Vicente took care of the logistical details.

After a long day, Don Vicente and his family finally arrived in San Pedro Tlaquepaque, where they found refuge in a spacious inn. After enjoying a hearty dinner, they retired to the rooms they had reserved. The excitement of the encounter with their cousin Atilano in Guadalajara was about to materialize, as their journey was nearing its conclusion.

However, when it came time to turn off the electric lights, they faced a dilemma. They didn't know how to do it, and in the darkness, Chilo and Tobias questioned each other about how to turn off those mysterious devices.

Tobias mentioned to Chilo that his father had asked the innkeeper, who had explained to them that the lights operated with something called "electricity." Perplexed, Chilo replied that he would use his new boot, which he had bought in Zapotlanejo, to turn off the light, having no idea how electricity worked (they didn't even notice the existence of switches).

The night passed without further incidents, and everyone slept peacefully. However, at dawn, while trying to take off the boot, Chilo realized that it had become deformed overnight and had become extremely small. To solve the problem, he opted to wear his "guaraches" instead of the boots. Ready to embark on the final stretch of their journey to Guadalajara, they continued on their way, carrying with them the unforgettable experience of their unexpected encounter with electricity.

The restless boys approached Don Vicente to ask if they had figured out how to turn off the enigmatic electric device. With a smile, Don Vicente confessed that they had not managed to solve the mystery of electricity. However, he mentioned that he had bought a ceramic jar in Tlaquepaque, and Tobias took the opportunity to share the curious anecdote of the deformed boots.

Don Vicente suggested the idea of acquiring new boots, considering that in Guadalajara there were many options of better quality. So, they resumed their journey early in the morning, advancing along a wide street. As they ventured further into the city, they came across tram tracks, something they found curious and unfamiliar.

They walked alongside their carts and horses, observing with astonishment the jaws of the trams that emitted sparks through the suspended wires in the air. However, an unexpected event took them by surprise. On a nearby corner, a tram passed by swiftly, throwing sparks and generating a deafening noise.

The reaction was immediate: SARIM, doña PETRA, and their companions were greatly frightened. Doña PETRA, riding her horse, stumbled and fell to the ground. The others, as they were close to doña LUPE's horse, also got scared, and some ran in their desperation. Laughter and screams mixed in a moment of confusion as they chased after doña PETRA's frightened horse, circling around the carts.

The unforgettable experience in the streets of Guadalajara left its mark on them, but they did not lose their spirits, continuing their journey with stories to tell and their adventurous spirit intact. With the care of a rider adjusting his saddle, Don Vicente prepared the saddles for the women. Amidst the commotion, he didn't even realize that Lolita was behind his horse.

Almost on the verge of falling, the ladies held onto each other, while Don Vicente positioned himself behind doña Lupe. He didn't feel much fear, but he was worried that, with the scare, the ladies might fall. He shouted determinedly, "Stop, old lady, stop! It's nothing, just a contraption." The tram passed, the cables crackled, and everyone recovered from the surprise.

Chilo and Tobias, who had taken refuge on the railings of nearby houses' windows, tried to climb onto the roofs through the gutters. However, when the tram moved away, they returned to solid ground. Meche, with his innate calmness, quickly reassured doña Petra, who was already recovering from the scare. He had experienced a similar situation when he was sent on a mission with Don Atilano in the past, but he had never thought to share that experience until now when everyone was scared.

When they overcame their initial amazement, they continued their journey and reunited with their cousin Atilano. The encounter was a cause for joy, as they had not seen each other for years. After a brief rest at his house, they set out to take care of the livestock, although they didn't have much space in the corral, as they had brought numerous animals.

Between Animals and Memories: A Man's Life and His Land

In a time of changes and challenges, my father, Don Vicente, lived a life marked by his love for his land and animals. In his narrative, he takes us on a journey through the memories of his ranch, his family, and his hermit life, which, despite being idyllic, was disrupted by the political circumstances of the era. With the help of Don Atilano, a loyal friend, my father found refuge in an inn located half a league away, on Calle Gigantes, near the parish of San Juan de Dios.

This place became a temporary sanctuary for him and his family, offering them peace and security in turbulent times. Don Atilano, always ready to help, assured my father that there was nothing to worry about. He provided them with accommodation, and the next day, he set out to show them two houses he had found for their possible new residence.

This is the story of how my father, Don Vicente, and his family faced the challenges imposed by the government of Calles, a time that forced thousands to change their lives. Through his words, we immerse ourselves in a narrative full of nostalgia, resilience, and the unbreakable connection to his land and his people.

Destiny Amidst Revolutions: A Love Story

In the turbulent times of the reconcentration, a popular saying comes to life: "Every cloud has a silver lining." This phrase perfectly reflects the story of my parents, whose courtship was strengthened amidst the adversities of early 20th-century Mexico. My Grandmother Chila and my Uncle Rafael, my Grandfather Antonio Martín del Campo's brother, lived in Guadalajara, just like my parents during this time. The city became a refuge and a meeting point for our family, marked by loss and resistance. My Uncle Miguel had passed away, and this painful event coincided with a second reconcentration.

Tragedy also touched my grandmother María, my father's mother, and my grandfather, who moved to Guadalajara. In a twist of fate, my uncle Liborio died in Palo Alto, California, the victim of a tragic accident with a bull in the stable where he worked alongside my uncle Eulogio. This stable, owned by a Portuguese family, was a well-known place in our family history. Meanwhile, my uncle Silviano, the eldest of the siblings, faced his own challenges, working in an environment marked by tension and politics.

The era of Plutarco Elías Calles had left a complicated legacy, and it wasn't until the arrival of Lázaro Cárdenas in 1934 that significant change was glimpsed. The year 1932 was particularly noteworthy. Despite interruptions and challenges, my parents' love continued to flourish. This year marked not only a turning point in Mexico's political history, with the end of the Cristero Rebellion and changes in national leadership, but also a decisive chapter in my family's life, where love emerged victorious amidst uncertainty and change.

WARNING!

Not everything written here is one hundred percent verified, but it is a collection of memories from individuals, books read, and other forms of information gathered throughout the life of Liborio Gutierrez.

CHAPTER 21

Reflections on Human Existence Made by God

In contemplating the essence of human existence, we recognize its tripartite nature: the body, spirit, and soul, each with its derivatives united in three aspects: "will," "mind," and "emotion." These three live within the human being.

The Body: consists of the physical and physiological, coming with will, mind, and emotion. The emotional will comes from the spirit united with the soul.

The Spirit: is the essence that is born with the body, whether rational or irrational. I refer to every animal of any species, and every species of animal has a "mind," "will," and "emotion." It has been said that 23 million animal species have been discovered, and studies have been conducted by scientists on more than three million species, each born with its spirit at the will of God.

"The Soul," united with the "Body" and the "Spirit," is an exclusive gift bestowed upon humanity by the divine will. It is a breath of God infused directly into our body and spirit. With this, He makes us like Him, giving us reason and intelligence. With it, He gives us the will to create wisdom. One is not born with wisdom; it is gradually created from birth, according to the will and desire to develop it, acquiring knowledge of things.

Free Will: As God gives us free will, He leaves us free in our own will and reason. We manage the body and soul with the "Spirit." The "Body" and the "Spirit" are united with the instinctive spirit, which belongs only to the irrational animal. The human being who reasons well with justice comes closer to the knowledge of God. Education plays a pivotal role in this journey, shaping individuals into noble, enlightened beings with virtuous character. "And at the same time, a being can be excellent and, at the same time, a despicable and horrendous being or it can be an ignorant and uneducated person but, at the same time, be a magnificent human being with good feelings. I strive to come a little closer to the truth and wisdom of God.

(Reflection on thought) Knowledge enriches thought, and knowing the truth of things is to communicate with logic and thus know God. Thus, to know more..."

Eternity

Eternity is a subject of controversy for human beings. Eternity is the representative of the Supreme Being on Earth and in life, an invaluable gift to us that is united in each person with the soul and spirit. With the intelligence and reasoning of the soul, we must think that after our human life, we enter our true eternal reality. From this world, you cannot take anything material, only the spiritual and your conscience. It is said that the conscience is the file of the path through your life, whether short or long, but you have to present it to God, and it will be judged by Him.

We never seriously think about using intelligence and waste time thinking that we will have a bodily end. Some people do not think that this life is a vain illusion; the days are counted like a shadow. It happens that we reach the end of the same goal, awakening from the dream of corporal life and entering eternal life.

"In reality, which is Eternal Life, controversial and which is the very reason for consciousness, 'Consciousness' is what directs the destiny of each one and adds up the facts, taking the product of it at the end of the body, which is then examined by the Supreme Judge who is God. How pleasant it is to find the appropriate answer and even more so when it is timely. The value of the human being before the eyes of God holds a significant place in His eyes. We have the proof with our own sight; He gives us reason and our own decision and gives us the freedom to save ourselves or condemn ourselves. He gives us a 'conscience' that we move and make according to our way of acting, for we have to necessarily present it to God."

"Advice to Seek God:" Seek and serve Him with all your heart and good disposition, because He examines all consciences and distinguishes every intention and thought. So, if you truly seek Him, He will allow you to find Him, but if you turn away from Him, He will reject you forever.

"Wisdom" (Reference: Wisdom [Biblical Book] 3:17-18): The beginning of "Wisdom" is the sincere desire to instruct oneself, and having the desire to instruct oneself is already loving wisdom. To love it is to obey its laws, and to obey its laws is to ensure eternity and glory.

God, Small in His Greatness

God, with His wisdom and will, formed the greatness of the infinite and its coordination. Yet, paradoxically, He is also present in the minutest of living organisms, like the molecules inside cells. It is said that a molecule is so small that it is up to a million times smaller than a cell, and the cell has to be seen with a microscope because it cannot be seen with the naked eye.

And even more, the greatness in volume of the cells of the human body is similar in greatness in volume to the stars of the universe. To count them, very powerful telescopes are needed. In books, it is said that the human being has 10 trillion cells, not millions but trillions. Trillions of neurons that serve as a communication network to coordinate activities, and each neuron is surrounded on average by some cells called neuroglias.

"The Milky Way," with its multitude of solar systems, millions of stars, and planets, is a testament to the vastness of the cosmos. Imagine how many galaxies there are in the universe. Countless. That's why I say that God, with His power and wisdom, is small in His greatness. A very significant and tangible miracle we have is that the life of the human being, at the beginning of our conception, each one of us is a single cell, from the union of a man and a woman. Through the divine will, we are 70 trillion cells, sustained by the nourishment of food, water, and air. All this is a small reason to know more about God and be close to Him and know His immense infinite capacity.

Another Significant Miracle

The process of body change, with eating three times a day adds something to prevention. We are capable of changing or recovering a complete body every seven years. Plant and animal cells become our own cells, either in our own blood, bones, and tissues. It is amazing how blood is transformed.

Thought: It is exciting to explore the paths of the Lord, the Creator of all things. And it is even more exciting when one enters them, although we know that we will never reach the goal. But it feels nice when we see the light, even if it is from afar. Almighty Father, keep me while I can be useful as a manifestation of your love on Earth.

The Holy Trinity in the Human Being: Air, The Sun, The Water, and The Air

The Sun - God: The eternal light. God gifted us a part of his light, turning it into matter and representing it with the sun, a source of earthly life. Without the sun, how could we live?

The Water - Represents Christ: Source of spiritual life. God sent His son so that through baptism we cleanse ourselves from all sin, and with his great martyrdom on the Cross, his shed blood achieved the salvation of our souls. Water is also a source of bodily life; without water, we could never live.

The Air - Compared with the Holy Spirit: How could we live without air? Never! We do not see it, but we feel it. The air nourishes us physically, and it is essential to think well and develop spiritually. Our intelligence and the Holy Spirit also nourish us spiritually so that we have our intelligence clear and our reasoning free, able to develop our sentimental decisions that make us palpitate clearly. Also, although we do not see it, it is with us representing the Holy Trinity as a gift that God gave us.

Faith is to believe that God is an infinitely perfect spiritual being, owner and creator of all things. It is to believe with all your soul, with all your heart, and with all the forces of your thought. Faith is to believe in the Holy Trinity: God the Father, God the Son, and God the Holy Spirit. In one true God and three distinct persons. How? Without wasting time trying to decipher this mystery, the human being does not have that capacity of intelligence. To believe unconditionally.

Faith in God is Blind

Faith is also to believe that under the Holy Spirit, Jesus was baptized in the river Jordan and immediately, in the form of a dove, when the heavens opened to Saint John the Baptist, a dove appeared and a voice said: "THIS IS MY BELOVED SON," in a voice in which I have all my trust.

Faith is the word of God, first transmitted to the prophets, and then Jesus to his disciples through his gospels. It confirms that God came down to Earth in his son Jesus Christ.

Faith is this other mystery that God, with His will, wanted the prophecy of the coming of the prophet Elijah, who was taken to heaven, to be fulfilled. God allowed him to incarnate in Saint John (Matthew 11:14-15).

Another mystery was and is the Transfiguration on the mount, when Jesus took Peter, Simon, John and when they saw this miracle: Jesus transformed into a celestial body alongside the prophet Elijah and Moses.

Faith includes believing that when Saint John the Baptist's head was cut off and his spirit left his body, it returned to its original state, which was the Prophet Elijah.

Faith is also to believe that on the third day after his death, Jesus resurrected and that after forty days he went to the outskirts of Jerusalem, took his disciples, blessed them, and said: "Go throughout the world to preach my gospel." Immediately the heavens opened, the angels descended, and he ascended with them to the kingdom of his Father (John 14:49-51).

This mystery is very important; it is to believe that God chose a Virgin named Mary so that his son would incarnate here on earth through the Holy Spirit in body.

And finally, it is to believe that God, with his infinite will and love, took the soul of His Ever-Virgin Mary, mother of Jesus Christ, to heaven. Mary was also chosen by God as the best mother on earth so that in heaven she would represent humans.

Faith also involves believing in the immense motherly love that Mary has for us on Earth. God gave her the power to help us in all our needs. Tirelessly, she protects and helps us and, as a mother, it is not her role to represent Justice, she only knows of LOVE and more LOVE, which she immensely has for us and is constantly interceding for us so that God does not punish us so severely. She cries and suffers greatly when we behave badly and even more when she sees that constantly her children are falling into "Hell" every day. That is why, lately, God has given her permission to appear on "Earth" very often to tell us to behave well, that we make her suffer a lot and that we make her son suffer a lot when we behave badly, and she does not want God to send us to the darkness forever.

God's Love Has No Color

An important reflection on this topic is to think and learn that the color of people or their appearance does not make humanity good or bad. "Evil" comes from feelings and "goodness" is the same. Sentimental decisions have neither color nor appearance, so we must try not to make mistakes. "I repeat," neither "color" nor appearance should be confused and thus avoid mistakes that may be irreparable. Humanity is made by God of different figures and skin colors; we are all His exclusive children, very different from other animals.

They have only spirit, and we are distinguished as His exclusive children, why? Because only from Him is our "SOUL." From there comes the "reasoning," the "intelligence" He gave us, something that other animals do not have. That is why God gave us the power and authority to be owners... Of all the species of animals that exist on Earth, according to scientists, there are 23 million animal species. Continuing with the human theme, no matter what color skin you have, God loves us all equally, and that's why I say, God's love has no color.

The negative effects of certain actions become evident, such as when one consumes a lot of liquor and wakes up the next day with stomach discomfort, or in other words, "hangover." She began to react upon realizing that this was not good in this life or for the afterlife. She wanted to separate from Lies, but she couldn't because Lies wouldn't let her. But one day, Integrity, her sister, came to visit her and convinced her that she was doing things wrong with Lies. It wasn't easy to separate from him; it requires great effort and sacrifice, but in the end, she managed to get away from young Lies and Traps, and thus returned to being the same Honesty.

Wisdom and Malice

This advice is dedicated to my son José Gutiérrez, about a request he made to me after I sent him the thought below about wisdom. He found it very brief and wanted me to write something more extensive on this topic, that is, this thought here.

The beginning of "Wisdom" is to have the sincere desire to instruct oneself, and to have the sincere desire to instruct oneself is already to love wisdom. To love it is to obey its laws, and to obey its laws is to ensure eternal glory. Intelligence and wisdom come from God, so they must be loved. Wisdom is something very great, with many years of learning and a lot of experience on the path of life.

At the beginning, when you are born, you are born with thought and instinct, and your intelligence grows like an orange; at first it is green and small, the days pass and it grows until it matures. Intelligence matures... Along with intelligence, "Malice" is very necessary for the long road of life. "Malice" is like when you have a new idea to go to the mountains for a season, where you know there are hills, bad roads, possibly storms, and mud. The day comes to go, suppose for a vacation, but you take the indispensable, less what is necessary. You arrive at the mentioned mountain, and you encounter a very strong storm, and the road is pure dirt with many fords and a lot of mud.

The moment comes when you get stuck and cannot get out of the mud. You start thinking that you forgot to buy chains for the tires, so you wouldn't have gotten stuck, and you also start thinking that you are missing several things that you forgot to put in the truck that you were going to need for prevention. What does that mean?

It's called lack of "Malice." Malice develops in thought and intelligence. "Malice," if you had it in mind, would have helped you think that you had to buy chains for the wheels in case of getting stuck. There are people who are born almost without malice, and these people need help, someone who teaches them little by little what malice is. There are people who are born with developed malice from childhood, they reflect it because it comes from family inheritance, and others pick it up through blows and failures, that's part of the learning of the long path of life to arrive with good "Wisdom." Failures and setbacks are necessary to manufacture victories and enjoy them better. "Malice" can save you from many dangers. For example, it can save you from not drowning in water, from a car accident, from a bad marriage, or from poverty; it can also help you. Youth do not forget to donate malice.

Advice: Travel
"PROVERB: He who travels much knows much, he who has much experience thinks wisely, he who has not undergone trials knows little, but he who has traveled becomes very smart. In my travels, I have seen many things and I know more than I tell. Many times, I have been in danger, but thanks to my experience, I came out without problems.

Advice: Selfishness in Your Knowledge
The main goal of life is not knowledge but action. If you have knowledge, you must realize it by "Reasoning" your knowledge. Without action, no one benefits, and you create a latent and conscious selfishness that neither helps you nor others.

Happiness and Wealth - ADVICE - What I Have Learned

I have learned that in this world, to seek happiness, one must educate oneself spiritually and act ethically, wherever you find yourself socially. Seek economic prosperity in a good way so that God may increase your financial wellbeing to ensure a comfortable life for you and your loved ones. And if your prosperity flourishes, you can help others beyond your family nucleus. Helping others creates a very strong wall that no one will think of jumping over to harm you. Thus, in your circle, there will be no reason for suffering, and if there is any enemy out of envy (which there always are), they will think twice before attempting to jump over it. You create the wall with your good will, and that's how one of the motives is realized, creating an economic treasure and a treasure of happiness for this world and the next one too.

CHAPTER 22

Questions

THE QUESTION: In the resurrection of the dead, will the living and the dead be transformed into celestial bodies? It is assumed that there will no longer be hunger, so how is it that many will sit down to eat with Abraham, Isaac, and Jacob? Will it be in the same sense as one eats in Heaven, or will it be on Earth already transformed? As I await the fulfillment of these prophecies, I embrace faith, trusting in the wisdom of our Heavenly Father. Though comprehension eludes me, my steadfast belief remains steadfast.

Misguided and Unrestrained Distortions

The degeneration of your person and your soul that gradually goes unrestrained in evil begs the question: How does one regain control? It has to start with impulse and will, to make an effort to control yourself and control the bad, misguided, sentimental, impulsive, and degenerate distortions. If no effort is made to control these bad habits, a frenzy of satisfaction in the bad and the wrong begins. If not controlled in time, it is like a malignant disease like gangrene, which leads to death if you do not pay attention. That is the soul: you sicken it with sin and, if you do not pay attention, it kills the soul and there is no other remedy that leads to condemnation. God gives you the freedom to save yourself or condemn yourself. When you are born, God gifts you a soul that comes with reason and intelligence.

Advice for Young People

When you are young, you develop physically and perceive daily life, learning from the environment in which you live. Life teaches you two paths: the first is the environment that seeks you, pursues you, and sometimes even attacks you to enter that environment. The second environment is the one you have to seek, and if you find it, do not let go of it, because it is a normal and morally upright environment. The first one seeks you to teach you a false treasure, but as you are young, you do not notice what is false nor do you know what is false. On the path you are traveling, you discover exciting things, and as most young people like everything that is exciting, that is where the danger lies.

Almost the first thing you will encounter are vices, alcohol, drugs, and women of ill repute. If you don't know how to reject them, or you don't want to because curiosity enters, that's where it doesn't work! You join a useless club and put a brake on your intelligence, you don't let your wisdom develop and you lose the opportunity to be a great, useful, powerful, or famous person, and to be able to help your family and your neighbor. But even so, there is always hope for recovery.

Will, decision, and courage are the best remedy to recover and thus start a new life, reviving the good dreams that were almost dead. The other path teaches you what is good. This one does not seek you; you must seek it. The good is normal, the normal has its level even on all sides. When you leave that normality and if you want to return to it, you have to look for it, if you have the desire to return. When you decide to look for it, it's because it was the best path for you and for everyone.

When You Are Born and You Are Lucky

When you have good parents, it is logical that they teach you what is good. When you start to have the use of reason, you perceive what is good, because your parents, who are good, teach you. When you reach the age of eight, that's where the danger lies; you start to think for yourself. The most dangerous age is when you reach thirteen years old; from there on, until you are interested in knowing what is good and right, you also start to distinguish what is bad or incorrect. There are some young people who begin to reason and perceive that they are doing wrong and develop the desire to enter the right path and recognize that they are hurting those who love them, and they are also hurting themselves. And there are also those who reach the age of 40 and are not interested in knowing what is good and right; the blows of life become an addiction, a masochism, and these in one way or another end soon.

Wealth and its Double Obligation

If you are rich by inheritance or luck, you become doubly rich: rich in economy and responsibilities. You have the obligation to grow your wealth and not squander it. Help your family, your close relatives, and your neighbor, as if buying your ticket to Heaven. Before helping anyone, you must be sure that they will not squander the help.

If the help serves to increase their economy, they must do the same as was done to them, helping others with the same voluntary condition, with God. No obligations are needed, but good will and desire. And do not forget God, who is the most important partner. When one is doing well, one does not need much, but if something is lacking, remember God to continue in the activities of His worship and representations on earth, in a good way and with love.

"*Diligence is the author of good luck.*" - Benjamin Franklin
"*Years ago, our parents brought to this continent a new nation conceived in liberty and dedicated to the proposition that all men are created equal.*" - President Abraham Lincoln, Nov. 19, 1863, USA.
"*Any time is the best time to do things right.*" - Martin Luther King
"*Cowards die many times before their deaths.*" - William Shakespeare
"*Hunger is the best sausage.*" - Miguel de Cervantes
"*All that glitters is not gold.*" - Miguel de Cervantes

The Light of the Soul

Try to keep your light, if it is distant, search for it and get as close as you can to your soul. If you already have it, share it so that it spreads like an epidemic. True men are tested in difficult moments. He who can smile when everything goes wrong is because he already knows who to blame. Resentment kills the soul. A smile is the foundation of happiness and health.

"*The memory of the past and grudges sicken your soul and don't let you prosper.*" - Liborio Gutierrez
A bad man knows how to receive a benefit, but not how to return it. Evil is not what enters a man's mouth, but what comes out.
"*I discovered that beauty is not discovered with the eyes, but with the heart. A man of few words is the best man. Your mind is the house of a great treasure. It is good that there are mice so that no one knows who eats the cheese.*" - Unknown author
"*The greatest wisdom is knowing oneself.*" - Galileo.
"*Love is the key that opens the door to happiness.*" - Liborio Gutierrez.
I compiled these sayings for my son, José, and his family at Christmas 2008.
"*Happiness depends on oneself.*" - Aristophanes.

"*I only fear my enemies when I start to see that they are right.*" - Unknown author

"*The only symbol of superiority that I know is kindness.*" - Unknown author

"*The only failure is the one who does not learn from his mistakes.*" - Unknown author

"*Love is not a feeling; love is a decision. To have a good future, you need to know the past.*" - Ted Kennedy

"*Defend the just and the correct, protect the humble, the loser, the innocent.*" – Richard, the Lionheart

"*Patience is half of science.*" - Socrates

Joy is a word to describe LOVE, and LOVE is a word to describe Joy. Triumph is not the destination, but the journey. Love is a two-way street, but there is always someone who doesn't know how to count. My intention in writing these ideologies of mine is something of God. I have compiled in my mind along my extensive path in life, exploring the world and the paths that lead to the "Golden Castle of Happiness." Sometimes, the Holy Spirit of God illuminates me to write about Him and about us, who are His children, like Him. I say this because He gave us a breath of His soul and, as a result, we could live happily in "Paradise" if we wish. I assure you that He makes it possible for us to want to go with Him. However, sometimes someone comes to disturb our good intentions.

They tell us about another more beautiful palace, and we believe it because we are weak and make mistakes. What happens is that we fall into misguided distortions that we encounter. It's like the mud where we get stuck, and sometimes you can get out of there, but also sometimes you stay there forever. The simple and straightforward things in the daily life of man are chained in the great power of God. His simplicity makes him powerful and intelligent. Simplicity combines with intelligence to strengthen faith in God. Therefore, with "FAITH," man becomes the richest in the world, because there is not enough money that can buy faith. Faith is free, and there are many ways to acquire it, for example, through wisdom. But where is wisdom found?

Knowledge of Nature and Faith
With the desire to know nature, it is the same as being close to God. This is achieved through three means: Through books or scriptures. Through the verb and the word. With these three things, faith is strengthened. These paths lead you to the deserved reward of faith and bring you closer to happiness, which is equivalent to being close to God.

Proverbs from the Bible
Wealth attracts multitudes of friends, but the poor even lose their friends. With a gift, all doors are opened, and one reaches important people. He who loves money always wants more, and he who loves wealth never thinks he has enough. This is also a vain illusion, because the more you have, the more you spend. He who works, eats little or much, always sleeps well. In contrast, the rich, their riches do not let them sleep. Life and death depend on the tongue. Those who talk a lot will suffer the consequences. Gossips are like Chinese jewels, but they do not penetrate to the deepest depths.

Something of God
The things of God are simple and straightforward. He who walks in this way lives, he who strays from them endures and contentedly complicates them, is where man begins to suffer and make others suffer.

Alcoholism

Even if you haven't had the will to leave alcoholism, you are aware that you have suffered tremendously. And even more so if you get neurosis which sometimes adheres to alcoholism. It's much more suffering, because with neurosis, even what you don't eat makes you sick. And all you want is to mistreat others, and those who suffer the most are those who are closest to you: your family, children, wife, or your friends, who are the ones who love you the most. But with all this, there is always hoped to remedy the evil. Will and more will to leave the addiction. Studies say that the alcoholic is born an alcoholic; it's like a pile of wood that's ready to start a bonfire. And it's just about lighting the match. Others are born as green wood, although they set fire to them. Many matches do not light.

Thoughts and Proverbs OMEL Recommendation of Religions

"Religion" is where man tries to find God and sometimes does not find Him. In the Gospel is where man should seek God. Do not allow any religion to stand in the way of your salvation and burden you with severe fanaticism. - Unknown author

Wealth

First, face the true reality: birth. The true birth is a rebirth after being born physically and undergoing a corporeal and spiritual trial. God gives us free will to face the journey of our physical life, with countless temptations, sometimes irresistible, in forbidden satisfactions. Some resist them because they were prepared to resist them, and others, even if they were not prepared, have great will and vision to resist them, to distinguish them, and to know what is good and bad. The bad thing is when you hurt your neighbor and make him suffer, but you also hurt yourself and in the long run, you pay the consequences.

The Joy of Life

If you want to have a joyful and peaceful life, you must follow these six pieces of advice. But first, you need to understand their meaning. The first three are from a professor friend, "Robert Ward": Try to do all things right. Do everything the best you can. Treat others with respect. And this is my way of thinking: three things every human being should have: Unconditional love for God. Have humility in all your interactions. Love everything you do for others. - Liborio Gutierrez

God did not send you to this world to suffer. He sent you to enjoy joy in this life. Suffering is created by yourself or is a bitter gift caused by your peers. Sometimes, it is necessary to run like a champion.

The Five Simple Rules to Be Happy
- Free your heart from hatred.
- Free your mind from worries.
- Live simply.
- Try to give more and expect less in return.

No one can go back and make a new beginning, star. No one can start from now and make a new ending. God does not promise days without pain, laughter without sorrow, sun without rain, but He does promise strength for the day, comfort for tears, and light for the path. Disappointment is like a road with fords that lowers the spirit a bit, but then you will enjoy the straight path without problems. But don't stay on the scattered path for too long; try to move on as soon as you can. - Guatlo

If you feel discouraged for not having what you've fought for, rejoice because God has thought of something better for you. When something happens to you, whether good or bad, consider what destiny is trying to tell you.

These are logical events that must happen to teach you to laugh more and cry less. You cannot make someone love you. What you can do is love someone; the rest depends on the other person wanting to fulfill your desire. The measure of love is how much you take without measuring it.

In life, it is very rare to find the person you truly love and who loves you in return. When you have them, never let them go because you will never have such an opportunity in life again. It is better to lose your pride for someone you love than to lose the person you love because of your pride. We spend a lot of time searching...

"Never abandon an old friend; the friend gets much better when he is older."

www.ingramcontent.com/pod-product-compliance
Lightning Source LLC
Chambersburg PA
CBHW051936290426
44110CB00015B/2003